RAPID READING
MADE SIMPLE®

Revised Edition

BY

JOHN WALDMAN, Ed.D.

**Associate Professor, English and Communication
Director, the Reading Laboratory, Pace University,
New York City**

MADE SIMPLE BOOKS
®
DOUBLEDAY & COMPANY, INC.
GARDEN CITY, NEW YORK

Library of Congress Cataloging in Publication Data
Waldman, John, 1911–
    Rapid reading made simple.
    (Made simple books)
    1. Rapid reading. I. Title. II. Series.
LB1050.54.W34   1981   428.4'3   80-2632
ISBN 0-385-17484-5 (pbk.)   AACR2

ACKNOWLEDGMENTS

Although it is impossible for me to mention by name the many scholars and teachers whose research in reading has made this book possible, I wish nevertheless to acknowledge my indebtedness to them.

I wish also to acknowledge the copyright permissions generously given by the following publishers:

CHAPTER ONE:

"The Fairy Tadpole" from *The River of Life*, by Rutherford Platt, © 1956. Reprinted by permission of Simon and Schuster, Inc.

Excerpts from "Does Anyone Have Time to Think?", Norman Cousins, © March 26, 1955. Reprinted by permission of *The Saturday Review*.

CHAPTER TWO:

Paragraph entitled "Books" from "Good Reading for the Millions," by Richard J. Crohn; from *The Wonderful World of Books*, © 1952, by Alfred Stefferud. Reprinted by permission of *The New American Library of World Literature*, and Houghton Mifflin Co.

CHAPTER FOUR:

"The Caliphate" from *A Child of the Century*, by Ben Hecht, © 1954, by Ben Hecht. Reprinted by permission of Simon and Schuster, Inc.
"May 1908" from *The Journals of Arnold Bennett*, © 1932. Reprinted by permission of The Viking Press, Inc.

CHAPTER SIX:

"Speaking of Books," by J. Donald Adams, © Nov. 20, 1955. Reprinted by permission of *The New York Times Book Review*.

CHAPTER SEVEN:

Excerpts from *A Basic History of the United States*, by Charles and Mary Beard, © 1960, by Doubleday & Company, Inc. Reprinted by permission of Doubleday & Company, Inc.

CHAPTER NINE:

"A Teacher Looks at Reading," by A. B. Herr from *The Wonderful World of Books*, © 1952, by Alfred Stefferud. Reprinted by permission of *The New American Library of World Literature*, and Houghton Mifflin Co.

CHAPTER TEN:

Paragraph entitled "The Passive Reader" from "A Little Learning" in *New World Writing, Ninth Mentor Selection,* © 1956. Reprinted by permission of Howard Mumford Jones.

CHAPTER ELEVEN:

"The Art of Beginning Where You Are," by Sophie Kerr from *The Arts of Living,* © 1950, 1951, 1952, 1953, 1954, by The Conde Nast Publications, Inc. Reprinted by permission of Simon and Schuster, Inc.

CHAPTER TWELVE:

"Calculating Machine" from *The Second Tree from the Corner,* by E. B. White (Harper & Brothers). Copyright 1951 by E. B. White and first published in *The New Yorker.*

"How the Men from Mars Ruined a Quiet Evening" by Ben Gross, from *I Looked and I Listened,* © 1954. Reprinted by permission of Random House, Inc.

CHAPTER THIRTEEN:

"Develop Adequate Habits of Concentration" from *Effective Reading,* by Homer L. J. Carter and Dorothy J. McGinnis, by permission of The Dryden Press, Inc. Copyright 1957 by The Dryden Press, Inc.

"It's Never Good Enough" from *Emotional Difficulties In Reading,* by Beulah Kanter Ephron, © 1953. Reprinted by permission of The Julian Press, Inc.

CHAPTER FOURTEEN:

"Sociality" by Jurgen Ruesch. Reprinted from *Communication: The Matrix of Psychiatry,* by Jurgen Ruesch & Gregory Bateson. By permission of W. W. Norton & Company, Inc. Copyright 1951 by W. W. Norton & Company, Inc. "The King's English in a Democratic World" by Charlton Laird from *The Miracle of Language,* © 1953. Reprinted by permission of The World Publishing Co.

CHAPTER SIXTEEN:

Excerpt from "The Sponge of the Present," by Elizabeth Bowen, © June 20, 1953. Reprinted by permission of *The Saturday Review.*

"Birthday Party" by Katharine Brush, © 1946. Originally published in *The New Yorker.*

CHAPTER EIGHTEEN:

Paragraph entitled "The Reading of Adults" by Lester Asheim, from *Adult Reading,* The National Society's Fifty-fifth Yearbook, Part I, © 1956. Reprinted by permission of National Society for the Study of Education.

ABOUT THIS BOOK

Speed up your reading! Increase your comprehension! Learn both how to concentrate and how to remember! Improve your study skills! You can do all of these things if you try!

You may have heard these encouraging remarks expressed before in a great variety of ways. Now you are hearing them again. Perhaps you have a question or two concerning such optimistic statements.

For example, you may ask: *How can I become a more efficient reader on my own?*

Or: *If I have been reading in a certain way for years, how can I change now?*

An answer to these questions can be stated quite simply.

The way to read both faster and better is to read, *read*, **read**,—**faster and better.** The method works, too, in most cases.

Why are we reading specialists so sure that this application of common sense will prove effective?

The reason is not hard to find.

Most people read at a miserly 20 to 25 percent of their capacity. This leaves a generous 75 to 80 percent of unused ability. As a result, we can well afford to be confident.

Even if the vast majority of readers improved only up to 50 percent of their unused capacity, they would be reading at approximately two and a half times their former rate—**a gain of 150 percent.**

In many instances a significant gain in comprehension would be an added reward. Furthermore, both concentrating and remembering would be strengthened.

A convincing amount of objective evidence shows that the reading rate of the general literate population of the United States over sixteen years old is around 250 words per minute. Comprehension is approximately 70 percent. This is about the sixth grade grammar school level.

Nevertheless, without being aware of it, most people have a reading potential of double, or triple, or even quadruple that rate, with no sacrifice of comprehension.

This book will help you to achieve your potential.

HOW TO USE THIS BOOK

Individuals approach books in various ways.

Some people start at the beginning of the first chapter of a book and continue right on to the end in one or two sittings. Others may look at the last chapter first in order to learn the author's conclusions.

Still others may spread a book in the middle to take the stiffness out of the binding, get absorbed in some eye-catching phrase, and read from the middle onward.

Any one of these and many more procedures may be appropriate for your purpose on a particular occasion. As your purpose changes you may find it useful to vary your procedure.

If you are to get the maximum benefit from the pages to follow, however, you must carry out all instructions carefully. The ability to understand and follow directions will be a real test of your inborn intelligence.

You should read this book a chapter at a time, in the order presented.

Work out the exercises as you proceed, and try to hold to **one** of the three suggested schedules which follow:

1. **ONE CHAPTER A WEEK, WITH ACCOMPANYING DAILY STUDY ACTIVITIES. TOTAL TIME FOR PROGRAM: 18 WEEKS. —OR**

2. **TWO CHAPTERS A WEEK, WITH ACCOMPANYING DAILY STUDY ACTIVITIES. TOTAL TIME FOR PROGRAM: 9 WEEKS. —OR**

3. **THREE CHAPTERS A WEEK, WITH ACCOMPANYING DAILY STUDY ACTIVITIES. TOTAL TIME FOR PROGRAM: 6 WEEKS.**

In any communication skills program of self-improvement, whether in writing, speaking, or reading, systematic practice over an extended period of time is most effective. **Remember that time works on your side.**

A program to improve your reading efficiency taking less than six weeks is therefore not advisable.

Try to plan a certain amount of time each day for practice. Apply yourself wholeheartedly to the readings and assignments. **You will succeed.**

Once you complete this book, you may wish to dip again into various chapters from time to time as a refresher. On your first time through, however, **Take Each Chapter In Order, Following Instructions Carefully As You Can.**

HOW DO YOU BEGIN?

Arnold Bennett, the famous British novelist and one of the greatest self-help writers who ever lived, answered this question for all time.

How do you begin?

Said Bennett: Dear sir, you simply begin. There is no magic method of beginning. If a man standing on the edge of a swimming-bath and wanting to jump into the cold water should ask you, "How do I begin to jump?" you would merely reply, "Just jump. Take hold of your nerves, and jump."

CONTENTS

CHAPTER FOUR

CHAPTER FIVE

CHAPTER SIX

CHAPTER SEVEN

CHAPTER EIGHT

CHAPTER NINE

CHAPTER TEN

CHAPTER ELEVEN

CHAPTER TWELVE

CHAPTER THIRTEEN

CHAPTER SEVENTEEN

THE MATURE READER

CHAPTER EIGHTEEN

MOVE AHEAD RAPIDLY—TEST YOURSELF

CHAPTER ONE

AN INTRODUCTION TO THE ART OF READING

Does it matter to you how well you read?

You must answer this question for yourself. It is important that you **do** answer it.

A strong desire to improve your reading is essential for success with this book.

The remarkable feat of communication called **reading** is too often merely taken for granted. A whole process of evolution, ages long, had to occur before the human eye could follow along the complex arrangements of lines and curves that eventually formed the letters of the alphabet.

Coordination of eye, hand and brain had to reach a high point of development for man to use these letters in combinations expressing meaningful messages.

Neither birds nor fishes, though they may have extraordinary vision, can read a book.

Reading is a uniquely human skill as well as an art, the basic equipment of every person who has received elementary schooling. Yet, amazingly, few use it to top capacity.

Most use it to only a small fraction of their capacity.

People put a coin in a slot for a juke-box tune, twist the car radio dial for the news, push a button for a television show, glance carelessly at the captions in a picture magazine, run their eyes hurriedly over newspaper headlines.

This kind of activity may put you on the receiving end of modern communication, but it's the type of receivership that leads directly to mental bankruptcy.

You may honestly feel that it is only a lack of time that keeps you from doing more reading. **The chances are it is really a lack of reading skill.**

A frequent symptom of this lack of skill is not only slow reading but also poor comprehension. You can't concentrate when you read. You can't remember what you read.

Most of the wisdom of the world has been handed down to us in print. Nevertheless, it remains locked up in print for all but a minority of the population.

Some thoughtful people pessimistically believe that reading in our modern world is fast becoming a lost skill as well as a lost art.

Perhaps it **does** matter to you, however, how well you read. You may be keenly aware of your needs and desires for becoming more efficient. You may genuinely want to do something about it.

You can do something.

TESTING YOURSELF

Reading Rate and Comprehension. In a personal program of reading improvement, your first steps are to be directed toward discovering your present abilities.

To help you measure where you stand now and also your later progress on the highway of better and faster reading, you will test yourself at regular intervals. The tests are in CHAPTER TWO, CHAPTER TEN, AND CHAPTER EIGHTEEN.

The first section of each test is designed to measure your reading speed in words per minute. Comprehension is measured by the number of answers correct out of twenty multiple-choice questions.

General directions are to note your reading time for these tests as measured **in seconds,** then find your reading rate by consulting the TABLE FOR DETERMINING READING RATE IN WORDS PER MINUTE in the Appendix.

Vocabulary. The second section of each test will measure your vocabulary strength under speed conditions. Your score is determined by counting the number of correct items in a multiple-choice word test. You are expected to complete thirty items in five minutes.

Paragraph Analysis. The third section of each test consists of a single paragraph followed by three multiple-choice questions. One question will ask for the main idea of the paragraph. Another question will ask for one of the details supporting the main idea. A final question will ask for an inference or implication which may be drawn from the paragraph.

Answers to reading tests, vocabulary tests, and paragraph analyses will be found in the CORRECTION KEY TO TESTS in the Appendix.

Progress Chart. Since you will measure your progress in relation to past performances, try to take all the tests under as nearly the same conditions as you can. Pick a time of day when you seem to work best. Keep a careful record of all results in the PERSONAL PROGRESS CHART, also found in the Appendix.

A NOTE ON ACHIEVEMENT

You may wish to know what scores you should achieve in the initial speed and comprehension exercises. No absolute standards can be set for each individual. You might keep in mind, however, the estimated median reading speed and comprehension level of the general literate population noted in the PREFACE.

This estimate, based on wide testing, is 250 words per minute for moderately easy reading material, with 70 percent comprehension—approximately the sixth-grade grammar school median.

Of more significance to you should be the relationship of your own scores to each other. Every time you enter the results of the tests and exercises in your PERSONAL PROGRESS RECORD, make comparisons.

Reading achievement is thus to be measured for each individual by reading progress.

THE PROGRAM

All the chapters in this book, with the exception of the test chapters, contain *developmental* reading material to provide a program of self-improvement as follows:

1. EXPLANATORY DISCUSSIONS
2. READING EXERCISES
3. DAILY STUDY ACTIVITIES

The term **developmental** is used to describe a planned sequence of study intended for the average reader who wishes to become a better reader. Discussions are based upon authoritative research findings. Much of the information has been successfully used in college classrooms.

The reading exercises as well as the daily study activities are also based on material planned for classroom groups and adapted for self-study.

QUESTION AND ANSWER

A question may arise here which should be answered at once. Can you be expected to do as well on your own as you would in a group?

The answer is, unequivocally, **yes.**

ON YOUR OWN IN READING

You can embark single-handed on a self-improvement program in reading with notable results.

In a classroom group, a reading specialist might impose certain disciplines. **You can do the same.**

He would also enforce deadlines for fulfilling study assignments. **You can do the same.**

He would perhaps interpret some of the material and suggest ways to tackle specific problems.

But you can do all of these things for yourself if you read each discussion in this book carefully and follow directions to the best of your ability.

Like millions of other literate Americans, you undoubtedly have a much higher potential than your present level of reading performance indicates. You must also have an ambition to realize this potential or you would not have come even so far as the first chapter of this book.

If you are willing to examine your attitudes toward reading and change them if necessary, improvement will follow.

If you are willing to substitute good habits for bad habits in reading, improvement will follow.

If you are willing to practice the skills of reading systematically and regularly, improvement will follow.

Furthermore, all of this improvement, leading toward your full potential of reading ability, will be achieved by you on your own.

TIMING YOURSELF

Accurate timing is important.

As you proceed with your reading improvement program you will constantly measure your progress by a comparison of your different reading rate scores.

You may expect these scores to vary widely.

Previous knowledge on the subject of the reading selection, personal likes and dislikes, even your subjective feelings at the time may affect your reading rate.

Over a period of weeks, however, your gains will be significant and measurable.

For timing yourself, you may use an ordinary watch or clock **with a sweep second hand.** Try to start your reading just as the second hand marks an even minute. Note the exact time. Then check the watch or clock when you finish reading.

Jot down immediately the total time elapsed in seconds.

A space for this time in seconds is provided at the end of each test and each reading exercise.

Some readers may wish to use a professional stop watch. In this case, release the starter when you begin to read an exercise and check your time in seconds when you stop reading.

Jot down immediately the total time elapsed in seconds.

Keep firmly in mind that if you continue your work systematically, your reading speed will eventually reach an effective and efficient level.

Don't get discouraged, however, if your recorded scores suddenly level off, or even go down temporarily. Some persons fail to improve immediately in spite of all efforts. Others improve rapidly at first and then seem to freeze at a certain point.

Such patterns of learning are to be expected.

COMPREHENSION

Many persons who speed up their reading hold their own in comprehension. They seem to get exactly as much out of their reading at a faster rate as they did at a slower rate, though of course it takes less time.

Others do actually increase their comprehension surprisingly as they increase speed. This is likely to happen with the syllable-by-syllable or word-by-word reader who is suddenly and dramatically released from his faulty habits and begins to read by absorbing ideas instead of meaningless word segments.

Still others discover that their comprehension drops off alarmingly during their early attempts to increase speed. If this happens to you, take it in your stride. With continued practice at your faster reading rate, your comprehension will gradually come up again to its original level and may even go higher.

In certain circumstances you may find it definitely an advantage to sacrifice a little comprehension for the sake of covering a lot more ground.

PRACTICE SESSION

You will now attempt a brief practice session. This will help to acquaint you with some of the procedures of test-taking. These introductory exercises are divided into three parts: **timed reading and comprehension, vocabulary quiz, and paragraph analysis.**

Make sure that you are in a comfortable spot for working with book and pencil, that you have a timing device of some kind, and that you won't be interrupted for at least the next fifteen minutes.

Directions. Note the exact time, then begin to read the short article which follows at your usual reading rate. Remember that you are to answer questions about the material.

When you finish, note the number of **seconds** it has taken you. Write this information in the space provided. Go on at once to answer the questions. Do not look back at what you have just read.

At the completion of the test, you will find further instructions. Follow them carefully.

Are you ready?

Time Yourself and Begin

THE FAIRY TADPOLE

By RUTHERFORD PLATT

If anything alive on earth indicates the possibility of animal life on other planets, where air pressures are cruel, it is the dark-brown, thick-shelled winter eggs of the fairy tadpole.

You can cook these eggs at 200 degrees Fahrenheit—only twelve degrees below boiling—for an hour, and the embryo lives. You can glaciate them at 360 degrees below zero Fahrenheit—a mere 100 degrees from absolute zero—and the embryo lives. You can keep these helpless, dead-looking little brown eggs in an air pressure of .000001 millimeters—only a whisper away from a complete vacuum—and the embryo lives.

The fairy tadpole is the most energetic water animal I have ever seen. It is three-quarters of an inch long, with a bowl-like shell, a powerful tail, and 100 legs all whipping at terrific speed while the body twists and bends in the agony of its urge to go somewhere.

It is unthinkable that such life is possible in a temporary fresh-water puddle at the face of the great North Pole. The puddle is water melted by twenty-four hours per day of sunlight on the glacier's surface. Icy cold, it has but a few weeks of existence and will suddenly freeze solid and be hard as steel for thirty-six weeks of the year. Yet this inhospitable water contains these lively things fashioned with leaf-like swimming feet which also act as gills.

How did the fairy tadpole get there? How does the creature survive months and months of the polar night, when temperatures are forty, fifty, and sixty degrees below zero? How does it escape the crushing expansion of the freezing pool? Where does it go with all those feet to take it?

The fairy tadpole's life span is compressed

into a few weeks in clear ice water clinking with ice cubes.

Life begins for the fairy tadpole in the mid-July sun-melt. Then the delicate shell of its egg bursts and the fairy tadpole matures in a day or so. If it is a female it looks around for a male, which it promptly embraces. Then the couple swims around locked in each other's legs for several days. After that the female fairy tadpole carries a clutch of eggs in a fan-shaped pocket on segment number eleven of her abdomen for a day or so.

Then she drops these eggs to the bottom of the water puddle and immediately goes after another mate. The eggs hatch so fast that sometimes the contents break out and are on the go before the eggs have time to leave the fan-shaped pocket of segment eleven.

If no mate is encountered she makes eggs anyway and puts them in her pocket and drops them. This is another rare case in which young are produced without benefit of a male. By using both polygamy and independence the fairy tadpole can lay six clutches of eggs in several weeks and up to 250 eggs per clutch. So life goes on.

In late August, at the moment when the midnight sun first dips below the northern horizon, a shadow passes across the reflections of the pool, and in its wake the water stiffens. The sole inhabitants of this outpost of life dive. The female fairy tadpole mixes some dark-brown stuff like fast-drying glue with the egg shells of the last clutch. She drops them between stones, from which the water will drain before it freezes, so that they will not be crushed by ice. Already a thick slab is congealing overhead to keep out drying winds. Using an infinitely tiny trace of water and oxygen, her unhatched progeny will sleep for nine sunless months in deep, sub-zero temperatures, until the Arctic sun comes up again and melts the ice into puddles next July. As the limpid water becomes rigid, the incongruous little animal vanishes, having succeeded during her frantic last moment in creating the most indestructible seed of animal life known on earth.

Time in seconds———

Directions: Select the best answer and place the appropriate letter in the parentheses.

1. According to the author, a single clutch of fairy tadpole eggs might number as many as (a) 150; (b) 200; (c) 250; (d) 300. ( )
2. The fairy tadpole matures in (a) a day or so; (b) a week; (c) several weeks; (d) a month. ( )
3. A final clutch of eggs is often (a) hatched unassisted by the male; (b) held throughout the polar night in the fairy tadpole's bowl-like shell; (c) hatched in a fan-shaped pocket in the fairy tadpole's abdomen; (d) dropped between stones to prevent them from being crushed when the water freezes. ( )
4. The author's main idea is that (a) Arctic nights are extremely cold; (b) the existence of the fairy tadpole indicates the possibility of animal life on other planets; (c) fairy tadpoles are extremely energetic in their movements; (d) polar regions are warm enough in mid-July to support animal life. ( )
5. You might infer from this brief article that (a) fairy tadpole eggs are edible; (b) the author has seen the fairy tadpole in action; (c) all the information about the fairy tadpole comes from books; (d) ice will never destroy a fairy tadpole egg. ( )

VOCABULARY

Directions: Read each definition and underline the word which fits it most closely. Do not linger on any one item, and try to complete this quiz in **one minute.** Your score will be based on the number correct within the time limit.

Time Yourself and Begin

1. Make level with the ground
   (a) erode; (b) raze; (c) plane; (d) curtail; (e) entail.

2. Act of breathing
   (a) intake; (b) oxidization; (c) vitality; (d) respiration; (e) vapor.
3. Keep from being effective
   (a) prejudice; (b) foil; (c) impair; (d) sully; (e) delay.
4. Not false or a substitute
   (a) authentic; (b) raw; (c) adulterated; (d) jeweled; (e) valuable.
5. Lack of caution and discretion
   (a) speed; (b) imprudence; (c) intolerance; (d) flair; (e) impulse.
6. Skill or talent for a particular thing
   (a) knack; (b) trait; (c) luck; (d) dextrose; (e) performance.

Time in seconds_____

PARAGRAPH ANALYSIS

Directions: Read this paragraph once. Then answer the questions about it. Try to complete the entire exercise within five minutes.

Time Yourself and Begin

THOUGHT

By NORMAN COUSINS

Thought is the basic energy in human history. Civilization is put together not by machines but by thought. Similarly, man's uniqueness is represented not by his ability to make objects but to sort them and relate them. Other animals practice communication; only man has the capacity for comprehension. Displace or eliminate thought, and the species itself has as little claim on survival as the dinosaurs with the four-foot skulls and the pea-sized brains. The impotence of the brute alongside the power of the sage is represented by thought.

Directions: Select the best answer and place the appropriate letter in the parentheses.

1. The main idea of this paragraph is that (a) dinosaurs could think in spite of pea-sized brains; (b) man's uniqueness is an ability to make objects; (c) human thought is the basic energy of civilization; (d) civilization is the result of man-made machines. ( )
2. The author states the skull size of dinosaurs as being (a) 1 foot; (b) 2 feet; (c) 3 feet; (d) 4 feet. ( )
3. You might infer from this paragraph that the author believes that man's survival depends on (a) machines; (b) time to think; (c) brute force; (d) civilization. ( )

DIRECTIONS FOR SCORING

Reading Rate. To find your reading rate in words per minute for the first selection, turn to the TABLE FOR DETERMINING READING RATE IN WORDS PER MINUTE in the Appendix.

Answers to Questions. Check the answers to the multiple-choice questions for the timed reading selection, the vocabulary quiz, and the paragraph analysis in the CORRECTION KEY TO PRACTICE TESTS, found at the end of this chapter.

Progress Chart. Reading rate and comprehension scores should be entered in the space provided.

STUDY ASSIGNMENT

Your study assignment is mainly concerned with preparation for the tests and exercises which will help you to increase your skill in the art of reading.

You are asked first to **review.**

Go back and read carefully all of the directions given to assist you with your developmental plan of reading improvement.

Begin with the **Preface.** Note once again the instructions on how to read this book. Check carefully the procedures described in this chapter for obtaining accurate time **in seconds** and how you convert this into **words per minute.**

If you like, you may try once again the brief practice sessions to further acquaint yourself with the testing methods that will be used in future chapters.

Another assignment is of extreme importance. You are asked to begin immediately to extend the reading you do outside of the pages of this book. Spend at least five, or ten, or even fifteen more minutes a day in reading than you have done in the past.

Also, you are asked to broaden your outside reading. Experiment with books on topics you don't ordinarily attempt. For example, if you are a steady newspaper reader, try some magazine articles. If you read only fiction, try nonfiction. Whatever you read, try to read more.

After you have reviewed this chapter and feel that you are thoroughly familiar with the testing procedures, turn to the next chapter.

CORRECTION KEY TO PRACTICE TESTS

"The Fairy Tadpole"	Vocabulary	"Thought"
1. c	1. b	1. c
2. a	2. d	2. d
3. d	3. b	3. b
4. b	4. a	Comprehension
5. b	5. b	____ %
Rate:	6. a	
____ w.p.m.	Number of Vocabulary Items Correct	
Comprehension		
____ %	____	

CHAPTER TWO

TEST YOURSELF

You are now going to give yourself a test to determine your present reading rate and comprehension level, your vocabulary strength, and your ability to analyze paragraphs.

Make sure that you are in a comfortable spot for working with book and pencil, and won't be interrupted for at least the next half hour.

A timing device of some kind, either a watch with a sweep hand or a stop-watch, will be needed. **Accurate timing is important.**

The general directions are as follows:

Note the exact time, then begin to read the article at the rate you ordinarily use for a non-fiction piece in a magazine. **Remember that you are to answer questions about it.**

When you finish, note the number of **seconds** it has taken you. Write this information down **immediately** in the space provided at the end of the article.

Continue then to answer the questions **without looking back at the article.**

When you have completed the questions, go on to the vocabulary section, timing yourself again as directed.

After you have completed the vocabulary section, continue with the paragraph analysis.

At the completion of the entire set of test exercises, you will find further instructions. Follow them carefully.

Are you ready?

Warning: If you are not ready, stop right here and postpone taking the test until you are prepared and consider the test-taking conditions favorable.

Time Yourself and Begin

THOMAS WOLFE

Almost everyone who has written about the American novelist, Thomas Wolfe, has made some reference to "the Wolfe legend." Perhaps it was his size which helped to create many of the stories about him and thus sustain the legend. Six feet six inches tall and weighing over two hundred and fifty pounds, he was indeed a giant of a man.

Wolfe's whole personality, moreover, seemed to carry out the idea of bigness. At thirty-five he boasted that he had written more words than any other living writer his age. He loved to eat steaks and his capacity for them was enormous. Eccentric behavior, associated with a thatch of unruly black hair, wild staring eyes and waving arms, further contributed to the legend.

Here was a Paul Bunyan in the flesh, except that this American giant had a weakness. Wolfe stammered.

One story he told on himself went as follows. At a very late hour, he was stretched out on a divan in the apartment of James Thurber, the writer and cartoonist. Although he had overstayed his welcome, Wolfe was enjoying another drink. Finally his host politely asked him to leave.

Wolfe was indignant at this treatment, and according to his own account complained belligerently, "Is this what you call h-h-hospitality?"

Nevertheless, he was persuaded by other guests to leave.

A week or two later, Wolfe saw one of Thurber's cartoons drawn on the wall of a restaurant patronized almost exclusively by writers. In the drawing a huge brute of a man with Wolfe's features was being confronted by one of Thurber's timid souls standing on books piled on a chair. The caption said: "Mr. Wolfe, if you don't leave at once, I'm going to throw you out!"

Born on October 3, 1900 in Asheville, North Carolina, Thomas Wolfe was the son of W. O. Wolfe, a stonecutter and monument shop proprietor, and his wife, Julia Elizabeth Westall Wolfe. Almost every detail of young Tom's early life was later recorded in his first novel. He described every member of his family, father, mother, sisters and brothers, with biographical accuracy. He even called his fictional twin brothers Benjamin Harrison and Grover Cleveland, the given names of his actual twin brothers.

When he was not yet sixteen years old, Wolfe left home to enter the University of North Carolina at Chapel Hill.

Many stories are told of him during these carefree days as an undergraduate. All the evidence points to the fact that he was well-liked. One former schoolmate has described him affectionately as a "long, gangling, awkward, stammering, grinning, lovable fellow with the mountains written all over him."

Wolfe's contemporaries are said to have particularly loved him for his good fellowship. If the students needed someone to give a humorous speech at a smoker, or a rousing pep talk at a football rally, or a poetry reading at a tea party, the call went out for Tom Wolfe. He had a reputation as a wit.

One account of his college days has him dashing off a poem to be read at a student club meeting, arriving fifteen minutes late, and being fined twenty-five cents. He then without hesitation offered the convincing excuse that his lateness was caused by his literary effort. A reading of his poem proved his point. As a result a motion was solemnly made and carried that the fine be lifted because of the excellence of the poem.

Although Wolfe later pictured himself in a novel as being a suffering martyr at college, the evidence contradicts this. Actually, those were happy days. He was a successful student and he seemed to enjoy himself and his success.

Upon receiving his diploma, Wolfe selected Harvard University for his graduate work.

The Harvard period, from 1920 to 1923, was of immense significance in the development of Thomas Wolfe. It was during this time that he first prepared himself for a writing career. Furthermore, it was during this time that he discovered the vast world of books. At Cambridge, he was exposed not only to one of the world's finest libraries, but also to one of the world's most brilliant faculties.

This was the time of Professor George Pierce Baker's celebrated 47 Workshop in playwriting. And it was the time of other famous literary courses taught by such distinguished men as A. N. Murray, John Livingston Lowes, Chester Greenough, G. L. Kittredge and Irving Babbitt.

Wolfe plunged into graduate work with all his tremendous drive and energy. He read incessant, voraciously. If an assignment stated that certain works of a certain poet or dramatist were to be read, Wolfe would attempt to read everything the writer had ever published. Amazingly enough, he remembered a great deal of what he read. His memory was remarkable. Wolfe claimed that he had inherited this trait from his mother.

In spite of his scholarly diligence, he still found time for "mighty laughter and abounding energy which would cause him to split a door with his fist." He also had time for an occasional illegal drink (it was during prohibition), an evening at a well-known steak house in Boston, or a date with a young lady from Wellesley.

Upon completing his M.A. thesis at Harvard, Wolfe registered in the placement bureau for a position as a teacher. He really didn't want to teach. He had his mind set more on peddling the plays he had written in Baker's 47 Workshop. Arriving in New York, he tried to impress Broadway producers but failed. He accepted instead an appointment to the English faculty at Washington Square College, New York University.

Wolfe enjoyed the classroom work. At the same time he yearned for the day when he would not have to earn his living by teaching freshman composition. Almost every spare moment found him in his furnished room in Greenwich Village working on a novel. His friends said that he would often devote himself so diligently to his work that he would lose all sense of time.

His first novel was finally completed. The first publisher it was offered to, however, turned it down. Wolfe was living abroad when a second publishing company accepted the work. A letter from the editor of the company brought him hurrying back to New York.

Then came nearly an entire year of working with the unwieldy manuscript to get it into book form. Six days before the 1929 Wall Street crash which ushered in the Great Depression, Wolfe's work was published. This was *Look Homeward, Angel*.

Fame arrived for the author almost immediately.

Wolfe did not rest on his laurels. If anything, he drove himself harder than ever. Page after page of manuscript was produced by him in almost a frenzy of activity. He did resign his teaching position, however. But wherever he went, from a Brooklyn basement to Europe and back to Manhattan, he wrote twelve to fourteen hours a day. His editor commented that the original manuscript for his second novel, *Of Time and the River*, published in 1935, was two feet high, and this was but a part of the work he had turned out.

In May of 1938, Wolfe accepted a lecture engagement at Purdue University for the Annual Literary Banquet. He was not a good speaker and he knew it. Another one of his stories on himself was of how a friend had laughed at the idea of his being paid to speak publicly. "You don't know how to deliver a speech," the friend said.

"No," Wolfe replied, "but I can d-d-do a lot of stammering for th-th-three hundred dollars."

No one was aware, of course, that the Purdue affair was to be Wolfe's final public appearance. Shortly after, in Seattle, he came down with the illness which was to result in a journey back across the country for an emergency operation at Johns Hopkins.

He died on September 15, 1938.

Although he had titled a novel, which was published after his death, *You Can't Go Home Again*, a bitter comment on the way he had been reviled by his townspeople for his autobiographical first novel, nevertheless he arrived once again in Asheville—for burial. As the college friend said, "the mountains were written all over him." And it was in the mountains he found his final resting place.

The literary critics have never agreed on whether Wolfe was a great American novelist. They have generally agreed that he was a genius. But at least one critic upon evaluating his work insisted that "genius is not enough." All of his works have been alternately praised and condemned.

Perhaps time will tell. So far time has been good to Wolfe's memory. His books are found on every library shelf in the country. They are almost a required reading experience for young people.

Every now and then someone or another begins to look more closely at "the Wolfe legend."

More often than not, they discover that what was said about him was not legendary, but true.

Time in seconds——

Directions: Select the best answer and place the appropriate letter in the parentheses.

1. Thomas Wolfe once said that he had (a) eaten more steaks than any man his age; (b) written more words than any man his age; (c) read more books than any man his age; (d) walked more miles than any man his age. ( )
2. Wolfe was best known during his undergraduate days for his (a) poetry; (b) wit; (c) appetite; (d) football playing. ( )
3. When Wolfe reached manhood his height was (a) six feet; (b) six feet two; (c) six feet four; (d) six feet six. ( )
4. Before he reached his sixteenth birthday Wolfe entered (a) the University of North Carolina; (b) the University of South Carolina; (c) Chapel Hill College; (d) North Carolina State University. ( )
5. Wolfe is best known to the American public as a (a) poet; (b) biographer; (c) legend; (d) novelist. ( )
6. Wolfe was born in (a) 1800; (b) 1890; (c) 1900; (d) 1910. ( )
7. Wolfe's good fellowship at college was attributed to his (a) love of good food and drink; (b) willingness to participate on short notice; (c) skill as a poet; (d) superior intelligence. ( )
8. You may infer from the account of Wolfe's life that he was (a) extremely sensitive about his speech defect; (b) boasted about his speech defect; (c) tried to overcome his speech defect; (d) accepted good-naturedly his speech defect. ( )
9. Wolfe had twin brothers named (a) Benjamin Harrison and Grover Cleveland; (b) Benjamin Harrison and William McKinley; (c) Grover Cleveland and Theodore Roosevelt; (d) Grover Cleveland and Benjamin Franklin. ( )
10. Wolfe was at Harvard University for (a) one year; (b) two years; (c) three years; (d) four years. ( )
11. The Harvard period was of immense significance because it was there that Wolfe (a) met a Wellesley girl; (b) decided on a career; (c) discovered the world of books; (d) started to drink heavily. ( )
12. The famous 47 Workshop at Harvard University was conducted by a distinguished professor named (a) Babbitt; (b) Kittredge; (c) Murray; (d) Baker. ( )
13. Wolfe's teaching appointment was at (a) New York University; (b) University of Washington; (c) University of the State of New York; (d) George Washington University. ( )
14. Wolfe's father was a (a) shop proprietor; (b) school teacher; (c) restaurant owner; (d) small farmer. ( )
15. The manuscript of Wolfe's second novel was a stack of paper (a) one foot high; (b) two feet high; (c) three feet high; (d) four feet high. ( )
16. The first novel was entitled (a) The Wolfe Legend; (b) You Can't Go Home Again; (c) Of Time and the River; (d) Look Homeward, Angel. ( )
17. Wolfe spent the five years after the publication of his first novel in (a) classroom teaching; (b) travel abroad; (c) piling up more manuscript; (d) lecturing. ( )
18. He was stricken with what proved to be a fatal illness when (a) at Purdue University; (b) in Seattle, Washington; (c) in a Brooklyn basement; (d) at Johns Hopkins. ( )
19. One of the following statements most closely describes the feeling of the literary critics about Wolfe: (a) Wolfe was a genius; (b) Wolfe wrote works of genius; (c) Wolfe was a great American novelist; (d) Wolfe will always be required reading for young people. ( )
20. Wolfe died when he was (a) 35 years old; (b) 37 years old; (c) 38 years old; (d) 40 years old. ( )

VOCABULARY TEST I

Directions: Read each definition and underline the word which fits it most closely. Do not linger on any one item. Try to complete the test within five minutes. Your score will be the number correct within this time limit. For purposes of comparison with later scores, you may consider that 28-30 is excellent, 25-28 fair. Under 25 shows a need for intensive vocabulary study.

Time Yourself and Begin

1. To wet thoroughly
(a) downpour; (b) undulate; (c) drench; (d) merge; (e) swirl.

2. Meeting of members of a group or organization for a special purpose
(a) convention; (b) board; (c) conversation; (d) lodge; (e) agenda.

3. A definite plan of action
(a) map; (b) survey; (c) summary; (d) reaction; (e) policy.

4. Money derived from work, rent or interest
(a) capital; (b) profit; (c) income; (d) gross; (e) gain.

5. To move in a trembling way(?)
(a) quiver; (b) whimper; (c) rustle; (d) implore; (e) frighten.

6. Done of one's own free will
(a) impromptu; (b) voluntary; (c) decisive; (d) immediate; (e) purposive.

7. Payment of a debt
(a) claim; (b) settlement; (c) revenue; (d) honor; (e) allocation.

8. Result of multiplying one number by another
(a) aggregate; (b) multiplicand; (c) total; (d) factor; (e) product.

9. An upright shaft or support
(a) buttress; (b) tower; (c) pediment; (d) column; (e) bulwark.

10. Story handed down by tradition
(a) legend; (b) narrative; (c) epic; (d) chivalry; (e) idyll.

11. A state or ruler connected with another by treaty
(a) partisan; (b) ally; (c) combatant; (d) protagonist; (e) colleague.

12. Part of a bell that strikes against the side
(a) toll; (b) belfry; (c) knell; (d) clangor; (e) clapper.

13. A journey undertaken for discovery or exploration
(a) expedition; (b) cavalcade; (c) safari; (d) excursion; (e) mission.

14. Repayment for damage or loss
(a) compensation; (b) guilt; (c) fine; (d) clearance; (e) award.

15. Well-known because of character or accomplishment
(a) pompous; (b) personality; (c) famous; (d) candidate; (e) successful.

16. To follow as a result of another happening
(a) pursue; (b) ensue; (c) conclude; (d) deviate; (e) detour.

17. A sound expressing disapproval or contempt
(a) plaudit; (b) yelp; (c) critique; (d) hiss; (e) discord.

18. Movement in a forward direction
(a) procedure; (b) acceleration; (c) trail; (d) anticipation; (e) progress.

19. Highest point
(a) altitude; (b) apex; (c) angle; (d) arcanum; (e) arch.

20. Containing nothing whatever
(a) rarefied; (b) pure; (c) formless; (d) void; (e) ethereal.

21. Acknowledgment of payment
(a) account; (b) discount; (c) invoice; (d) receipt; (e) credit.

22. An introductory speech or writing
(a) anecdote; (b) preface; (c) homily; (d) diatribe; (e) dedication.

23. Measurement of distance northward or southward from the equator on the earth's surface
(a) tropics; (b) polarity; (c) latitude; (d) knots; (e) trajectory.

24. Human organ of voice
(a) palate; (b) larynx; (c) diaphragm; (d) chord; (e) vibrator.

25. A decrease in size or amount
(a) reduction; (b) division; (c) merger; (d) liquidation; (e) loss.

26. Apparatus for steering a ship
(a) bridge; (b) helm; (c) log; (d) gyroscope; (e) navigation.

27. Enter by force
(a) counteract; (b) attack; (c) invade; (d) march; (e) besiege.

28. Concentrated or extreme in effect
(a) intense; (b) pugnacious; (c) disastrous; (d) apathetic; (e) fulsome.

29. Having sides of equal length
    (a) equine; (b) isosceles; (c) parallel; (d) equilateral (e) cubic.
30. A dull, heavy sound
    (a) roar; (b) blow; (c) thud; (d) blast; (e) dirge.

Directions: Read this paragraph once and then answer the questions about it. Try to complete the entire exercise within five minutes.

BOOKS

By RICHARD J. CROHN

Experts in the book business estimate that there are over 17,000 retail bookstores in this country and perhaps another 1,000 stores that sell books in addition to other merchandise. Paperbound books, however, are sold at more than 100,000 outlets today—newsstands, drug stores, stationery stores, cigar stores, supermarkets, variety stores, department stores, airports, bus and railroad terminals, and, of course, bookstores. Wherever magazines are sold, you are likely to find paperbound books. It is this marriage of book publishing and magazine distribution, combined with low prices and attractive packaging, that has made it possible to sell millions of books in areas where virtually no books may have been sold in the past. It would be hard to find a community in this country today that does not have paperbound books available at prices within the reach of everyone. As a result, millions of people who may never have had the opportunity or inclination to visit a bookstore (if they were lucky enough to have one locally) are now regular book purchasers.

Directions: Select the best answer and place the appropriate letter in the parentheses.

1. The main idea expressed in this paragraph is that (a) the book business is booming at present; (b) book publishing and magazine distribution are "married"; (c) millions of people are now buying books who never bought them before; (d) paperbound books are sold everywhere except in bookstores.　　　　( )

2. According to the author, outlets for paperbound books number more than (a) one million; (b) one hundred thousand; (c) fifteen hundred; (d) one thousand.　　　　( )

3. It might be inferred from this brief passage that the author (a) approves of paperbound books; (b) disapproves of paperbound books; (c) feels that paperbound books are a temporary fad; (d) feels that paperbound books will eventually replace magazines.

DIRECTIONS FOR SCORING

Reading Rate. To find your reading rate in words per minute for the reading selection, turn to the TABLE FOR DETERMINING READING RATE IN WORDS PER MINUTE in the Appendix.

Answers to Questions. First, check the answers to the twenty multiple-choice questions for the timed reading selection in the CORRECTION KEY TO TESTS, found in the Appendix. Multiply the number you have right by five to get your comprehension score in percentages. For example, if you had thirteen correct out of twenty, set down your score as 65%.

Finally, check the answers to both the vocabulary test and the paragraph analysis test.

Important Note: Please do not look ahead at the answers to subsequent tests and exercises. A casual glance at the correction key will not matter, but a deliberate attempt to study and remember answers will defeat the purpose of accurately measuring your progress over a period of time.

Progress Chart. Reading rate and all comprehension, vocabulary, and paragraph analysis scores should be entered in the places provided in your PERSONAL PROGRESS CHART, found in the Appendix.

SOME WORKING TOOLS

You have already used two important working tools if you have seriously attempted to make this book an effective instrument of learning: a pencil and a watch with a sweep hand (or a stopwatch).

Now more tools and materials will be required as you go along. Plan to get these easy-to-obtain and relatively inexpensive items before you continue. A checklist follows:

1. Small notebook
2. Large notebook (or diary)
3. Pack of 3 x 5 white index cards (plain or ruled)
4. Egg timer, a kitchen timer, or a stopwatch
5. Desk dictionary

STUDY ASSIGNMENT

Word Recognition. Your first study assignment is to make a list of any words you believe you have failed to recognized upon sight. Do not think at this time of the *meaning* of these words. Instead, consider the *form*, note whether or not the words begin with vowels or consonants, count syllables, observe spelling. **Say Them Aloud.**

Some words unfamiliar to you will perhaps be found in the vocabulary test. But include also in your listing words taken from any passage you have read so far.

Keep the listing in a small notebook, or preferably on separate 3 x 5 file cards. Print them in large letters. For example, if you happen to select the word "diatribe" as one you are unfamiliar with, print it in your notebook (one word to a page) or on a separate card.

Look at these words from time to time. Repeat them aloud. Look up the pronunciation in your dictionary, if necessary.

Further instructions concerning the use of these word cards, which will involve the use of a dictionary, will be given in later chapters.

CHAPTER THREE

THE WONDERFUL READING MACHINE

As your eyes follow this line of print across the column and down the page, you may feel that they move continuously. This is not so.

Reading is instead characterized by a **stop—start—stop—start** movement of the eyes. You see words or phrases or short sentences only **at the instant** when your eyes stop.

At this instant, your brain is busily engaged in organizing the complicated data presented to it through the lines and curves of printers' type.

You are not merely **seeing**, you are **reading**.

How the eyes and brain of a human being accomplish this amazing feat is not exactly known to science. The process may be described somewhat as follows:

Light rays from the printed page enter the clear, transparent window of the eye called the **cornea** (see the illustration below). These rays then pass through the small round hole in the **iris** known as the **pupil** of the eye. As they enter the **lens** the rays are bent and brought into relatively accurate focus on the **retina.**

This produces an image instantaneously transmitted by impulses along the **optic nerve** and then through various brain centers.

Vision actually takes place in the brain and the images are interpreted there. Here also the impulses from your two eyes are coordinated into a single picture. Again, science doesn't quite know how it's done.

Sometimes things go wrong with the process. Human eyes are rarely perfect instruments. But the brain often makes up for any deficiencies in sight.

Seagulls may have remarkable vision—but a seagull can't be taught to read.

Only a human being can follow the printed symbols on this page, group them together in a certain way, and extract information from them.

Endowed with the capacity to read, you almost feel obliged to read well.

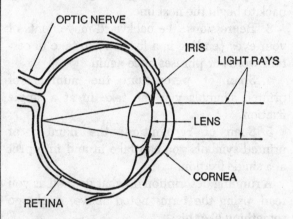

People who don't read well often blame it on their eyes. This may produce a mild anxiety which further distracts them as they read. The eyes feel even more tired and strained. Print becomes blurred. Headaches are likely to occur.

Individuals may actually become quite ill, yet not even remember that it all started when they originally blamed their eyes for difficulty in reading.

The difficulty is far more likely to result from lack of skill than from lack of good eyesight.

Tough and resilient, the eyes are actually one of the most efficient sense organs in the human body. Barring accident or disease, they are ready for a long lifetime of steady use.

Slight differences in the structure of one or both eyes may cause any one of several ocular problems. But these are all usually solved by glasses.

THE READING PROCESS

Several terms may help you to understand the activity of your eyes and brain when you read. These terms need not be learned but simply noted as follows:

1. **Fixations:** the pauses your eyes make to take in a certain portion of the printed line.

2. **Return sweep:** the smooth operation of your eyes when you complete one line and go back to begin the next line.

3. **Regressions:** the backward movements of your eyes (ending in a fixation) to take in certain words or phrases once again.

4. **Span of perception:** the number of printed symbols you can take in at a single fixation.

5. **Span of recognition:** the number of printed symbols you can take in **and interpret** at a single fixation.

A running description of what goes on as you read, using the terms noted above, might go something like this:

Beginning a paragraph with a **fixation,** your eyes follow along a line of print with stop—start—stop—start jerky movements.

Each time your eyes stop you have a certain **span of perception.** Actual reading occurs during these brief pauses, or **fixations.**

Your **span of recognition,** or your ability to understand and interpret a certain group of printed symbols, may equal your **span of perception,** or the number of symbols your eyes can take in at a single glance.

At the end of each line, your eyes race swiftly back to the beginning of the next line in a re- **turn sweep.**

Occasionally, however, your eyes go back further to look again at a word or phrase. This is a **regression.**

INSTRUMENTS AND DEVICES

Mechanical ways to analyze eye movements have been available since the beginning of the century.

The most advanced method makes use of a special movie camera which records **fixations, return sweeps,** and **regressions** on a photographic film.

Another class of machines includes those constructed to pace or control reading speed. An adjustable bar or shutter or a beam of light is lowered at timed rates over the printed page. You may accelerate or slow it down as you wish.

A third group of machines includes instruments and devices for exposing words or other visual material on a screen for controlled periods of time as brief as one-hundredth of a second. They are all based on the principle of a **tachistoscope** (literal meaning: **viewing swiftly**), an apparatus invented years ago by psychologists for experimental work in vision.

The highest development of the tachistoscopic method is a type of motion picture film designed to present reading selections by flashing consecutive phrases on a screen.

BOOK-CENTERED PRACTICE

Although many of the exercises which follow in this book are based on tachistoscopic methods, it would not be accurate to say that book-centered practice and machine-centered practice in reading will produce identical results.

In fact, research studies are not conclusive on the relative merits of one as against the other.

Evidence exists, however, that although machines may stimulate some individuals to spec-

tacular initial gains in reading efficiency, book practice is much more likely to result in steady and relatively permanent gains.

Without question, the emphasis has lately shifted from machines to books in college and university reading centers, in commercial reading laboratories, and in business and industry training programs.

Think about what you are reading. Forget about what your eyes are doing.

Search for meaning on the printed page. Let your eye movements take care of themselves.

In any acceleration of your reading and improvement of comprehension it is your own efforts that determine the results, not the mechanical means employed.

The person who pushes a button and then sits back patiently expecting a machine to improve his reading is bound to be disappointed.

Even this book, or any other book on self-improvement which takes the form of discussions, tests and exercises is a kind of machine made of paper and ink.

And you can't expect it to work miracles by itself.

Your own individual effort is required. Motivation, purpose, drive, alert eyes and brain, and your own *will* to better yourself are all needed.

Keep in mind always that the most remarkable reading machine ever developed is **you— You Yourself.**

SEEING AND READING

Before going ahead with the next part of this chapter, make sure you will not be interrupted for fifteen minutes, and have your timing device handy.

Instructions: As every schoolboy knows, light exists. And the human eye is sensitive to light. These are scientific certainties. In the article which follows, these certainties and some problems which may arise are discussed in simple nontechnical terms. The moment you finish reading the article, jot down your time **in seconds** in the space provided. Then answer the questions.

Time Yourself and Begin

YOUR EYES

Four ocular difficulties account almost completely for the fact that about two out of every three people in the United States wear glasses.

These difficulties may be briefly described as follows:

1. Hyperopia, or far-sightedness.

When you are reading at close range, parallel rays of light from the printed page pass through the lens of each eye and theoretically come into focus **behind** the retina.

The retina may be compared to the sensitized film in a camera, where focusing normally occurs. Print thus appears blurred. Words some distance away, however, on a billboard or a traffic sign, may be in perfect focus.

To correct for close reading, glasses are usually required.

2. Myopia, or near-sightedness.

Parallel rays of light from the printed page in this case pass through the lens of each eye and come into focus **in front** of the retina.

The reader has only to bring the page closer to get the proper focus. This may not be a handicap at all for reading.

The extreme myope often lives in a visible world measured by the length of his arms, and this may result in a pattern of activities which can be performed efficiently within those limits. Near-sighted persons should be and often are excellent readers. Glasses are usually required for focusing on far objects.

3. Presbyopia.

This is a common type of far-sightedness caused by a gradual hardening of the lenses of the eyes. Accelerated after people reach forty or forty-five years of age, this condition is correctible by glasses.

4. Astigmatism.

Caused by imperfections either in the outer covering of the eyeball or in the lens, astigmatism is also caused by the muscles being out of balance.

Twelve muscles, six for each eye, must coordinate. When you read, the parallel rays of light from the printed page going through the lens of each eye must not only be brought into focus but also converge to produce a single image. If the muscles are weak, they will tire quickly and the reader will have to strain his eyes to keep the print from blurring.

Eye exercises may be helpful in such cases to tone up the muscles.

Sometimes the muscles do their job too well and cause the eyes to cross slightly. This may produce a blurred, double image.

Both of these varieties of muscular imbalance can usually be corrected by exercises or glasses.

An exaggeration of the muscle condition occurs in convergent or divergent **squint.** This is a condition when an eye is permanently turned either inward or outward. Then the individual may have a social problem but **not necessarily a reading problem.**

The physical operation of reading is in fact simplified for the person who squints. He uses but one eye at a time for reading. When this eye tires, he merely shifts to the other one. Either way, the brain obligingly suppresses images received with the eye that is idle at the moment.

A partial list of possible causes for eye troubles might include local conditions such as glaucoma, cataract, or conjunctivitis, as well as general conditions such as anemia, diabetes, or high blood pressure.

The list might be continued with innumerable other things such as abuse of the eyes, improper diet, incorrect glasses, and even lack of sleep, sunshine and fresh air.

Are you abusing your eyes when you read a great deal?

Not at all, according to the best medical judgment. The more you use your eyes the better they are. If your eyes tire, you can give them a quick rest by focusing on a far point. A conventional reading break for a student is ten minutes out of every hour. Five minutes out of every half-hour might be even better.

What about the controversial subject of reading in bed?

The consensus of ophthalmological opinion is that if you are comfortable and have adequate light you can read under almost any circumstances.

In a condition known as **aniseikonia,** each eye receives a different size image and thus may cause print to blur. Everyone has this condition to some extent, since no two eyes in a pair are absolutely identical in size or shape. In some persons there is a marked difference.

Although sometimes things go wrong with your eyes, in most instances they are corrected either by your brain or by man's ingenious invention—spectacles.

Everyone should have at least one examination by an ophthalmologist. If you are under forty or forty-five, you will probably need no more than a single visit unless you have definite symptoms of eye trouble.

Over forty or forty-five, you will probably need to have regular examinations, depending on the advice of your doctor.

A brief vocabulary lesson on eye specialists might prove helpful at this point.

Remember, an optician grinds optical lenses; an optometrist examines your eyes and fits you for glasses; and an ophthalmologist (or oculist) is a medical doctor, who examines your eyes and can both prescribe medication and perform operations.

Eye troubles are sometimes caused by the lack of a proper diet.

Vitamins A, B₁, B₂, and C have all proved essential for the health of the eyes. A deficiency of vitamin A, found in fresh leafy vegetables, butter, eggs and milk, may not only result in night-blindness but also inflammation of the cornea.

Deficiencies of the vitamin B group may result in a variety of eye impairment diseases due to nerve or muscle weakness. Whole yeast and liver are two rich sources of the B group.

A deficiency of vitamin C, found in highest concentration in fresh or frozen citrus fruits and juices, may have a serious effect on the eyes by causing rupture of capillaries.

Although specific needs for vitamins are highly individual, doctors can usually determine these needs and prescribe accordingly. Regular medical check-ups as well as regular eye check-ups are thus advisable.

General good health ordinarily means good eye health, whether you have to wear glasses or not.

No evidence exists that eyes wear out from hard use.

It is questionable whether, when you complain of "tired" eyes, it is actually your eyes that are tired. More often it is your brain.

Many persons who feel, after a day in the office, that their eyes could not possibly take in another column of figures or line of print, will then go home and spend the evening comfortably racing through a mystery novel or western.

A healthy nervous system, adequate light, any modern book type used by publishers today, and corrective glasses (if needed) will provide perfect conditions for your eyes to do their part.

The rest is up to you, to improve your communication skills and speed up your reading.

Time in seconds———

Directions: Select the best answer and place the appropriate letter in the parentheses.

1. The estimated number of people who wear glasses in the United States is (a) one out of every two; (b) one out of every three; (c) two out of every three; (d) two out of every five. ( )

2. The medical term for far-sightedness is (a) hyperopia; (b) astigmatism; (c) presbyopia; (d) myopia. ( )

3. The article states that (a) eye exercises do more harm than good; (b) all difficulties can be cured with eye exercises; (c) exercises may be helpful in toning up eye muscles; (d) eye exercises may cause squint. ( )

4. Reading in bed is considered as (a) all right if you have reading comfort; (b) not harmful if done by candlelight; (c) dangerous under all circumstances; (d) not a topic for discussion since it is controversial. ( )

5. Printed words may seem blurred on the page to readers with aniseikonia because (a) the image is focused behind the retina; (b) the image is focused in front of the retina; (c) the lens of the eye has hardened; (d) each eye receives a different image. ( )

6. The number of muscles coordinating a pair of eyes is (a) six; (b) eight; (c) ten; (d) twelve. ( )

7. One of the following statements accurately reflects the views of the article on nutrition and eye health: (a) everyone should take a vitamin pill daily; (b) regular medical check-ups give the doctor an opportunity to determine your vitamin needs and prescribe accordingly; (c) vitamins can always be obtained in proper amounts if you eat three meals a day; (d) vitamins have little relation to eye health. ( )

8. According to the article, a complaint of "tired" eyes may actually mean (a) a serious need for glasses; (b) a sign that a medical examination is needed; (c) a lack of sufficient vitamin C; (d) a tired brain. ( )

9. The article defines an optician as one who (a) grinds lenses; (b) fits you for glasses; (c) is an M.D.; (d) is the same as an ophthalmologist. ( )

10. The article carries the strong implication that (a) most reading problems are the result of

eye difficulties; (b) human eyes are hard-working instruments of sight which, barring accident or disease, will give a lifetime of service; (c) balanced meals will help you to speed up your reading; (d) all anyone needs to improve reading is a book with clear type and adequate light.   ( )

DIRECTIONS FOR SCORING

Reading Rate. To find your reading rate in words per minute for the article entitled "Your Eyes," turn back to your time in seconds as noted in the space provided. Then look for your wpm rate in the TABLE FOR DETERMINING READING RATE IN WORDS PER MINUTE.

Answers to Questions. Your ability to recall material you have read as well as to comprehend it is being measured. If you wish, you may reread the article and then look over and make any changes in your answers you feel necessary. This permission is granted in this instance since, although the material on eyes is presented in a popular style, unfamiliar terms might block comprehension.

Check your answers in the CORRECTION KEY TO EXERCISES.

Progress Chart. Reading rate and comprehension scores should be entered immediately in your PERSONAL PROGRESS CHART.

ANOTHER WORKING TOOL

In order to help you increase both your **span of perception** and your **span of recognition**, a series of exercises will be present throughout this book using numbers, words, phrases, and short sentences.

Most readers of this book have the capacity to see at least four related words, totaling some 24 letters, and spaces, **at a single fixation.** Many readers, with practice, will be able to see and comprehend even more than this.

Instructions: Cut out a rectangular opening in a 3 x 5 file card according to the measurements given below.

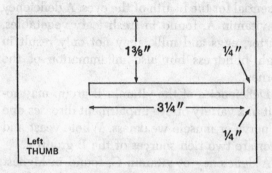

Directions for Using Eye-Span Card. Place the card between thumb and forefinger of the left hand. (Left-handed persons will use the right hand.) Center the card in the column so that the first asterisk in each eye-span exercise appears in the center of the rectangular opening. Then move the card rapidly downward past the digits, words, phrases or sentences (as the case may be) to the next asterisk.

Follow instructions carefully for each exercise.

Note: You may practice these exercises without using the cut-out card, if you prefer. You simply lower a 3 x 5 card down the column as you would a descending shutter. The cut-out card is more effective, however, since it keeps your eyes focused on the material to be read.

EYE-SPAN EXERCISES

Instructions: Most people can see a four-digit number at a glance and remember it long enough either to say it aloud or write it down. In this exercise, you will begin with a single digit and work up to four digits. Write down the numbers on a separate sheet of paper. Move your card rapidly from one asterisk to the next. Do not linger on the number.

Begin

```
        *
        7
        *
        1
        *
        3
        *
        8
        *
        5
        *
        9
        *
        6
        *
       27
        *
       17
        *
       83
        *
       79
        *
       42
        *
       69
        *
       71
        *
      339
        *
      373
        *
      738
        *
      717
        *
      883
        *
      962
        *
      534
        *
     9336
        *
```

```
     4217
        *
     1743
        *
     5283
        *
     6152
        *
     8235
        *
     6381
        *
```

Many people can also handle longer sequences very easily, seeing and recalling them without effort. One reason may be that constant practice with telephone numbers has made the three-and-four-digit sequences a familiar one to a great section of the population.

Even some of the small children in our modern society are skilled in looking up numbers in a telephone directory and remembering them long enough to dial.

This ability to look up information quickly and accurately for immediate use is of extreme importance in efficient reading.

Before going on to the sequence, you are first to answer certain questions concerning the telephone numbers in sequence of three-and-four numbers.

Allow yourself only one minute for the task.

Below you will find five questions. The answers to the questions are in the sample section of a page torn from an old directory which follows. At the end of the sample section are five questions and spaces for the answers to the questions.

Instructions: Read the first question; look for the answer in the directory; place the answer in the correct space. Then go back and read the second question, and proceed as before.

Time Yourself and Begin

Sanner G. T. r 1950 W Market 569-8160
SanSoucie V B r 1350 2nd 569-6462
Santymire Charles L r 365 E Phila 717-3257
Sargen Gertrude L chiropodist
   Rosenmiller Blvd. 879-5234
Sauder H R r 1412 MtRose av 689-6908
Saul Chas F r R D 5 247-5512
Saul Spurgeon L r 553 Ogontz 751-9563
Saunders Earl H r R D 7 288-3006
Sauppee Anna M Mrs r 731 S George ...439-7258
Sauppee John E r 118 W King 953-4112
Sawyer John L Rev r 747 Madison 247-2431
Sayers Pete r 216 W Jackson 569-3441
Saylor Blair & Bro cigars candy who ret
   41 N Geo 288-1349
Saylor Bros whol 7 S Belvidere 717-7123
Saylor C C r 1023 W Princess 879-0458
Saylor C E r 108 N Penn 288-6151
Saylor D E r 722 W Phila 879-4378
Saylor George A r 347 E Poplar 439-3425
Saylor H O coal & ice 601 Hay 249-2140
Saylor H O r 1017 E Phila 832-4467
Saylor Joseph W r 100 N Findlay 879-0010
Saylor LaMont Z ins 7 S Belvidere 717-7123
Saylor Leona R r Lincoln Hiway 953-3706
Scarborough John H r 1418 W Market ..214-9538

1. What is the telephone number of G. T. Sanner?

2. What is the telephone number of a coal and ice dealer?

3. What is the number of the Saylor who is in the insurance business?

4. What is the Reverend John L. Sawyer's number?

5. What is the number of a chiropodist?

Answers:

1. _____
2. _____
3. _____
4. _____
5. _____

Time in seconds_____

EYE-SPAN EXERCISES CONTINUED

Five digits:

69154
31257
65279
35448
39238
42184
51215
32341
43527
43326
24316
17571
59141
72357
34186
29162
42487
79694
46123
37272

Six digits:

*

595717

*

343143

*

452145

*

257696

*

127212

*

536154

*

926692

*

384571

*

252585

*

492578

*

296521

*

674967

*

796173

*

413181

*

531239

*

692768

*

796951

*

383127

*

423491

*

392639

*

STUDY ASSIGNMENT

Practice a few minutes each day, preferably at a regular time, with your Eye-Span Card. Write the numbers on a separate piece of paper. Do an entire series before you check for accuracy.

Through repetition you will, of course, eventually commit the numbers to memory. You are then urged to construct your own number tests, using a typewriter and plain white bond paper. Proceed as follows:

First strike the asterisk key, then double-space and write the number below. Double-space again and strike the asterisk, then double-space and write the next number below. Continue down the page.

For best results, prepare your material a day or so before you use it for practice.

Another suggested exercise requires a telephone directory and a dial telephone.

Select any number at random and as you quickly glance at it check it with a pencil mark. Then without raising the handset, dial the number. Refer back to the directory, then select the next number, tick it off and repeat the operation.

An easier variation of this exercise is to turn to the index of any book and let your eyes pick out any subject at random. Note the page quickly, then immediately turn to the page. Do this repeatedly, with your eyes going at random from topic to topic.

A final suggestion is to use your own ingenuity in discovering ways to improve both your number perception and your number memory.

Even the game of noting automobile license numbers as you ride along the highway may be helpful. So may practice in adding a column of figures quickly and correctly.

Or simply glance at a piece of statistical information in your daily newspaper, then close your eyes and answer the question: **What was that number?**

CHAPTER FOUR

YOUR READING AUTOBIOGRAPHY

Now is the time to stop and ask yourself a few personal questions.

Suppose you were a robot that could read. For eyes you probably would have a photoelectric cell which could take in messages and transmit them to your electronic brain to produce certain mechanical actions.

Hurrying up this "reading" process for the sake of efficiency would be simple enough. With only a few adjustments and dial settings you would immediately start to operate at any speed desired, within certain limits.

But you are a flesh-and-blood being, not a robot. To your reading improvement effort, as to everything else you undertake, you bring a whole background of personal attitudes and experiences.

Added to these is the very human characteristic of resistance to change.

Your present reading habits have a long history behind them. Changing these habits means, perhaps, changing ways of doing things that you learned early in your childhood and now take for granted as second nature.

This is seldom easy to accomplish.

It has already been pointed out that your program of self-help in reading improvement needs a strong motivation and persistence in carrying out the instructions contained in this book.

Another factor you will find extremely helpful is **insight**.

INSIGHT

You may at one time or another say to yourself something like this: I really want to read better and faster, but all my efforts seem blocked, somehow. Either I can't take in what I read, or I can't concentrate, or I can't remember, or I keep going back and back, or something else is always wrong.

You may have a strong urge to find out why there is such a difference between what you really want and what you actually have.

The first step is to get a true picture of both your strengths and weaknesses.

You must become aware of your **Self** in relation to your present capabilities in the art and skill of reading. You must try to understand your **Self** as well as accept your **Self**.

Through this self-awareness, and self-understanding, and self-acceptance may come the flashes of **insight** into your own problems so essential to self-improvement.

This chapter has been written to assist you with your task of self-evaluation.

KNOW YOURSELF

The initial reading test in CHAPTER TWO has perhaps already given you a general picture of your present level of reading.

Now you are asked to attempt, in writing, a picture of your reading self.

Since you will be writing for your own information and yours alone, you need have no feelings of reticence. The whole purpose of this continuing exercise in self-evaluation is to give you as much knowledge as possible about your habit patterns, communication skills, and attitudes of mind.

Once some of these things are known and understood, you will find them far less formidable, far easier to modify or change.

HOW TO PROCEED WITH SELF-STUDY

Take five or ten minutes each day to get down on paper, preferably in a notebook or diary, as much about yourself as you can. Start with your reading experience to date.

Continue adding to what you have written whenever any new idea comes to mind. Do this throughout the entire period you are working to improve your reading.

You may fill not only one notebook but several.

Of considerable importance, the very act of writing down your thoughts is likely to help you with your reading. Although reading specialists still have no conclusive objective data concerning the interrelationship of the communication skills, many are nevertheless convinced that the interrelationship exists.

That is, if you learn to read better, you will learn to write better. If you learn to write better, you will learn to speak better. If you learn to speak better, you will learn to read better.

And so on and so forth.[1]

Much of what you write about yourself may not seem to have any bearing at all on your reading problems. Yet it may lead you to remember other bits of information that strike you as having startling application.

Insight into your own problems, when it comes, is likely to come suddenly and unexpectedly.

At the end of this discussion you will find a suggested data sheet which may help stimulate your thinking about yourself.

Refer to it now. Then look at it again from time to time as you continue to read this chapter.

[1] Readers of this book who are seriously interested in the interrelationship of the communication skills and further self-improvement are referred to two other books in the series: *The Art of Writing Made Simple* and *The Art of Speaking Made Simple*. Later reference will be made to the book on vocabulary development entitled, *Word Mastery Made Simple.*

A PERSONAL CHECKLIST

If you have looked over the PERSONAL DATA SHEET you will have noted that the opening question asks if you ever have had eye trouble. Whether you have had or not, you might note the date on which you last had an eye examination and judge for yourself whether it's time for another.

Surprisingly enough, some persons have **never** had an eye examination by a qualified medical doctor.

Your general health might be noted next. A great many persons have reading difficulties because they are in a run-down condition. Your doctor can tell you if you are in one, and what to do about it.

Next, have you any particular mannerisms as you read?

Some individuals cannot read anything at all without muttering to themselves. If their family and friends are too polite to tell them they may even be oblivious of the habit.

Other readers move their lips silently.

Still others don't move their lips or make a sound, but are nevertheless vocalizing deep in their throats. Their muscles constantly strain to form each syllable of the printed words. Consequently they can never read any faster silently than it would take them orally, even for the simplest material.

Much of the mystery surrounding these and other individual habit patterns may be dispelled by a modest amount of personal research.

Are you a word-by-word reader?

Then, first, hands off!

If you have the habit of following a line of print with a guiding finger or pencil, stop it. Keep your hands off as you read, unless you are turning a page, for they will only slow you down.

Next, keep your head still!

Your eyes are efficient, hard-working instruments of sight which can easily follow printed words across a column or a page. Moving your head from side to side doesn't help them in the performance of their job. To break this habit, you might prop your elbows on a table, a book in front of you, and place your head firmly between your hands.

Finally, read silently!

Reading aloud and reading silently are two separate skills requiring quite different techniques. Every literate adult has a potential of becoming an efficient silent reader. Expert oral readers are rare.

Everyone learns to read aloud, however, before learning to read silently. As a child you were very likely praised for your oral reading and encouraged to read aloud for family and friends. Encouragement and praise are not easy to come by, especially for children. The act of reading aloud is thus often felt to be some special ability which needs to be guarded.

This is admirable as far as it goes, in the first stages of learning to read. A problem arises when the technique of saying each word separately is transferred to silent reading. What is good in one situation is not necessarily good in another.

The silent reader who lingers on each syllable of each word will have a hard time breaking through the barrier of the spoken word rate of reading, usually below 200 words per minute.

No matter what the type of material being read, or the purpose of the reader, the words-per-minute rate remains about the same in oral reading.

Sports page and editorial page, feature article and essay, comic book and textbook, popular fiction and the classics, *all* are read at the same rate orally.

Finger-pointing, head-moving, lip-moving and vocalization are the visible and audible signs of oral word-by-word reading.

More difficult to detect is inward vocalization.

In this instance, your vocal cords are going through all the motions of oral reading but without sound. This is a paradox which might be described as reading aloud silently.

Various methods can be used to determine whether or not you are vocalizing inwardly. For example, hold a finger across your lips as you read. Or touch your fingers lightly to your throat. Movement or vibration can easily be detected.

You may even notice that your throat feels tired after any sustained reading.

One trick that often proves helpful in both discovering and breaking the vocalization habit is to clench a pencil in your teeth as you read. You might even try gum chewing, which will perhaps tire your jaw but nevertheless keep your vocal cords rested.

Ask someone to observe you. Try every means you can think of to discover any signs of vocalization.

A full awareness on your part is almost essential in breaking this habit pattern.

WHEN ENGLISH IS A SECOND LANGUAGE

The next item on the checklist concerns the language or languages spoken in your home during your childhood.

You may wonder why such a question is relevant. For most readers of this book the answer will undoubtedly be English.

Nevertheless some people who have spoken and written and read English for as long as they can remember spent their infancy in a foreign language environment.

Words in any language which have a reality for an infant in the early formative years may continue to be full of deep meaning for him in adult life.

Such words are those connected with the intimacies of family life. They make a deep and lasting impression. They are said to be emotionally "loaded."

But what happens if a child is taken out of this foreign language environment at any time after the age of four, five or six and placed in another?

In order to get on socially with his playmates, his schoolmates and teachers, and later his associates in adult life, he must learn an entirely new set of words.

Meanwhile, those words he learned in babyhood, although charged with emotional meaning, become blocked off. (It is an observable fact in American life that most children who come from homes where a language other than English is spoken have a strong resistance to speaking anything but English outside the home.)

This blocking off of the language of early childhood experience may in some cases create an unconscious resistance to learning the second language well.

The result is often poor speech, poor writing, and especially poor reading.

Again, awareness of the roots of the problem may be of help in solving the problem.

Sometimes a deliberate return to the childhood language through foreign language study in school may result in an entirely new and improved approach to the second language, English.

INTERESTS

As you proceed with your reading autobiography you might consider **reading interests.**

Look back into your past as far as you can remember. Think about the things you have read. Reflect upon what you have liked and what you have disliked.

Write down the kinds of books or stories you have read. If you can recall titles, note them.

Try to answer the following questions:

Were you read to as a child?

Did you read aloud to others?

What were some of the details of your earliest reading?

Even minor and seemingly insignificant details may have some meaning for you in the light of further study in this book.

A close look at the reading habits of most people shows that they read a great deal less than you might expect. Furthermore, no concrete evidence indicates that the well-educated read more or read better than those with less education, ruling out complete illiterates.

Most people glance over a newspaper or two daily, perhaps read a magazine or two monthly, attempt a piece of full-length fiction or nonfiction rarely if at all.

Many cut their reading teeth on comic books and a few are still chewing away on this lean diet as adults.

Once a source of satisfaction to a great many people, reading as a means to a fuller, richer life is fast becoming a lost art.

Individuals often read now because they have to read—to hold a position, to pass an examination, to maintain social prestige. Occasionally they buy books they have heard talked about or subscribe to a book club that sounds interesting. Sensationalism also holds a strong attraction for the reading public.

But many persons are frequently discontented about reading because what should be a pleasure is actually a chore.

You might give more than a little thought to exactly *why* you read. This could provide a clue to why you want to read better and faster. If you list your dissatisfactions with your present reading methods, this may help you to formulate a goal.

A clear idea of your present reading needs plus a statement of your present reading shortcomings will equal for you a recognizable target to shoot at.

Perhaps no single cause will ever be found to explain why some otherwise alert, normal, efficient individuals cannot read well. Instead, a complexity of causes may exist.

Your continuing reading autobiography will give you a means of gaining valuable insight into the dynamics of these causes.

PERSONAL DATA SHEET

Name _____

Have you ever had eye trouble? _____

Describe: _____

_____

Date of last eye examination: _____

Date of last physical examination: _____

Mannerisms while reading:

Saying words aloud

Moving lips silently

Following words with finger or pencil

Nail biting

Teeth grinding

Hands constantly to face

Other

Comment on mannerisms: _____

_____

Have you any idea when you first began to have such mannerisms? _____

_____

Are they associated in your mind with any situation or incident? _____

_____

Language spoken in your childhood home: _____

If English is a second language, can you still read, write and speak your first language? _____

Can you remember any incidents connected with reading when you were a child? _____

_____

How would you describe your present reading ability?

Poor

Fair

Good

Comment: _____

_____

If dissatisfied with present ability, specify reasons:

_____

Do you enjoy reading? _____

If you have any feeling of resistance to reading, have you any idea when it began? _____

Do you feel that you received a satisfactory education? _____

If not, list reasons for dissatisfaction: _____

_____

_____

_____

Do you wish to continue your education? In what direction? Have you made concrete plans to do so? If not, why not? Comment fully: _____

_____

_____

_____

List three books you remember as having enjoyed more than any others in your whole life: _____

_____

_____

Do you still prefer that same type of reading matter? _____

List your reading preferences in general and if possible analyze the reasons for them: _____

_____

_____

_____

_____

_____

What, primarily, do you read for?

Information

Excitement

Relaxation

Identification with characters

Other

Comment: _____

_____

_____

Do your reading habits and/or mannerisms change depending on the type of book you are reading? Can you explain this? _____

_____

Write a description of yourself reading a book, giving details of your posture, attitude, expression, etc., etc., as if you were another person looking on.

What specifically do you wish to accomplish by carrying out the program outlined in this book? Describe in detail.

HOW OTHERS SAW THEMSELVES

Almost everyone finds it easier to write about personal experiences than about any other subject. Through setting down these personal experiences on paper, the writer often reveals more about himself than he perhaps intended.

Even though memory often plays tricks and what appears to be fact often is really fiction, yet the genuine "truth" about the person is often found between the lines of an autobiography.

Instructions: Below are three selections from personal histories by well-known authors of both the past and present. Read the passages rapidly but carefully. Time yourself as you read, and jot down your time in seconds in the space provided. Then answer the questions.

It is suggested that you do each exercise at separate times.

Time Yourself and Begin

THE DAYS WHEN I READ
By MICHEL DE MONTAIGNE

It is easy enough for a man to walk who has a horse at his command. The invalid is not to be pitied who has a cure up his sleeve. And such is the advantage I receive from books.

They relieve me from idleness, rescue me from company I dislike, and blunt the edge of my grief, if it is not too extreme. They are the comfort and solitude of my old age.

When I am attacked by gloomy thoughts, nothing helps me so much as running to my books. They quickly absorb me and banish the clouds from my mind. And they don't rebel because I use them only for lack of pastimes more natural and alive. They always receive me with the same welcome.

Yet I make as little use of them, at most, as a miser does of his gold. Knowing I can enjoy them when I please, I am satisfied by their mere possession. I never travel without books, either in war or in peace. Still, I often pass days and months without looking in them. "I'll read by-and-by," I say to myself, "or tomorrow, or when I choose." Meanwhile time slips away, and no harm is done. For you can't imagine how comforting it is to know they are by my side, to be opened when I will; and what a refreshment they are to my life.

They are the best provisions I have found for this human journey. And I am sorry indeed for the man of understanding who is deprived of them.

But reading books is as laborious as any other work, and can be as great a menace to the health. Neither should we be deceived by the pleasure of it, which is the same pleasure that traps the man of affairs, the miser, the libertine, and the ambitious. Books are pleasant enough; but if too much reading impairs the health and spoils our good humor—our most priceless possessions—we should drop it. Nothing we can gain from it will repay us for so great a loss.

In the days when I read a great deal, I used to lay a piece of glass on my page to remove the glare from the paper; and it gave my eyes considerable relief. Even now, at fifty-four years of age, I have no need of spectacles. I can see as far as I ever did, and as well as anyone else. True, if I read in the dusk I begin to notice that my sight is a little dim and weak. But, anyway, I always found reading a strain on my eyes, especially at night. They always tire quickly; and I could never stay long at a book, but was forced to have someone read aloud to me.

For my part, I like only easy and amusing books which tickle my fancy, or such as give me counsel and comfort. If I use them for study, it is to learn how to know myself, and to teach myself the proper way to live and die.

If someone tells me it degrades the value of the Muses to use them only for sport and pastime, I will answer that he little knows the value of pleasure—and it will be all I can do not to add that any other end in life is ridiculous. I live from day to day and, speaking with reverence, only for myself. When young, I studied for show; later, to make myself a little wiser; and now, for pleasure. And never for profit.

I do not bite my nails over the difficulties I encounter in a book. After one or two assaults I give them up. If I kept at them, I would only lose my time and myself as well; for my mind is good for only one jump. If I can't see a point at the first glance, repeated efforts will do nothing but make it more obscure.

If one book wearies me, I quickly pick up another. I never read except at such hours when the tedium of doing nothing drives me to it.

I am not much taken by the new books; the old ones seem to have more meat and sinew. Nor by the Greeks, for my judgment can't come into play when my knowledge of a language is rudimentary and weak.

Time in seconds———

Directions: Select the best answer and place the appropriate letter in the parentheses.

1. The author had no need of glasses at age (a) 34; (b) 44; (c) 54; (d) 64.   ( )
2. At the period when Montaigne wrote this section of his autobiography he states that he read mainly for (a) profit; (b) pleasure; (c) wisdom; (d) show.   ( )
3. If too much reading impairs the health the author suggests (a) laying a piece of glass across the page; (b) having someone read aloud; (c) reading in the dusk; (d) dropping it.   ( )
4. The main idea of this passage is that (a) reading books is an unhealthy pastime; (b) all books should be read for pleasure; (c) books are the best provisions for our human journey; (d) books are a certain cure for gloomy thoughts.   ( )
5. It might be inferred that Montaigne considered (a) a man without books an object of pity; (b) the old books are the best; (c) reading both pleasure and hard work; (d) all of the above.   ( )

Time Yourself and Begin

THE CALIPHATE
By BEN HECHT

And How Wondrous Were Its Words

It was Shakespeare I read first. I lay in my attic at night, eyes held to the blurring pages. The plots meant nothing. The characters were indistinguishable, even male from female. I had no idea who was king or clown, villain or hero, or to what purpose they battled and slew. But I met and recognized the nobility and precision of language. The words leaped from the paper and seemed to hang in the air like feats of magic.

The magic of words still remains for me. I prefer them to ideas. They are a more precious currency. No ideas have ever filled me with wonder. Phrases have. Ideas become quickly impoverished. Their value, never great, fades with usage: The word has a hardier mintage.

Phrases, not ideas, are the tools for re-creating life. Ideas lie on a perpetual rubbish heap, waiting to be salvaged, dusted off and flaunted anew as riches. The mind, searching pompously for truth, pokes among the fineries of yesterday, re-arrays itself in what it has outgrown, parades again in remodelings. The ideas of yesterday, today and tomorrow are the same, and they add nothing to the meaning of life.

It is phrasing alone that can bring fresh gifts to the spirit. When we describe accurately a mood, a mountain, a desire—when we put down with that combination of diligence and dream the words that are the true souls of things observed—we add to the stream of life.

On Reading Versus Writing

In the last ten years I have reread Dickens and Twain. They were as good as I thought them in my first encounter. They could not be better.

Two such jolly and bitter men! How these chuckling, weeping, roaring fellows haunted my pillow! What a carnival they unloosed in my attic room! It was not to be believed.

Schopenhauer declaims, "What palace ever rivaled in magnificence the dingy hole where Cervantes wrote *Don Quixote!*" We *read* the great storytellers in as fine a place.

Villiers de L'Isle-Adam, the Parisian writer, who lived like an alley cat, ate stale fish, went hiccuping and threadbare through fifty years of penury, who wrote with frostbitten fingers on cigarette papers, spoke from his hovel when dying: "Farewell. I have lived the richest and most magnificent of men."

We who read can die with a similar boast.

Shakespeare had been to me warriors and kings, plumed in words; earth and sky become a mirage of words and thoughts, like falling stars, swooping before my eyes. Twain and Dickens were cornucopias. Populations tumbled out of them.

I have always preferred reading fiction to writing it, not alone because it is easier. The sad thing about writing fiction is that unless one writes classics one writes in a closet. Nothing can disappear like a book. I remember reading some time ago an account of the origins of man. In it the author discussed the vanishing of the Neanderthal race, a species of human being who seemingly had ceased suddenly to exist, as if they had been spun off the earth by an accelerated movement of our globe on its axis. The Cro-Magnon race had popped up out of nowhere and taken its place. The author, a learned and unbiased man, debated from this whether the Neanderthal race had ever existed at all. That is how a book one has written can disappear.

I have written much fiction. The characters I made up are still alive, but they inhabit no world—only a closet. A foot beyond is limbo. They do not walk or caper in people's minds. They continue to utter their many fine sentences, to weep, joke and make love—but in the closet always. Like all writers who have

tried hard, I dream sometimes that the closet door will open.

Time in seconds_____

Directions: Select the best answer and place the appropriate letter in the parentheses.

1. Ben Hecht evidently felt strongly that the most precious currency in reading is (a) plots; (b) characterization; (c) ideas; (d) words.   ( )
2. "What palace ever rivaled in magnificence the dingy hole where Cervantes wrote *Don Quixote!*" was declaimed by (a) Shakespeare; (b) Dickens; (c) Schopenhauer; (d) Villiers de L'Isle-Adam.   ( )
3. According to Hecht, the Cro-Magnon race (a) never existed; (b) popped out of nowhere; (c) spun off the earth; (d) ate stale fish.   ( )
4. You might infer that Hecht (a) had no great opinion of himself as a writer; (b) had a high opinion of his fiction; (c) fervently hoped he would create a book that would endure; (d) had given up writing fiction for reading it.   ( )
5. You might also infer that he believed (a) reading makes the poorest man rich; (b) it is harder to read than to write; (c) no book every completely disappears; (d) ideas in books never fade.   ( )

Time Yourself and Begin

MAY 1908

By Arnold Bennett

Saturday, May 23rd.—In the afternoon I continued reading Lewes's *History of Philosophy*, which I have undertaken in all its bigness.

While reading it I was seized again with the idea of learning Latin decently; it was so strong that I could scarcely keep my attention on the book. Another example of the indiscipline of the brain.

Yet I have gradually got my brain far better under control than most people. Always haunted by dissatisfaction at the discrepancy between reason and conduct! No reason why conduct should not conform to the ideas of reason, except inefficient control of the brain. This that I am always preaching, and with a success of popular interest too, I cannot perfectly practise. It is the clumsiness of my living that disgusts me. The rough carpentry instead of fine cabinetry. The unnecessary friction. The constant slight inattention to my own rules. I could be a marvel to others and to myself if only I practised more sincerely. Half an hour in the morning in complete concentration on the living-through of the day, and I should work wonders! But this all-important concentration is continually interrupted—interruptions which weaken it; sometimes deliberately abandoned for concentration on matters of admittedly inferior importance! Strange! One can only stick to it.

It is humiliating that I cannot get through one single day without wounding or lightly abrading the sensibility of others, without wasting time and brain-power on thoughts that I do not desire to think, without yielding to appetites that I despise! I am so wrapped up in myself that I, if anyone, ought to succeed in a relative self-perfection. I aim as much from love of perfection and scorn of inefficiency as for my own happiness. I honestly think I care quite as much for other people's happiness as for my own; and that is not saying much for my love of my own happiness. Love of justice, more than outraged sensibility at the spectacle of suffering and cruelty, prompts me to support social reforms. I can and do look at suffering with scientific (artistic) coldness. I do not care. I am above it. But I want to hasten justice, for its own sake. I think this is fairly sincere; perhaps not quite. I don't think I scorn people; I have none of that scorn of inferior people (i.e., of the vast majority of people) which is seen in many great men. I think my view is greater than theirs. Clumsiness in living is what I scorn: systems, not people. And even systems I can excuse and justify to myself.

Time in seconds——

Directions: Select the best answer and place the appropriate letter in the parentheses.

1. Arnold Bennett's main concern in this entry from his *Journal* seems to be (a) the study of Latin; (b) fine cabinetry; (c) love of justice; (d) indiscipline of the brain. ( )
2. You might infer from this entry that the author was (a) a perfectionist; (b) a philosopher; (c) a carpenter; (d) a preacher. ( )
3. Bennett states that he would work wonders if he could only completely concentrate on the living-through of the day for (a) 15 minutes each morning; (b) 30 minutes each morning; (c) 45 minutes each morning; (d) 60 minutes each morning. ( )

DIRECTIONS FOR SCORING

Reading Rate. To find your reading rate in words per minute for each reading selection, turn to the TABLE FOR DETERMINING READING RATE IN WORDS PER MINUTE in the Appendix.

Answers to Questions. Check the answers to all of the questions in the CORRECTION KEY TO EXERCISES in the Appendix. Each question in the first two selections is valued at 20 percent. Each question in the final selection is valued at 33 percent.

Progress Chart. Reading rate (in words per minute) and comprehension (in percentages) scores should be entered in the places provided in your PERSONAL PROGRESS CHART in the Appendix.

STUDY ASSIGNMENT

The passages you have just completed may have given you a desire to read the complete autobiographies of these writers, or to read what other famous people have written about themselves in diaries, journals, or autobiographies.

Below you will find a brief selected listing of such works, many of them available in inexpensive paperback editions.

Read at least one of them during the next

few weeks as a study assignment. This may encourage you to add to your own reading autobiography.

The listing follows:

Benjamin Franklin's Autobiography and Other Writings. Houghton Mifflin; New American Library; Holt, Rinehart, & Winston; MacMillan.

The Autobiography of Michel de Montaigne, selected, arranged & edited by Marvin Lowenthal. Vintage Books, Inc.

The Journals of Arnold Bennett, selected and edited by Frank Swinnerton. Penguin Books.

The Life of Henri Brulard, by Stendhal. Vintage Books.

Summing Up, by W. Somerset Maugham. Penguin.

Walden and Other Writings, by Henry David Thoreau. Modern Library.

EYE-SPAN EXERCISES

Instructions: Using your Eye-Span Card, move it rapidly from one asterisk to the next. Do not linger on the number. This time instead of saying each number aloud, *think* the number. Then write it down.

Begin

✻

2

✻

72

✻

147

✻

6339

✻

54327

✻

384028

✻

9793364

✻

21694126

✻

717438831

✻

4955732398

✻

Directions: Note the number sequences which gave you trouble, if any. Then proceed to try another series below.

Begin

✻

4

✻

41

✻

272

✻

3663

✻

98366

✻

191924

✻

5569312

✻

69271334

✻

241167989

✻

5657154356

✻

Instructions: Check again to discover the sequence which gives you trouble. Then turn back to CHAPTER THREE and practice once again the eye-span exercises up through the six-digit numbers. Below are the final groups of practice exercises using digits.

Seven digits:

✻

4166936

✻

2429542

✻

4251967

✻

7269823
*

6364612
*

1954649
*

4851838
*

4143312
*

3219817
*

5217117
*

6424392
*

3725941
*

3452613
*

6491393
*

1358558
*

5912195
*

1695774
*

4935649
*

5927943
*

5658496
*

Eight digits:

*

64593212
*

94166963
*

72429552
*

74251967
*

17269823
*

87625731
*

54372983
*

94652748
*

25692748
*

17923816
*

94763128
*

74318546
*

36458137
*

73452962
*

59484236
*

78693512
*

62931283
*

52419728
*

14768936
*

58379412
*

If you find that you have little difficulty in handling eight digits, you may prepare your own sets of exercises using nine and ten digits, for nine-digit postal zip codes will become standard by the middle of the 1980s.

Some individuals with a high aptitude for number perception and number memory can do well with eleven and even twelve digits, a useful skill in an electronic era with all taxation record keeping based on social security numbers and 15-digit bank identifications.

Although in the next chapter you will proceed with words and in later chapters with phrases and sentences, for eye-span training, it has been demonstrated that digits provide valuable practice material.

CHAPTER FIVE

CASTING OUT DEMONS: WORD RECOGNITION

Consider now your method for **recognizing** and **attacking** a word you can't recall ever having seen before.

You almost certainly won't turn to a dictionary. Not at first, at any rate. Like most readers, you will probably attempt to guess what an unfamiliar word means by its position in the sentence.

Other people honestly admit that they turn to the nearest person for help: parent, wife or husband, friend, colleague, co-worker.

Few people confess that they just skip over the word and try to forget it ever existed—until they meet it the next time.

RECOGNITION AND ATTACK

Almost without thinking, you employ a variety of detective methods to learn enough about a new word so that you can face up to it.

First, you decide that it's a new word to you because, although it may be similar to other words you've met and recognized, it's not exactly the same. The **form** of the word is unique.

You may try to figure out the meaning by the **place** of the word in a phrase or sentence. This is the clue of **context.**

You may then attempt to take the word apart to see if any portion of it resembles another word. This is **structural analysis.**

You may try to figure out something about the word by the way it sounds when spoken aloud. This is **phonetic analysis.**

Form
Context
Structural analysis
Phonetic analysis

Any one or all of these methods may be applied in an instant. Almost in the same instant you attack the problem of the new and unfamiliar word and come up with a solution.

Or at least you come up with a solution which satisfies you for the time being as you continue your reading. The solution may be little more than a guess, but it is not exactly a wild guess.

Actually, you have brought not only present thinking but also past experience to bear on the problem.

Some readers are much better at recognizing and attacking new and unfamiliar words than others. Self-confidence helps.

Refuse to be a word coward. Stand up to the strangers you meet in the language. Don't let them stop you.

ROOTS AND PREFIXES

An invaluable aid to recognition and attack is a working knowledge of the most useful Latin and Greek roots of words in the language as well as Latin, Greek and Anglo-Saxon prefixes.

The following selected lists were drawn from *Word Mastery Made Simple*, by Dr. Arthur Waldhorn and Dr. Arthur Zeiger, of the Department of English, the College of the City of New York.[1] These roots and prefixes should be learned by identifying them first with current words familiar to you. Then look up in a dictionary the current words which are unfamiliar.

[1] A comprehensive alphabetical listing of roots, prefixes, and suffixes appears in Appendix B of *Word Mastery Made Simple*, by Arthur Waldhorn and Arthur Zeiger, Made Simple Books, Inc.

A List of Ten Most Frequent Latin Roots

Root		Current Words
	Meaning:	take, hold
cap		captious, caprice, captivate, capacity, capable,
cip		municipal, anticipate, principal, recipient, incipient
cept		precept, deception, inception, concept, accept
	Meaning:	make, do
fac		fact, factory, faculty, factotum, putrefaction
fic		benefice, pontifical, efficacy, co-efficient, edifice
fect		disaffection, refection, confection, infection, defective
	Meaning:	carry, bring, bear
fer		referendum, fertile, conifer, infer, vociferous, proffer
	Meaning:	end, limit
fin		definition, infinitive, finite, infinite, refine, final, finance
	Meaning:	send, throw
mit		emit, permit, commit, omit
miss		remission, submission, emissary, missile, missive
mise		demise, surmise, promise
	Meaning:	rule, straight, arrange
reg		regimen, regal, regiment, reign
rect		corrective, erect, director, rector, rectitude
rig		incorrigible
ress		dress, redress, address
	Meaning:	stand
sta		stable, equidistant, trans-

		substantiation, stanchion, stanza, distant
stat		statute, constituent, statuary, static, destitute
sist		desist, irresistible, subsist, persist
	Meaning:	look, see, appear
spec		species, specious, specimen
spect		introspective, perspective, retrospect, prospectus, circumspect
spic		perspicacity, conspicuous, auspicious, suspicion
	Meaning:	hold
ten		tenure, untenable, tenant, tenable, tenacious, lieutenant
tent		content, detention
tin		incontinent, abstinence, impertinent, retinue, pertinacity
tain		appertain, abstain, maintain
	Meaning:	see
vid		evident, provident
vis		vista, visible, revise, supervise, visage

A List of Ten Most Frequent Greek Roots

Root		Current Words
	Meaning:	man
anthrop		anthropoid, anthropology, misanthrope, philanthropic, anthropomorphic
	Meaning:	self
auto		autonomous, autochthonous, autocrat, autopsy, authentic, autobiography

bio	*Meaning:*	life
		biology, biography, biotic, biophysics, biogenesis
graph	*Meaning:*	write
		graphic, autograph, topographical, stenography, orthography, bibliography
hetero	*Meaning:*	different
		heterogeneous, heterodox, heterosexual, heteronym
homo	*Meaning:*	the same
		homogenized, homogenous, homologous, homonym, homosexual, homograph
log	*Meaning:*	word, speech, science
		logic, etymology, eulogy, prologue, epilogue, catalogue, philology, psychology, dialogue, apology, logarithm
phil	*Meaning:*	loving, friendly, kind
		philosopher, philanthropist, bibliophile, Philadelphia, philharmonic, philology, Anglophile, philter
soph	*Meaning:*	wise
		sophisticate, sophist theosophy, sophomore, philosophy
tele	*Meaning:*	far
		teleology, telepathy, telescope, telephone, telegraph, television, teletype, teleran (*tele*vision-*rad*ar-navigation)

The Ten Most Frequent Latin Prefixes

Prefix	Variants	Current Words
	Meaning:	to, toward
ad-		adduce, adhere, adjudicate, advertisement
	a-	ascend, averse, ascribe
	ac-	accede, accord, accrue, accumulate
	af-	afflatus, affect, affix, affiance
	ag-	aggregate, aggravate, aggrandize
	al-	allocate, allude, allot
	an-	annex, announce
	ap-	apparent, appendage, applaud
	ar-	arraign, arrive
	as-	assist, assemble, assign, assent
	at-	attenuate, attest, attendance
	Meaning:	together, with
com-		commodious, compendium, commerce, communal, compulsion
	con-	conductive, concatenation, configuration, congruent, contiguous, convolution
	col-	collusion, colloquy, college, collateral
	cor-	corroborate, correlate, corrode
	cog-	cognate, cogent, cogitate
	co-	coeducation, coefficient, coagulate
	Meaning:	from, down (negative meaning)
de-		declivity, delineate, deprecatory, desuetude, detritus, devious

dis- *Meaning:* from, away, apart (negative meaning) dissonance, dissect, dispel, disagree, distort, disperse

di-   divert, digress, diligent
dif- differ, diffuse, diffident

ex- *Meaning:* out, from, away
exigency, expatriate, expatiate, extemporize, extrinsic

Note:
  ex- is used with a noun to mean "former": ex-president, ex officio.

e-   educate, evoke, event, eliminate, elongate
ef- efficacious, effulgent, effect

in- *Meaning:* in, into, on
(used with verbs intrude, inure, incision, in-
and nouns) voke, inspire, invent, incline, intoxicate
il- illuminate, illegal, illiterate, illicit
im- import, imbibe, implore
ir- irrigate, irradiate

in- *Meaning:* not
(used with indecent, infallible, informal
adjectives)
il- illiterate, illicit, illegal
ig- ignoble, ignominious, ignorant
im- immodest, immoral, improper
ir- irregular, irrational, irreducible

pre- *Meaning:* before (in *place* or *time*)
precursor, precede, prevent, predict, predestination

pro- *Meaning:* forward, in favor of
promulgate, proceed, pro-

voke, progeny, profligate, pronoun, proficient, projector

re- *Meaning:* again, back
redolent, renaissance, relapse, refer, revoke, recede, retract, reincarnate, renegade, renege

The Five Most Frequent Greek Prefixes

Prefix	*Variants*	*Current Words*

a- *Meaning:* not, without
apathetic, asexual, agnostic, atheist, abyss, aseptic
an- anathema, anarchy, anesthetic, anomaly

apo- *Meaning:* away, off
apostle, apology, apostasy, apotheosis, apocryphal, apoplexy, apogee, apocope

epi- *Meaning:* upon, beside
epidemic, epidermis, epitaph, epithet, epileptic, epitomize, epilogue, epigram, episode
ep- epoch, epode
eph- ephemeral

para- *Meaning:* beside
paraphrase, parabolic, paranoia, parallel, paradox, parody, paraphernalia, paraplegic

syn- *Meaning:* with, together
synagogue, synod, synonym, synopsis, synthesis, syntax
sym- sympathy, symphony, symmetry
syl- syllogism, syllable

The Five Most Frequent Anglo-Saxon Prefixes

Prefix		Current Words
a-	*Meaning:*	at, in, on, to
		aground, ahead, asleep, atop, afoot
be-	*Meaning:*	throughout, over
		beshrew, bedaub, besmudge, bemoan, bespeak, besiege
mis-	*Meaning:*	error, defect, wrong, badly
		mistake, misspell, mislay, miscreant, misconduct
over-	*Meaning:*	over, beyond, above
		overalls, overwrought, overreach, overawe
un-	*Meaning:*	not
		undo, unethical, uninspired

SPELLING

All persons with normal learning capacities can constantly improve their ability to recognize and attack new and unfamiliar words. That is the first step in word mastery.

The next steps are to learn to spell them, pronounce them, and define them.

Consider first the problem of spelling.

Individuals don't usually have to be told if they are poor spellers. They have been hearing it most of their lives. What they would like to hear instead is a sure, easy way to become good spellers. Unfortunately, no panacea exists.

If the one best way to improve your spelling can be summed up in a single word, that word is a familiar one: **drill.**

Perhaps you need take only three minutes a day, or five minutes a day, or at the most ten minutes a day to conduct your drill sessions. But they must be conducted every day, day in and day out, without skipping, until you can note a significant improvement.

First, you should know something about your spelling weaknesses as well as your spelling strengths.

Can you **see** the word? That is, can you pick out a misspelled word if it is placed next to the same word correctly spelled? Can you pick out a misspelled word from a group of correctly spelled words?

If you can't, you need to improve your seeing skill, the ability to visualize in your mind's eye just how a word should look on paper with its correct spelling.

Can you **hear** the word?

This ability can be tricky. Everyone knows that words in English aren't necessarily spelled the way they sound. Among the exercises at the end of this chapter you will find one to test your ability to know how a word is spelled in spite of the way it sounds.

Can you **feel** the word?

This ability is often neglected when attempts are made to improve spelling. Yet if you stop to think a moment, you will realize how important it is.

How many words do you spell correctly in writing because your hand guides your pencil properly? You may not even be thinking about spelling. Still the word comes out the way it should.

An example of this is the spelling of your own name. Simple or complicated, you can always dash it off without thinking.

Another example is that of the proficient typist. The right fingers find the right keys automatically to spell the familiar words you know.

See the Word
Hear the Word
Feel the Word

Using three of your senses, **sight, hearing,** and **touch,** in coordination will aid you significantly in improving your spelling. No one knows why some people learn to spell easily and others don't. Hard as the language is, theoretically everyone can learn.

A few rules might help. However, in most instances learning the rules and their exceptions is more complicated than learning the words.

One easy-to-remember rule is often helpful, and that is **i before e except after c.** But even in this case, you must also remember several exceptions, including **either, neither, leisure, seize,** and **weird.**

Above all, develop what is known as **spelling consciousness.** Become aware of words in the language and how they are put together.

Play some of the currently popular games which give you practice in arranging letters to make words.

Don't hesitate to go to the dictionary for spelling advice. Even champion spellers are sometimes stumped and must turn to an authority.

Good speller or poor speller—you can always become a better if not a perfect speller.

PRONUNCIATION

Knowing how a word sounds and being able to reproduce that sound correctly when you speak the word may help you with your spelling. As you are perhaps aware, you must use this approach with caution.

Words in English are not always what they seem to be by the sound of them.

All you have to do is consider thoughtfully the pronunciation of a few words ending in "ough" to get the point. For example, say these words aloud: **rough, bough, through, though.**

A further illustration is George Bernard Shaw's famous spelling for **fish,** as follows: **ghoti.** (The **gh** as in **tough;** the **o** as in **women;** and the **ti** as in **nation.**)

Nevertheless, in spite of the dangers of relying too much on pronunciation, the generalization can be confidently made that saying words correctly helps you in spelling them correctly, and spelling them correctly helps your reading.

Listening to other speakers provides an excellent way to improve your pronunciation. Passive listening is not enough, however. Hearing is not necessarily listening any more than seeing is reading.

The important but often neglected communication skill of listening requires conscious mental effort. It also takes a certain amount of physical energy. But the rewards for active and discriminating listening are enormous in this electronic age.

When you turn on your television or radio set, you may very likely hear some of the best speaking voices in the nation, both from the platform and from the stage.

Listen with all your senses alert. Note how others use the language. Participate with your mind.

The intelligent viewer and listener can add immeasurably to his reading skill by making himself active instead of passive when he tunes in on a channel or station.

Dictionaries are also a valuable tool for correct pronunciation. Although over fifty sounds are used in speaking English, dictionaries have simplified these to about forty-three.

Take a few minutes to study the forty-three sounds and the symbols used to describe them in the chart below. You will then have no difficulty when you consult your dictionary on how to say a word correctly.

PRONUNCIATION CHART

ă	add, bat	f	fly, muff
ā	age, date	g	game, beg
â	air, bare	h	hit, hear
ä	arm, father	ĭ	it, dig
b	best, rub	ī	ice, mile
ch	chill, reach	j	jut, hedge
d	dim, bed	k	keep, bake
ĕ	ebb, bet	l	low, ill
ē	evil, bee	m	me, dim

n	no, in	sh	ship, passion
ng	ring, English	t	tin, night
ŏ	box, dot	th	thin, wrath
ō	oh, no	th	then, mother
ô	orb, ball	ŭ	up, dove
oi	oil, coy	ū	use, cue
ŏŏ	book, could	ûr	urn, purge
ōō	ooze, rude	v	vain, live
ou	out, how	w	we, away
p	pay, drop	y	yes, yellow
r	red, dry	z	zone, these
s	so, pass	zh	vision, pleasure

All of these forty-two symbols are composed of the letters of the alphabet, with a few unusual markings to differentiate them. The forty-third is also a letter, but turned upside-down as follows: ǝ

Known as the schwa, this symbol represents unstressed vowel sounds in the language. Thus it may at one time symbolize an **a**, another an **e**, or **i**, **o**, or **u**, depending upon whether or not the vowel is in an accented or an unaccented syllable.

For example, the symbol ǝ is used to indicate the following sounds:

> **a as in ago**
> **e as in hidden**
> **i as in charity**
> **o as in compare**
> **u as in crocus**

DEFINITION

If you discover that you are not readily recognizing and attacking words, immediate action is required. The action is simple and direct.

List the troublesome words. Break them down into syllables if necessary. Look at them. Say them. Think them.

If you have a spelling problem, note the words which are your personal demons. Look at them. Say them. Think them. And write the words until you can **feel** them in your fingertips.

If you have a pronunciation problem, practice speaking until you get the sound of the words in your ears. Listen to good speech whenever you get the opportunity.

Use the dictionary.

Finally, try not to halt or tremble before any word in the language. Approach all words with confidence, either genuine or assumed.

In this case, it's far better to be a fool rushing in attacking a word than an angel fearing to tread.

The next step is, of course, **definition.**

Learning the precise meanings of words and building a strong vocabulary is essential to effective reading. The entire next chapter is devoted to this activity.

But before you take up the important discussion on vocabulary, several exercises have been planned to help you with **word recognition and attack, spelling, pronunciation,** and **reading speed and comprehension.**

WORD RECOGNITION AND ATTACK EXERCISE

Directions: Look at the single word, preferably through your Eye-Span Card. Then move the card rapidly to the five words directly below, and pick out with your eyes the word that is exactly the same as the single word. **Do Not Say The Word Aloud.** Continue to the next single word and repeat the operation. Do not make any marks on the page, so that you can repeat this exercise daily for a week or two.

Begin

mill
mile mill milk mild mull

though
through thorough trough though thought

wide
wide wild wile wine wick

screen

scream screech screen spleen sheen

*

widow

window willow windrow widen widow

*

warning

warning waning worming warming wearing

*

guilt

quilt guilt guile guise built

*

sacred

sacred scarred scored scorned scared

*

bored

bared barred bored borne boded

*

spite

spirit spit sprite spill spite

*

fire

fire file fine fir rife

*

stuck

stock stuck stack stick stunk

*

white

white while whit with whither

*

angle

agile angel angle anklet ankle

*

tried

cried tired treed trice tried

*

statue

stature statue statute station status

*

trial

trill trail train trial triad

shine

shin sheen shone shame shine

*

write

while white write writ writhe

*

skill

skill skull skid kills shill

SPELLING EXERCISE

Directions: The list below contains many words almost all poor spellers and many good spellers find formidable. Many of them are examples of words which are not spelled the way your ear tells you they should be spelled. You might call them **super-demons.**

One letter has been omitted in each of the words. Supply the missing letter. Allow yourself five minutes for the task.

Time Yourself and Begin

d—scription	nois—ly
eig—th	obst—cle
gramm—r	permiss—ble
exist—nce	bal—nce
math—matics	d—cision
opt—mism	compar—tive
rep—tition	lonel—ness
sep—rate	propell—r
defin—te	prim—tive
bus—ness	d—spair
irresist—ble	expl—nation
disc—pline	priv—lege
occurr—nce	rar—fied
pleas—nt	vis—ble
conqu—r	dorm—tory
d—seases	lab—ratory
prep—rations	appear—nce
accomm—date	elim—nated
indispens—ble	promin—nt
r—diculous	sacr—fice
superintend—nt	diss—pation
resour—e	remembr—nce

persist—nt
hindr—nce
d—stroy
specim—n
persever—nce
gard—ner
p—rsue
bull—tin

cemet—ry
barb—rous
appar—nt
intell—gent
accum—late
vig—rous
def—nition
abs—rd

Check your answers with the dictionary. A score of 56 to 60 items correct in five minutes: **excellent;** 50 to 55 items correct: **good;** under 50: spelling may be a problem for you.

Practice the items you missed by placing a large capital in the missing-letter space. For example: **prepArations.** Study these words carefully, so that you can accurately visualize the key letter.

PRONUNCIATION EXERCISES

Directions: The words below are not only often misspelled but also often mispronounced. There is a connection. And the result of both mispronunciation and misspelling is likely to be inefficient reading.

In this exercise, look at the word, supply the missing letter, then say the word.

Begin

sec—etary
lib—ary
soph—more
chim—ey
gover—ment
Feb—uary
envi—onment
liter—ture
cand—elight
li—able
embroid—ry
e—corting
ruff—an
hund—ed
vet—ran

us—ally
temper—ment
stric—ly
w—arf
fam—ly
gen—rally
g—ography
ar—tic
quan—ity
reco—nize
visu—lize
valu—ble
can—idate
bound—ry
represent—tive

Check your answers with the dictionary.

Practice the items missed by placing a large capital in the missing-letter space. For example: **arCtic.** Study these words carefully, so that you can accurately visualize as well as pronounce them correctly.

Now try this exercise for practice in correct pronunciation. It is based on the phonetic alphabet adopted by the Armed Forces.

Instructions: Lower your Eye-Span Card from item to item. First, say the letter of the alphabet, then the phonetic equivalent. Check your accuracy immediately with the pronunciation guide. The accented syllable is in capital letters.

A	Alfa	AL fah
B	Bravo	BRAH voh
C	Charlie	CHAR lee
D	Delta	DELL ta
E	Echo	ECK oh
F	Foxtrot	FOKS trot
G	Golf	GOLF
H	Hotel	hoh TELL
I	India	IN dee ah
J	Juliet	JEW lee ett
K	Kilo	KEY ioh
L	Lima	LEE mah
M	Mike	MIKE
N	November	no VEM ber
O	Oscar	OSS cah
P	Papa	pah PAH
Q	Quebec	keh BECK
R	Romeo	ROW me oh
S	Sierra	see AIRRAH
T	Tango	TANG go
U	Uniform	YOU nee form
V	Victor	VIK tah /tor
W	Whiskey	WISS key
X	Xray	ECKS ray
Y	Yankee	YANK key
Z	Zulu	ZOO loo

Instructions: Dr. Samuel Johnson's brilliant reputation as a writer and a talker seems fairly well established after two hundred and more years. But it was as a dictionary maker that he first achieved success. The reading exercise tells you something about this famous Englishman.

Before you continue, however, you may wish to carry out a suggestion.

In the checklist of working tools to use in reading improvement given at the end of CHAPTER TWO, one of the items is an hourglass or egg-timer. A household gadget filled with sand which runs from one compartment to another in exactly **three minutes,** it will prove useful in the next series of reading exercises.

Try to complete the selection before the sand runs out.

(If you do not use the hourglass, time yourself as usual with a watch or clock.)

Time Yourself and Begin

SAM JOHNSON, DICTIONARY MAKER

The chief editor of a modern dictionary estimated that in the course of doing a job he consulted some 350 people, all specialists in various fields of knowledge. He made no estimate of the number of people who helped out with the clerical duties. Nor did he mention the many different kinds of mechanical equipment used, from electric typewriters to electronic calculators.

By way of contrast, consider Dr. Samuel Johnson's *Dictionary of the English Language.* This monumental work, which appeared on April 15, 1755, was essentially a one-man operation. Johnson did have some assistance for hand-copying his material. But most of the original labor was his own.

Published in two massive volumes weighing a total of 27 pounds, the book took nearly a decade to complete. Although not the first dictionary in English, it certainly was the most reliable and comprehensive. "Dictionary" Johnson, as the famous lexicographer was known at that period, earned his honorary title well.

When the idea of the work was first proposed to him Johnson immediately dismissed it as something he would never undertake. Shortly afterward, he was confidently predicting that he could accomplish the task in a matter of three years. At this point, one of Johnson's friends protested, arguing that the French Academy, consisting of forty members, took forty years to complete its Dictionary.

"Sir, thus it is," Johnson replied, with what must have been a twinkle in his eye. "This is the proportion. Let me see; forty times forty is sixteen hundred. As three to sixteen hundred, so is the proportion of an Englishman to a Frenchman."

The task actually took nine years. But Johnson never admitted that his estimate had been wrong. He intimated instead that he hadn't properly applied himself.

With an attic as his workshop, and a few hired copyists, he set about the work at hand. The result was a major achievement in English letters. Whatever else Dr. Johnson may be remembered for, the Dictionary will always stand out as a pioneering work which for the first time combined all the various elements required for a modern word reference book.

Inevitably, some weaknesses were noted in the work when it appeared, and they have fascinated generations of scholars ever since. Sam Johnson was a man of prejudices and perversity. His personal feelings both pro and con on certain subjects were often frankly injected into his word descriptions. If he was pompous on occasion, however, he was also witty. If his vocabulary was on the stuffy, old-fashioned side, his thinking was decidedly not.

Many of his definitions have been quoted for their humor, both intentional and unintentional.

In his famous definition of **oats**, for example, Johnson was obviously expressing his dislike of the Scotch. Oats, he wrote, is a grain which in England is generally given to horses, but in Scotland supports the people.

He also could look at himself with humorous detachment. For example, he defined a **lexicographer** as a writer of dictionaries, a harmless drudge.

An example of unintentional humor is perhaps best illustrated by his description of a **pie** as any crust baked with something in it. A **poetess** to Johnson was a she-poet.

Sometimes Johnson lashed out with fury in his definitions at what he considered injustice in the world. No one knew better than he the grinding effects of poverty. During his early days in London he had gone around the streets half-starving, ill-clothed and ill-shod.

He defined **excise** as a hateful tax levied upon commodities, and adjudged not by the common judges of property but by wretches hired by those to whom excise is paid.

Ignored by the wealthy nobleman, Lord Chesterfield, who had promised his financial support while the Dictionary was in the making but failed to provide it, Johnson gave vent to his feelings about the matter in a definition of **patron**. A **patron**, he wrote bitterly, is commonly a wretch who supports with insolence, and is paid with flattery.

Johnson himself was no flatterer. When Chesterfield tried to make up for his neglect by praising the Dictionary, he received instead of flattery a deserved rebuke in the form of still another definition of a patron. "Is not a Patron, my Lord," Johnson wrote, "one who looks with unconcern on a man struggling for life in the water, and when he has reached ground, encumbers him with help?"

Thanks to the genius and devotion of James Boswell, posterity has a record of many of the events that went into the making of the Dictionary. One day, after the tremendous job was completed, Boswell remarked to Johnson that perhaps he had not realized in advance what he was undertaking. The great man's reply was neither modest nor boastful, but instead a simple declaration of the truth.

"Yes, Sir," he said, "I knew very well what I was undertaking—and very well how to do it—and have done it very well."

Time in seconds———

Directions: Select the best answer and place the appropriate letter in the parentheses.

1. The preparation of a modern dictionary is (a) done solely by electronic calculators; (b) essentially a one-man operation; (c) accomplished by a huge clerical staff; (d) largely the work of consultants under a chief editor.   ( )
2. In preparing his *Dictionary of the English Language,* Dr. Samuel Johnson consulted (a) 150 people; (b) 250 people; (c) 350 people; (d) nobody.   ( )
3. When the idea of preparing a dictionary was first proposed to Dr. Johnson he (a) dismissed it as something he would not undertake; (b) confidently predicted that he could accomplish the task in three years; (c) remained thoughtfully silent; (d) said flatly that such a task was beyond his capacities.   ( )
4. It may be inferred from this account that Johnson's Dictionary was (a) the first dictionary; (b) the first dictionary in English; (c) the first modern dictionary; (d) the first modern dictionary in English.   ( )
5. The inevitable weaknesses of Johnson's Dictionary, according to this account, resulted in (a) a source of fascination for generations of scholars; (b) the withdrawal of the work from public sale; (c) ridicule being heaped on the author; (d) Johnson's complete eclipse as a writer.   ( )
6. It may be gathered from some of the definitions that (a) none of the work was original; (b) a humorous effect was Johnson's sole aim; (c) Johnson freely expressed his likes and dis-

likes; (c) all the humor in the work was un-intentional. ( )

7. It may be inferred from this account that while working on the Dictionary (a) Johnson went around the streets half starving; (b) Johnson was in no need of any financial assistance; (c) Johnson's patron, Lord Chesterfield, was liberal in his support; (d) Johnson had to struggle to make ends meet. ( )

8. The task of preparing the Dictionary actually took (a) three years; (b) six years; (c) nine years; (d) twelve years. ( )

9. That Johnson had a sense of humorous detachment is illustrated by his definition of (a) oats; (b) patron; (c) lexicographer; (c) excise. ( )

10. Dr. Johnson obviously took great pride in being (a) a lexicographer; (b) an Englishman; (c) a member of the French Academy; (d) a flatterer. ( )

DIRECTIONS FOR SCORING

Reading Rate. If you completed the selection within the three-minute time limit imposed by your hourglass, enter your score in the PERSONAL PROGRESS CHART as 275 words per minute. If you failed to complete the selection in the time allowed, **try again.**

If you timed yourself **in seconds** with your watch or clock, find your reading rate in words per minute by turning to the TABLE FOR DETERMINING READING RATE IN WORDS PER MINUTE.

Answers to Questions. Check the answers to the multiple-choice questions in the CORRECTION KEY TO EXERCISES.

Progress Chart. Enter all reading rate and comprehension scores in the PERSONAL PROGRESS CHART.

STUDY ASSIGNMENT

Review regularly the section on root words, prefixes, and suffixes, until you are familiar with them. If possible, look up more complete listings in a book on vocabulary.

If spelling is a problem with you, make a list of your personal demons. Study at least one each day.

Look at the word.
Pronounce the word.
Close your eyes and try to recall the word.
Spell the word aloud.
Write the word.
Feel the word.
Check the word.

Study the key to pronunciation. Check your dictionary for the key used. Note that in most dictionaries an abbreviated key may be found at the bottom of all right-hand pages.

Finally, add material each day to your reading autobiography.

CHAPTER SIX

THE HAT TRICK: WORD MASTERY

Successful men and women in business or the professions have good, hard-working vocabularies. Whether they know and use a great many words because they are successful or are successful because they know and use a great many words has never been exactly determined.

A direct relationship does exist.

A well-stocked storeroom of words also helps you to become a better and faster reader. Not only will you recognize and attack words more easily, you will also be able to define them. Your comprehension is high.

Definition is not easy, however, Exact definition of a word as it appears in a phrase or sentence is even more difficult. Some words in the language are slippery and elusive. In one context they will mean one thing, in another context another thing.

Simple words like **run** and **game**, for example have literally scores of different meanings and shades of meaning. A word is not really yours until you can spot it in most of its settings and describe it accurately.

Solitary synonyms are usually not accurate enough as definitions. Another word may not describe precisely the word you have in mind.

A further weakness of definition by synonyms is that you may know that two words mean approximately the same thing without knowing the exact meaning of either one.

FLASH CARDS

An effective way to improve your vocabulary is to keep a personal list of words on cards for frequent study. This is the method already suggested to you, which will now be described in more detail.

Hand-print the selected word on a standard 3 x 5 index card in large lower case letters. On the other side of the card, write a phrase or sentence containing the word exactly as it is used. Then below that note the dictionary definition.

For example:

egregious

The leading man in the play had an **egregious** lack of charm.
def. Conspicuous for bad quality; flagrant; gross.

A well-known teaching device, these flash cards are useful in the word-learning process. Write on separate cards all new and unfamiliar words that you come across. Look at a few cards regularly each day until you can define and use the words immediately without referring to the written definition.

Build your own pack of cards by adding to them at every opportunity. Discard those which contain words you have mastered.

What is mastery of a word?

Perhaps it comes when the word is firmly entrenched in your passive vocabularies of **listening** and **reading**.

Certainly you have achieved it when the word has become a part of your active vocabularies of **writing** and **speaking**.

Everyone operates with these four vocabulary groups, two passive (listening and reading) and two active (writing and speaking). Your listening and reading vocabularies combine to form your largest word store. Next comes your writing vocabulary, somewhat smaller. And finally comes your speaking vocabulary, smallest of all.

Building up a large reserve of words in your passive vocabularies inevitably means that some of them will turn up in your active vocabularies.

Once you use a word easily and correctly in writing or speech, either formally or informally, you can really call that word your own.

OTHER VOCABULARY ACTIVITIES

The regular use of flash cards is only one way to help you enrich your stock of words, and a supplementary way at that. Nobody as yet has devised a method or a course of study for increasing your word power which takes the place of direct experience.

An advertising executive once labeled direct experience "the hat trick." In this instance, the phrase means taking your hat off the shelf, putting it on your head, and then going out into the world to talk and listen to people.

A visit to another community, a trip by car to a neighboring state, travel by land, sea or air to distant places, all contribute to experience and thus expose you to new words.

New activities take you directly to the language of the new activities. A new position in the workaday world means a new set of words to learn. New friends and acquaintances have differing ways of expressing themselves.

How people think, feel, act, and talk may affect the way you think, feel, act, and talk.

The moment you take time out to leave a fa-

miliar beaten path and cross the street, you may add to your experience. You may also add to your stock of words. And, in turn, the new words themselves are likely to become a means of introducing you to still more experiences.

Another suggested method for vocabulary building is the regular use of prepared tests and exercises which are arranged in some order of either subject-matter or difficulty. Examples of this type of material are contained in many popular books on the market. Some of them will be listed at the end of this chapter.

Individuals who are addicted to crossword puzzles or to the increasing variety of word games appearing either in periodicals or on toy counters may find them helpful in a limited way for vocabulary improvement. Perhaps their greatest value lies in keeping people interested in words.

College instructors have frequently found that mere mention of the importance of a good vocabulary to scholastic achievement and professional or business success is enough to stimulate some students to apply themselves to word study, with notable results.

READING THE DICTIONARY

Many persons open a dictionary only when they wish to learn how a word is spelled, or for a definition quickly glanced at and just as quickly forgotten. Sometimes a dictionary is used to learn how a word is accented or pronounced.

Rarely does anyone turn to a dictionary as an interesting and absorbing book.

Yet for those who are often frustrated in their reading because they can't get the meaning of passages they would enjoy if they only knew what the words meant, regular sessions with a dictionary might be exceedingly helpful.

Various approaches can be used.

Some people take a word at random and then let that word lead them to another and so on.

Others choose a page a day, or a letter a week, and then ramble through the list learning those words which they feel will interest them. Any method you choose will bring good results, provided you are in a confident, receptive frame of mind as you read.

Words which are almost but not quite a part of your present word store are the ones likely to catch your eye. They are not complete strangers, but reside just outside the range of your attention. You have seen them or heard them but you still do not know them. The dictionary introduces them to you.

The most valuable kind of dictionary for these systematic explorations is a desk-size or college-type dictionary. Although the large, unabridged dictionaries are the choice of writers and scholars, they are usually forbidding to pick up and just read. The medium-size dictionaries are more practical for everyday purposes.

Many pocket-size dictionaries are available. Some of them have been thoughtfully compiled. Precious companions for the poor speller, these smaller works have a limited value for defining words exactly because of limited space.

Each type of dictionary, however, medium-size, large, or small, may at one time or another be the appropriate one to help you spell words, pronounce words and build your vocabulary.

The thesaurus, which defines words by their synonyms, is another reference work of some value, although it is not to be used in place of a dictionary. Helpful in setting your imagination to work because of the variety of words it groups around single ideas, concepts, emotions and acts, the thesaurus may start you out on a fruitful word hunt. The dictionary completes the search with a definition in detail of the exact word you are looking for.

Building a personal vocabulary from a skimpy word store into a sizable stock is not an easy task for adults. Words come rushing into your vocabulary until you reach your late teens. From then on your accumulation of words is a slow process.

Nevertheless, vocabulary building is a skill which you can develop and practice during your whole life. It means constant additions to both passive and active vocabularies through definition in detail. Methods may vary, but they all depend on or supplement "the hat trick," direct experience of one kind or another.

Wide reading, with careful attention to words and their settings and a dictionary always close at hand, is always a rich source of vocabulary-building materials. As a reader you have an almost limitless opportunity for vicarious experience, bound by neither time nor clime as you sit and turn the pages of fiction or nonfiction.

The whole wide world and even some areas beyond are the province of the written word, restricted only by the imagination and creative ability of the writer.

Going to books to reinforce your steadily increasing stock of words results in a remarkable spiral of self-improvement.

You increase your vocabulary by wide reading and you read better and faster when you increase your vocabulary.

READING EXERCISE

Instructions: A noted literary columnist gives his views of the kind of dictionary he would prefer for a small "desert island library." Maximum reading time, using the hourglass, is **three minutes.** Try to do it in less. Then answer the questions immediately. You may time yourself in seconds, if you wish.

Time Yourself and Begin

SPEAKING OF BOOKS
By J. Donald Adams

When I named my selections for a small desert island library a few weeks ago a correspondent suggested that I might well have found a place for a good dictionary. The suggestion was made in no unkindly spirit; simply on the grounds of usefulness and possibly enjoyment. I think he had a point. It would have to be, of course, a dictionary of ample dimensions; no pocket job would do, nor even one of those medium-sized affairs which are usually labeled as college editions. It would need to be as hefty as the Webster's International or the Shorter Oxford, and I think my choice would rest upon the latter, as the more interesting. It is more generous in its use of quotation, in its descriptions of origin and descent, and it satisfies our curiosity as to when a word first came into use.

In this matter of dating the appearance of words, I am goggle-eyed at the assurance with which the Oxford English Dictionary places a date after a word. More often than not, it is a very definite date: 1652, the O.E.D. will say, or 1728, or 1871. Being of a naturally trustful nature, I assume that the editors of the O.E.D. know what they are talking about, and that they have actually pin-pointed the arrival of that particular word upon the literary scene. If my trust is not misplaced, what labors of scholarship and research must lie behind each such entry! How many dull and uninviting tomes must have been plowed through before the editor in charge of that account could say with satisfaction to himself, and with reasonable credibility: This is it; this is the year in which the verb *canvass* came into the language, and sets down the date, 1508.

But his labors haven't ended there—not by a long shot. Words are tricky characters; they start out by meaning one thing and end up, quite often, by meaning its opposite. They begin shabbily and acquire glamour, or they take off by parading themselves in drawing rooms, only to end up in the gutter. I mentioned **canvass** because it happened to be the first word

I came upon which has had a varied history. The separate uses to which it has been put are amazing, or would be, if English were not such a contradictory and illogical language. The record of **canvass** is enough to drive a lexicographer to distraction.

Shortly after its birth it had a meaning approximate to the sense in which we now use it; to solicit, as support, votes, orders, contributions, etc. But not many years later it could mean, to toss in a canvas sheet, or to knock about, to beat or to batter. About the same time it was used figuratively to mean, to buffet in writing or to criticize destructively, and a little later, to bargain with. In the eighteenth century it came to mean, to sue for a thing. Today it means what it came to mean in 1812, to solicit the support of a constituency, or to ascertain the number of one's supporters.

Much of the interest which attaches to words derives from their history, and that is why the ordinary desk dictionary, although it serves a very useful purpose, should be supplemented in any library deserving of the name by a bigger one, in which there is room for history as well as current definition. Dictionaries would be still more interesting if they contained supplements devoted to phrases in common current use, with their equivalents in earlier periods. Like a lot of other people, I have been trying to establish in my mind when that popular, and to many ears, annoying phrase, "Goodbye now," came into common use. My guess is that it doesn't much antedate World War II; at least I cannot remember having heard it earlier.

Speculation as to why it came into being also interests me. My suspicion is that it was the natural outgrowth of the constant effort in English to find a satisfactory substitute for the finality of "Goodbye" itself. We have no established phrase, comparable to the French **au revoir**, the Italian **arrivederci**, the German **auf**

wiedersehn. Consequently we invent slang or colloquial phrases which do not live beyond the brief period in which they are commonly used; a short while ago it was "so long," which is not now often heard; now it is either "Goodbye now, or "I'll be seeing you." As often as not, in the streets of New York, and among men particularly, the parting words will be "Take it easy." Whether or not this last phrase is predominantly a New Yorkism, I am not sure. Certainly it might be accounted for as the natural product of a hurried, stressful time, in a hurried, stressful place. I find it difficult to place this one in time also; my guess would be that it is no more than ten or fifteen years old.

Curiously, forms of greeting seem to change less often than the phrases used for parting. Aside from the formal "How do you do" or the more casual "How are you," "Hello" still holds its own, though the monosyllabic "Hi" has taken over pretty completely among the small fry and has been rapidly spreading among their elders. These are matters, I contend, with which our dictionaries might properly concern themselves, and not make it necessary for us to consult more specialized works.

Time in seconds——

Directions: Select the best answer and place the appropriate letter in the parentheses.

1. J. Donald Adams states that the best dictionary for a "small desert island library" in his estimation is (a) a convenient pocket-sized edition; (b) any college edition; (c) the Shorter Oxford; (d) Webster's International. ( )
2. One important reason for his choice of a dictionary for an imaginary island is that it (a) is heftier; (b) dates the appearance of words; (c) is useful and enjoyable; (d) can be easily packed and stored. ( )
3. Mr. Adams finds placing dates on words to be (a) an exact pin-pointing procedure; (b) beyond belief; (c) a waste of an editor's time; (d) within reasonable credibility. ( )
4. The verb **canvass** came into the language, according to this article, in (a) 1508; (b) 1608; (c) 1708; (d) 1812. ( )
5. Evidently the word **canvass** (a) has held its meaning throughout its history; (b) began with one meaning and ended with another; (c) after many changes, now means the same thing as it originally did; (d) changed meanings over the years and is now obsolete. ( )
6. Dictionaries could be improved, suggests Mr. Adams, by (a) being shortened; (b) being made more hefty; (c) supplementing definitions with word histories; (d) keeping definitions up-to-date. ( )
7. He apparently feels that a college edition dictionary (a) serves a useful purpose, but should be supplemented; (b) serves no useful purpose; (c) serves perfectly for the imaginery desert island library; (d) serves perfectly under all circumstances. ( )
8. The phrase "Goodbye now" is probably considered by Mr. Adams as (a) annoying; (b) a satisfactory substitute for **au revoir**; (c) an established farewell in the United States; (d) obsolete. ( )
9. Forms of greeting in English seem to change (a) more than phrases for parting; (b) rarely, if at all; (c) less than phrases for parting; (d) steadily toward the single word "Hi." ( )
10. Mr. Adams evidently believes that dictionary makers (a) often are driven to distraction by certain words; (b) are not to be trusted on dating words; (c) live a hurried, stressful life; (d) part from their friends by saying "Take it easy." ( )

DIRECTIONS FOR SCORING

Reading Rate. If you completed the selection within the three-minute time limit by your hourglass, enter your score in the PERSONAL PROGRESS CHART as 300 words per minute. If you failed to complete the selection in the time allowed, **try again.**

If you timed yourself **in seconds,** follow directions as in other timed selections.

Answers to Questions. Check the answers to the multiple-choice questions in the CORRECTION KEY TO EXERCISES.

Progress Chart. Enter all reading rate and comprehension scores in the PERSONAL PROGRESS CHART.

VOCABULARY EXERCISE—I

The most popular type of vocabulary exercise is the multiple-choice test using synonyms. You are given a test word followed by several other words, one of which is related to the original word. One weakness of this type of definition has already been pointed out: **you may know that two words are related without knowing the meaning of either one.**

You may also know the test word and the test synonym and use both of them correctly. To make sure that this is the case, however, you are advised to **look up the words in your dictionary** after you have taken the test. Then figure your score. All the words in this test were drawn from a college freshman English textbook and have a frequency of occurrence of at least once in every million words you read.

Directions: Read each test word and then underline the synonym which fits it most closely. Do not linger on any one item. Try to complete the test within **five minutes.** Your score will be the number correct within this time limit. For purposes of comparison with later scores, you may consider 28-30 is excellent, 25-28 fair. Under 25 shows the need for intensive vocabulary study.

Time Yourself and Begin

1. *vociferous* (a) subdued; (b) angry; (c) profane; (d) noisy; (e) insistent.
2. *ephemeral* (a) permanent; (b) effeminate; (c) interesting; (d) roundabout; (e) transitory.
3. *opulent* (a) wealthy; (b) sleepy; (c) obese; (d) wasteful; (e) impoverished.
4. *magnanimous* (a) offensive; (b) inflated; (c) unselfish; (d) majestic; (e) spectacular.
5. *eminent* (a) overflowing; (b) vivid; (c) outstanding; (d) insistent; (e) soon.
6. *inevitable* (a) truthful; (b) ambiguous; (c) insecure; (d) worthy; (e) unavoidable.
7. *manifest* (a) obscure; (b) tenacious; (c) well-fed; (d) willing; (e) unmistakable.
8. *nurture* (a) upbringing; (b) tenderness; (c) agriculture; (d) beauty; (e) leadership.
9. *exigency* (a) exhaustion; (b) requirement; (c) ingenuity; (d) humility; (e) fear.
10. *vehement* (a) impetuous; (b) urbane; (c) discourteous; (d) stern; (e) uncouth.
11. *blatant* (a) dark; (b) blasphemous; (c) bland; (d) flattering; (e) noisy.
12. *audacity* (a) impudence; (b) curtness; (c) boldness; (d) loudness; (e) simplicity.
13. *supercilious* (a) melancholy; (b) arrogant; (c) superficial; (d) cowardly; (e) dangerous.
14. *exemplary* (a) problematical; (b) certified; (c) excusable; (d) model; (e) noble.
15. *incredulous* (a) skeptical; (b) interesting; (c) dull; (d) showing concern; (e) desirous.
16. *acquiesce* (a) approach; (b) obtain easily; (c) consent quietly; (d) mourn; (e) question.
17. *diabolical* (a) clever; (b) round; (c) insulting; (d) menacing; (e) fiendish.
18. *tumultuous* (a) uproarious; (b) melodious; (c) persuasive; (d) multitudinous; (e) stormy.
19. *opprobrious* (a) subservient; (b) aggressive; (c) disgraceful; (d) lackadaisical; (e) sober.
20. *sordid* (a) glaring; (b) depressing; (c) implausible; (d) senseless; (e) ignoble.
21. *frivolous* (a) serious; (b) stubborn; (c) obnoxious; (d) silly; (e) smooth.
22. *prodigious* (a) abundant; (b) enormous; (c) extravagant; (d) stingy; (e) productive.
23. *indefatigable* (a) untiring; (b) dispirited; (c) clumsy; (d) overweight; (e) deaf.
23. *querulous* (a) insistent; (b) complaining; (c) questioning; (d) strange; (e) talkative.
25. *languor* (a) loud ringing; (b) disbelief; (c) rage; (d) sluggishness; (e) intenseness.
26. *despicable* (a) unworthy; (b) contemptible; (c) painful; (d) tyrannical; (e) immoral.
27. *reminiscent* (a) futuristic; (b) remembering; (c) flowering; (d) reviving; (e) intelligent.

28. *crucial* (a) contrite; (b) decisive; (c) impulsive; (d) uncertain; (e) special.
29. *compatible* (a) self-satisfied; (b) deep; (c) capable; (d) harmonious; (e) appreciative.
30. *tenacious* (a) stubborn; (b) firm; (c) porous; (d) abrasive; (e) pleasant.

DIRECTIONS FOR SCORING

The answers to Vocabulary Exercise—I on the previous page can be found in your dictionary.

If you did not complete the items within the five-minute time limit, do this now. All words which you missed should be entered on flash cards for further study.

When you have completed checking and scoring, go to the next test.

VOCABULARY EXERCISE—II

Directions: The exercise below is patterned exactly after the 30-item vocabulary tests which measure your reading improvement progress at regular intervals.

You are to read each definition and underline the word which fits it most closely. Do not linger on any one item. Try to complete the exercise within **five minutes**. Your score will be based on the number correct within this time limit.

Time Yourself and Begin

1. Too familiar to be interesting
   (a) vulgar; (b) trite; (c) stagnant; (d) repetitious; (e) trivial.
2. Prepare for publication
   (a) transcribe; (b) edit; (c) proofread; (d) type; (e) revise.
3. Outward appearance
   (a) aspect; (b) bearing; (c) mask; (d) disguise; (e) deportment.
4. A rude, boisterous girl
   (a) minx; (b) shrew; (c) coquette; (d) hoyden; (e) vixen.
5. Not inclined to do something
   (a) latent; (b) retired; (c) quiescent; (d) loath; (e) impassive.
6. A search that usually involves a journey
   (a) quest; (b) foray; (c) excavation; (d) survey; (e) retinue.
7. Having the characteristics of old age
   (a) despotic; (b) morbid; (c) senile; (d) pathetic; (e) nostalgic.
8. Constantly industrious
   (a) laborious; (b) assiduous; (c) tireless; (d) provident; (e) abstemious.
9. Speak slightingly about someone or something
   (a) dispute; (b) disprove; (c) allege; (d) disbar; (e) disparage.
10. Enriched by gifts
    (a) endowed; (b) opulent; (c) funded; (d) treasured; (e) receptive.
11. Yield in order to gain time
    (a) defer; (b) retrench; (c) succumb; (d) recapitulate; (e) temporize.
12. Abandonment of a legal right or claim
    (a) resignation; (b) waiver; (c) abdication; (d) severance; (e) renege.
13. An alliance between two or more persons, parties or nations for a mutual purpose
    (a) league; (b) armistice; (c) partisanship; (d) truce; (e) charter.
14. To display boldly
    (a) depict; (b) predominate; (c) flaunt; (d) flagellate; (e) tantalize.
15. To chatter meaninglessly
    (a) brag; (b) babble; (c) rave; (d) tattle; (e) rant.
16. To avoid something considered undesirable
    (a) vacate; (b) scorn; (c) shun; (d) sneer; (e) repulse.
17. An indistinct sight
    (a) outline; (b) blur; (c) vestige; (d) apparition; (e) vision.
18. An indirect reference to anything
    (a) slander; (b) hearsay; (c) allusion; (d) paraphrase; (e) reflex.
19. Get value out of something for one's own advantage
    (a) improve; (b) appraise; (c) depreciate; (d) exploit; (e) market.
20. Easily disgusted or offended
    (a) squeamish; (b) discriminating; (c) haughty; (d) susceptible; (e) neurotic.

21. A small shoot or twig on a plant or tree
    (a) spindle; (b) freshet; (c) bud; (d) vine; (e) sprig.
22. Using more words than necessary
    (a) prolific; (b) compulsive; (c) verbose; (d) garbled; (e) bombastic.
23. A person who pretends to be something he is not
    (a) knave; (b) contender; (c) impostor; (d) upstart; (e) scoundrel.
24. To thicken or solidify
    (a) deepen; (b) compress; (c) agglutinate; (d) inure; (e) coagulate.
25. Standing for something else
    (a) surrealist; (b) symbolic; (c) significant; (d) fraudulent; (e) semantic.
26. A wasting away from lack of use or nourishment
    (a) atrophy; (b) liquidation; (c) aversion; (d) neglect; (e) infirmity.
27. A person despised by society
    (a) pariah; (b) criminal; (c) paragon; (d) servitor; (e) vagrant.
28. To speak evil of someone
    (a) betray; (b) bespeak; (c) malign; (d) chide; (e) harry.
29. Pertaining to the stars
    (a) nebulous; (b) ethereal; (c) astral; (d) luminous; (e) lunar.
30. Full of courage and spirit
    (a) sturdy; (b) intrepid; (c) brazen; (d) versatile; (e) sprightly.

DIRECTIONS FOR SCORING

Check the answers to the vocabulary questions in the CORRECTION KEY TO EXERCISES in the Appendix.

Enter all your scores in your PERSONAL PROGRESS CHART.

If you did not complete the vocabulary items within the five-minute time limit, do this now. All words which you missed should be entered on flash cards for further study.

A score in this vocabulary exercise of 28 or over can be considered excellent; 25-27 items correct, good; and 24 or under correct, an indication that intensive work with flash cards and a dictionary is needed.

SELECTED PAPERBOUND WORD BOOKS

Instant Vocabulary, by Ida Ehrlich. Pocket Books, Inc.

New Guide to Word Power, by Norman Lewis. Pyramid.

Six Weeks to Words of Power, by Wilfred Funk. Pocket Books, Inc.

Word Power Made Easy, by Norman Lewis. Pocket Books, Inc.

Word Mastery Made Simple, by Arthur Waldhorn and Arthur Zeiger. Made Simple Books, Inc.

Your Words Are Your Magic, by Beth Brown. Pocket Books, Inc.

PAPERBOUND DICTIONARIES

American Heritage Dictionary of the English Language (Dell)

Funk and Wagnall's Standard Dictionary (NAL/Signet)

The Merriam-Webster Dictionary (Pocket Books, Inc.)

The Oxford English Dictionary (Avon)

The Random House Dictionary (Ballantine)

The Scribner-Bantam English Dictionary (Bantam)

Webster's New World Dictionary of the American Language (Popular Library)

Webster's New World Dictionary of the American Language (New American Library)

WORD RECOGNITION AND ATTACK EXERCISE

Directions: Look at the single word, preferably through the Eye-Span Card. Then move the card rapidly to the five words directly below, and pick out with your eyes the word that is exactly the same as the single word.

Do Not Say The Word Aloud.

Continue to the next single word and repeat the operation. Do not make any marks on the page, so that you can repeat this exercise daily for a week or two.

*

whither
whether whither wither either whiter

*

beater
beater beaten better bleater later

*

porch
porch parch perch pitch patch

*

complement
compliment clement confident complement comment

*

eclectic
electric elective celeriac elliptic eclectic

*

partial
practice particle partisan partial practical

*

depreciate
depreciate deprecate delegate deprivation appreciate

*

seminary
seminal seminary cemetery secretary centenary

*

predilection
prediction perdition perfection predilection election

*

equitable
equivocal equable equal equitable equivocate

*

gregarious
pregarious egregious querulous grievous garrulous

*

consecutive
conserve consecutive costive consent consulate

*

insulate
isolate insular isolation insulation insulate

*

affected
afflicted affected effected reflected deflected

*

towed
towed trowel toured toned towel

*

tribute
tribute tribal tribune tribunal trident

*

danger
dander danger dangler bandage badinage

*

topical
topical typical tropical tropic stoical

*

antipathy
antimony sympathy anticipate articulate antipathy

*

ingenuous
ingenuous indents ingenious unguents engender

STUDY ASSIGNMENT

To help you consciously speed up your reading when you look at any printed material— your daily newspaper, magazine articles or books—try this exercise occasionally using your 3 x 5 card.

Lower the card on the column on page you are reading **line by line.** Continue down the page in this way as rapidly as you can.

You may vary this technique by using the top edge of the card. As you lower the card the printed material will be exposed **line by line.** This technique permits you to **regress,** but it will also draw your attention immediately back to the exposed line.

Both of these methods require a certain amount of self-discipline. You yourself are in effect acting somewhat like a mechanical device. With a consistent application of these methods reading speed gains are likely to be not only **made** but also **held.**

You are furthermore urged to consciously speed up your reading even when you are not using the 3 x 5 card down the page.

Continue adding to your reading autobiography.

Study conscientiously your vocabulary flash cards.

CHAPTER SEVEN

HOW TO READ A PARAGRAPH

Your own reading, for no matter what purpose, will have a great deal more meaning for you if you think of it as an important part of the process of **communication.**

Communication may be defined as the transmission of messages between human beings.

A diagram to help you visualize the communication process is so simple that you can jot it down for yourself.

At the left of a sheet of paper, draw a circle to represent the **sender** of a message. At the right, draw a circle to represent the **receiver.**

Then connect the two circles by a straight line. This will represent the channel.

When a message is sent, the information it contains is theoretically fed into the left circle, where it is encoded, or given expression, in print, speech, or gesture. Out goes the message over the line.

At the other circle, the message is received and decoded, or interpreted, so that the information may be used, acted upon, or simply enjoyed. It may also be ignored, of course.

Consider the act of reading a single paragraph appearing in print.

The writer has encoded his thoughts by expressing them in appropriate words, which have been published. The paragraph itself is the medium of communication (made up of paper and printers' ink), represented by the channel on the diagram. You read the paragraph, decode the printed words in your mind, and thereby get the intended message.

A similar transmission of ideas takes place between a speaker and a listener, a demonstrator and an observer.

This is all very simple and yet all very complicated. Because as you know and everybody else knows, even the most elementary piece of information contained in a single paragraph often does not reach its destination in its original form. Or even if it does, it may not be at all understood by the receiver.

Often it is the sender's fault if the message fails to carry effectively.

Fuzzy thinking is expressed in weak writing, faulty speech, or inappropriate gesture. This may place such a handicap on the intended message that all meaning is lost by the time it reaches the receiver.

Your daily life is flooded by such messages. They drum into your ears, overflow your mailbox at home and in the office. They drone, blast, or flash out on your television screen.

In other instances, the failure of communication is caused by what electronic engineers call "noise."

NOISE

Noise may be defined as anything which interferes with the transmission of a message once it goes out over the line. Thus noise may be "snow" on a TV screen, or static on the radio. Noise is also loud conversation in the room when you're trying to see and hear a program.

A typographical error in a newspaper, a break in a movie film, inferior acoustics in a theater, all can be considered noise.

Even a misspelled word in a business letter will be noise to the critical reader.

When reading is thought of as a communication skill, the failure of messages to arrive is often the sign of a poor receiver. A clear main idea, supported by details clearly expressed in a paragraph of print—not just hastily thrown together, but revised, edited, proofread and placed on the page with care—may be lost on the inefficient reader.

Transmission excellent in this case, with noise at a minimum. Reception: Nil.

This book is concerned throughout with increasing your capacity to receive such messages.

SENTENCES AND PARAGRAPHS

Improving your **word attack** and **recognition** as well as your **vocabulary** are some of the ways you can become a better receiver of printed and written messages.

The ability to analyze sentences and paragraphs quickly is another way.

You don't need to take every sentence in a paragraph apart to see how it ticks. Knowing how to parse or diagram a sentence may be helpful but it is not essential.

You should, however, have a grasp of certain features of the grammar of a sentence in English.

It may come as a surprise to you that you know a lot about it already. Otherwise you wouldn't be able to communicate with your fellowman at all.

You may not know the terminology. But you do know how to handle what the terms stand for.

Descriptive English grammar tries to present all the facts about the language gathered from systematic observation. How you speak and write is a part of the total picture.

From this observation you learn that three levels of language usage exist, although they may merge on many occasions.

As they appear in print, they are briefly as follows:

1. **Formal level of usage,** found in many quality magazines and often on the editorial page of a newspaper.

2. **Informal level of usage,** found in popular magazines and in the news sections of most newspapers.

3. **Colloquial level of usage,** found in pulp magazines and some tabloid newspapers.

Books in print, both fiction and nonfiction, may be written on **any one** or **all** levels of usage.

Descriptive grammar is therefore far from being a set of hidebound rules. Instead, it is an attempt to describe English as it actually operates in your life and in the lives of those around you.

Whenever you speak or write you do so in sentences or fragments of sentences, though you probably seldom stop to analyze them consciously. And every time you communicate in the English language you make use of a feeling for **word order.**

This feeling is acquired almost with the air you breathe as a child.

Individuals who learn English as a second language often have difficulty with this at first, but actually the sense for **word order** can be learned by anyone.

It is of especial importance for those who are trying to increase reading efficiency to be aware that English sentences repeatedly fall into a standard pattern to carry the reader's attention forward as follows:

actor → action → goal

Stated in another way, you may call the **actor** part of the sentence the **subject.**

The action part is the **verb** (or **linking verb,** in some instances, such as *be, feel, seem, etc.*) and is contained in the **predicate** of the sentence.

And finally, the goal is either a **direct** or **indirect object,** or, in the instance of a **linking verb, a complement.**

In this brief description, you can discover all you need to discover about the underlying pattern of the typical English sentence to help you with your reading.

Of course, these bare bones of a sentence are usually clothed in **modifiers** of various kinds as well as the extra refinements of **phrases** and **clauses**.[1]

Occasionally, too, the word order is inverted for reasons of writing style.

But the familiar skeleton is still there if you're skillful enough to discover it.

One example may point this up for you.

Joe struck Jack.

Here is a simple enough statement, with the **actor** (Joe), **action** (struck), and **goal** (Jack) clearly stated.

Now build up this sentence, based on the original word order, and you will see how the essential information is carried within the standard pattern.

In a wild, stick-swinging battle for the puck at the end of a championship hockey game, Joe Dosideau, of the visiting Quebec team, accidentally struck Jack LeBlanc, of Saskachewan, over the right eye and sent him to the dressing room for five stitches.

No matter how you present this information —and it can be said in a dozen ways—the underlying word order pattern will always tell you one thing. **It is poor Jack who gets the shiner!**

The efficient reader will discover this underlying pattern no matter how complicated the sentence may appear to be.

You might take a few minutes each day to pick out and underline the **actor—action—goal** words in the sentences you read. Any item on the front page of your newspaper will provide material. Note especially the position of the words in the sentence.

Note also the position of sentences in a paragraph.

A paragraph, you will observe, usually contains one main idea, often stated in the first sentence. Supporting details follow in succeeding sentences. For a new main idea, you may expect a new paragraph.

The sentence containing the main idea is sometimes called the topic sentence.

TOPIC SENTENCES

Although almost everyone was taught about topic sentences at some point or another in early school years, the teaching was customarily applied to **writing** paragraphs, not to **reading** them.

To refresh your memory, paragraphs do not always have the topic sentence as the first sentence. They may be organized so that a series of sentences with supporting details will lead up to a final summarizing sentence. Some paragraphs have topic sentences at both beginning and end. Sometimes they are in the middle.

Occasionally, you will find paragraphs without a topic sentence. In this case, either the main idea is implied or the paragraph may contain merely a series of details to develop the theme.

The value to a reader of being able to analyze quickly and accurately the construction of a paragraph is obvious. In an instant, the main idea is picked up and the supporting details are covered in rapid succession.

Or the experienced reader will move ahead swiftly taking in all of the supporting details and then linger a moment longer over a summarizing statement containing the main idea.

In material on a familiar subject, the reader often will find the bare statement of the main idea to be sufficient, supplying from personal experience or memory the details, comparisons, statistics, or whatever else is needed to support the main idea. This is especially the case in reading books or articles on your own trade, business or profession.

PURPOSE

Your *purpose* in reading certain types of printed material, in particular nonfiction prose

---

[1] Readers who wish to pursue further study in English grammar are referred to *English Made Simple*, by Arthur Waldhorn and Arthur Zeiger, Made Simple Books, Inc.

of a factual nature, also will determine how you approach each paragraph.

In preparing for an **essay-type examination** or a **platform speech** you might wish to read for main ideas so that you can grasp the larger concepts. This will give you an opportunity to read widely on the subject since you can cover more ground when you do not concern yourself too much with details. The details can be filled in from information you already have.

In preparing for an **objective-type examination** or a **group discussion** you might wish to read not only for main ideas but also for the supporting details. This will supply you with a stock of incidental facts about the subject at hand.

An entire later chapter will be devoted to the various techniques of reading textbooks for study.

A good way to complete your grasp of paragraph structure is to go directly to printed material and analyze the paragraphs used by professional writers. Some of them will be difficult to take apart. Many will appear intricate because the main idea is implied and not stated.

Most of the paragraphs, however, will contain the statement of the main idea in the first sentence. Just this knowledge in itself will help you to speed up your reading.

Next you can begin to look at the larger elements, the position of paragraphs in the entire work. Here again a certain order of arrangement may be used by the writer which can be analyzed quickly by the reader.

Some of these orders of arrangement will be discussed in CHAPTER EIGHT.

PARAGRAPH ANALYSIS EXERCISE

Directions: This exercise consists of ten paragraphs taken from *A Basic History of the United States,* by Charles A. Beard and Mary R. Beard. Following each paragraph are three multiple-choice items. The first item asks you for the location of the topic sentence in the paragraph, if any. The second item asks you for the main idea of the paragraph. The third item asks you for a piece of factual information contained in the paragraph. In each case you are to read the paragraph, then go on to answer the questions by underlining your choice. You may look back if you wish. Try to complete this exercise within **ten minutes**.

Time Yourself and Begin

A BASIC HISTORY OF THE UNITED STATES

I.

In far-off times it had been written: "Blessed are the meek for they shall inherit the earth." As if to fulfill the law, Henry VII, King of England, established in 1497 a claim to the continental domain in which the history of the United States was to unfold. Thus he took title to a great portion of the earth for the English people long before anyone, even in England, knew that the voyage of Columbus from Spain across the sea to the West Indies in 1492 had broken the path to a vast new world.

1. Identify the topic sentence: (a) first; (b) last; (c) middle; (d) first and last; (e) none.
2. King Henry VII was, according to the passage, (a) a grasping monarch; (b) an adventurous monarch; (c) a mild monarch.
3. The claim of King Henry VII was made in the (a) fourteenth century; (b) fifteenth century; (c) sixteenth century.

II.

Cabot reached Cape Breton Island in 1497 and there planted the standard of the English King, supposing that he had come upon the east coast of Asia. With news of this discovery he went back to England. The next year Cabot was sent out again, on a second voyage, to explore further. This time Cabot sighted the east coast of Greenland but his sailors mutinied against pushing as far north as he wished to go. Turning south, he scouted the shore to a point in the neighborhood of Chesapeake Bay. Unable, however, to find a rich people with goods for profitable trade, he returned to England deeply disappointed.

1. Identify the topic sentence: (a) first; (b) last; (c) middle; (d) first and last; (e) none.
2. Cabot's voyages resulted in his attaining a feeling of (a) high accomplishment; (b) deep disappointment; (c) bitter frustration.
3. Cabot planted the standard of the King of England on (a) Cape Breton; (b) Greenland; (c) the east coast of Asia.

III.

Besides encountering the strange aborigines, the first English settlers found themselves in the presence of new and wide variations of climate. In their old home they had been accustomed to a moderate temperature. Now they had before them a great range of climate from the cold coasts of Maine to the hot savannahs of Georgia, with all the gradations from the far North to the deep South. To the exigencies of these variations, all the immigrants, from the British Isles as well as the Continent, had to adapt their economy and ways of living. Wherever the colonists set to work in clearing land for tillage, building houses, sowing and reaping, and producing the commodities required for living, they had to take into account the conditioning element of climate.

1. Identify the topic sentence: (a) first; (b) last; (c) middle; (d) first and last; (e) none.
2. The main idea of this paragraph is centered on (a) the strange aborigines; (b) the climate; (c) the English settlers.
3. The immigrants were from (a) the Continent of Europe; (b) the British Isles; (c) the British Isles as well as the Continent.

IV.

In the forests were also wild animals in a great variety, the furs and skins of which were useful for domestic purposes and profitable for export. In the forests was wild game for food—

turkeys, deer, rabbits, and squirrels, for instance—and more meat and more kinds of meat could be procured than the plain peoples had ever enjoyed in the Old World, at first without asking the permission of any lord or gamekeeper or poaching secretly on private preserves. In the forests were nuts, berries, grapes, and other wild fruits available to agile climbers and pickers, aids to a balanced diet and free as the air.

1. Identify the topic sentence: (a) first; (b) last; (c) middle; (d) first and last; (e) none.
2. The best title for this paragraph would be (a) The Riches of the New World: (b) How to Hunt Wild Animals; (c) A Balanced Diet.
3. It is noted that through exportation, profits might be gained from (a) wild fruits; (b) furs and skins; (c) meat.

V.

In Pennsylvania the proprietor had the right, like the proprietor of Maryland, under his charter, to lay out and sell great estates, manors, in his colony and he did in fact lend some encouragement to great landlordism. But most of Pennsylvania was divided into farms that could be tilled by their owners aided only by one or a few extra laborers, if any. Furthermore large numbers of pioneers simply settled on the frontier without asking the permission of Penn or anybody else. Thus farming on a small or moderate scale became the general rule in Pennsylvania agriculture.

1. Identify the topic sentence: (a) first; (b) last; (c) middle; (d) first and last; (e) none.
2. The main idea in this paragraph is contained in a statement about (a) William Penn; (b) Maryland; (c) Pennsylvania.
3. The land owners at this time could till their farms with the help of (a) one or two laborers; (b) no laborers; (c) other landlords.

VI.

On farms and plantations from New Hampshire to Georgia men usually made and repaired farm implements—plows, sleds, wagons, and hoes. Out of furs and skins they made shoes, hats, and caps. Out of wood they fashioned furniture, churns, spinning wheels, and looms. Where wrought iron was available they manufactured nails, shovels, and chains. At the same time women generally turned their skills and wits to making cloth, rugs, soap, candles, bedding, coverlets, tablecloths, and garments. They also operated processing plants, in which bread was baked, meat was packed, fruits and vegetables were dehydrated and preserved, and butter was churned.

1. Identify the topic sentence: (a) first; (b) last; (c) middle; (d) first and last; (e) none.
2. The best title for this selection would be (a) The Self-sufficiency of the New England Farmer; (b) The Farm Women; (c) A Day in the Country.
3. Out of wood the early American farmer made (a) shoes; (b) looms; (c) plows.

VII.

The early newcomers to America were under obligations to look about for objects of commerce almost as soon as they landed. The first ship which deposited settlers in Virginia carried home a cargo of wooden staves prepared for it under the direction of Captain John Smith. Lumber and its by-products became commodities for export from Virginia before settlers in that colony learned to produce, cure, and pack tobacco.

1. Identify the topic sentence: (a) first; (b) last; (c) middle; (d) first and last; (e) none.
2. The early settlers were obliged to look for the following almost as soon as they landed; (a) tobacco; (b) forests; (c) objects of commerce.
3. On a return voyage, the first ship to reach Virginia's shores carried home (a) Captain John Smith; (b) wooden staves; (c) tobacco.

VIII.

The dissemination of knowledge and ideas, news, information, and misinformation was facilitated by the rise and growth of a colonial postal system. As early as 1639 the legislature of Massachusetts made provision for a local post office and this example was followed by other colonies as they grew in size and population. Under a royal patent of 1692 an intercolonial postal service was established as a private enterprise. Fifteen years later it was taken over by the English government and developed under successive postmasters general, Benjamin Franklin assuming that office in 1753.

1. Identify the topic sentence: (a) first; (b) last; (c) middle; (d) first and last; (e) none.
2. The principal thought in this passage deals with (a) the postal system; (b) royal patents; (c) Benjamin Franklin.
3. Benjamin Franklin assumed the office of postmaster general in (a) 1629; (b) 1692; (c) 1753.

IX.

The growing body of federal officers engaged in enforcing the new laws under Washington's executive direction was supplemented by a new federal judiciary. By the Judiciary Act of 1789, Congress established the Supreme Court prescribed by the Constitution and a federal district court in each state, with a set of officials and agents for each court. Washington appointed as Chief Justice John Jay, who had battled for the ratification of the Constitution; and all the other judgeships he filled with men having a similar attitude toward the new order.

1. Identify the topic sentence: (a) first; (b) last; (c) middle; (d) first and last; (e) none.
2. The main idea in this paragraph is (a) the growing body of federal officers; (b) the Judiciary Act of 1789; (c) the appointment of John Jay as Chief Justice of the Supreme Court.
3. The federal judiciary was established by (a) the Congress of the United States; (b) George Washington; (c) John Jay.

X.

As an outcome of the stirring and converging forces at work in the United States the little

Union formed by the original thirteen states on the seaboard—the Union now continental in extent—was becoming national in its ideas and feelings, even in the South as pro-slavery secessionists learned from the number and vigor of their opponents in their very midst. It is true that nowhere in the Constitution of the United States did the word "nation" or the word "national" appear. In their secret convention at Philadelphia in 1787 the framers of the Constitution at first resolved that they were seeking to establish a government "national" in all departments; but they struck out the word "national" from their resolutions, thinking, no doubt, that it would disturb advocates of states' rights. Nevertheless Madison, Jay, and Hamilton used the fateful and prophetic words in *The Federalist*. Washington, Jefferson, and Jackson repeatedly referred to the United States as a "nation" and to its great interests as "national." Although as late as 1850 it was still customary in popular usage and in prayers for divine blessing to speak of "these" United States, events were outrunning the language. In the travail of the democratic insurgency these states were fusing into an American nation—one and indivisible.

1. Identify the topic sentence: (a) first; (b) last; (c) middle; (d) first and last; (e) none.
2. The main idea in this passage can be stated in the single word (a) secessionism; (b) nationalism; (c) statism.
3. The framers of the Constitution (a) never once used the word "national" in their resolutions; (b) used the word "national" in the final draft; (c) used the word "national" in an original draft but then struck it out.

DIRECTIONS FOR SCORING

Reading Rate. Although ten minutes was the time limit suggested for the paragraph exercise just completed, fifteen minutes is considered **good**, and twenty minutes, **fair**. Over twenty minutes is considered slow for this type of material. These reading rate evaluations are based on a comprehension score of not less than 21 items correct out of 30.

Answers to Questions. Check the answers to the multiple-choice questions in the CORRECTION KEY TO EXERCISES.

Progress Chart. Enter your comprehension score in the PERSONAL PROGRESS CHART.

READING EXERCISE

Instructions: Electronic brains are remarkable "thinkers," but they still rely on man for direction. Even that lowly form of life the octopus can use its brain in ways a robot cannot. Read this selection in **three minutes or less.** Answer the questions immediately.

Time Yourself and Begin

THE OCTOPUS AND THE ROBOT

Deep-sea explorers who have observed the octopus at home on the ocean's floor tell of its strange behavior in certain situations. If confronted by a large enough object, something the size of its enemy the dogfish or, even larger, a scientist in a diving helmet, it will retreat and change color, turning first a dusky shade of white or red and then a mottled pattern of light and dark. Although this masquerade will hardly intimidate the scientist, it is quite likely to scare the dogfish away.

On the other hand, if the confronting object is a crab, the octopus, aware of a potential meal, will hurl itself in pursuit, and with perfect aim seize the target in its tentacles.

Again, the octopus (which, incidentally, is also called the devil fish and is much sought after by fishermen from the Mediterranean to the Sea of Japan, to be sold as a table delicacy) will behave in just the same way if it is observed instead through the glass walls of a tank in a marine laboratory. A poke from a stick results in a change of color. A crab tossed into the tank soon becomes a meal.

But what makes the octopus act with such consistency, so that food calls forth one sort of response and an enemy another? Can this creature think? Does it have a brain, that is, that enables it to size up a situation and then behave as intelligently as possible for its own survival? Yes, say the scientists. It is a very elementary sort of brain, but it is sufficient for the octopus.

Now consider a guided missile known as the Falcon, developed since World War II and highly prized by the United States Air Force. Six feet long and weighing a hundred pounds, this electronic robot loaded with explosives can be launched from a jet fighter. Once a target has been selected, the Falcon will find and destroy it. If the target should change its course it makes no difference; the Falcon acts as if it has a brain and uses it.

Only, the Falcon's "brain" is easily understood by man, since he himself made it. The brain of the octopus is for the most part still a mystery. Nevertheless, a comparison of the two is found useful by scientists who do research on human brain processes.

Professor J. Z. Young, of University College, London, for instance, makes the point that noting resemblances between the unknown (the brain of an octopus) and the known (an electronic "brain") may be a step toward comprehension of a further unknown (the living human brain). Such analogies, though not to be taken literally, help to explain more clearly the direction in which modern study of the brain is moving.

"We still cannot describe exactly how the nervous system works in the octopus," Professor Young says, "but we find it helpful in trying to do so to speak of the actions of its brain as an engineer would describe the parts of a guided missile."

The behavior of both octopus and robot is regulated by *feedback*. That is the principle according to which the action of a machine (or an organism) is controlled by its own results. Many examples of feedback may be found in the human nervous system as well as in the giant electronic computers used in science and industry, but a simple, familiar illustration will serve here: the governor used on steam engines. As the engine reaches a certain speed, centrifugal force makes the whirling governor rise and automatically shut off steam. Consequently, the engine slows down; whereupon the governor lowers and turns the steam on again.

Naturally, feedback systems vary greatly in complexity. Those in the much-publicized electronic "brains" are highly complicated; so is the system by which the octopus can turn the color of a red brick when it spots an enemy. But far more complicated, in fact beyond present comprehension, is the process within the human brain. What happens, say, when a man falls in love with a beautiful girl, so that for a considerable time afterward her presence or her image or her voice has a marked effect on his behavior?

This ability of the brain to select and react to slightly different shapes and sounds is a remarkable evolutionary achievement, and no one has as yet succeeded in explaining it.

A baby learns at an early stage to focus its eyes, move them together, and follow along lines, especially continuous lines that make an object stand out from its background. Certain patterns soon become more familiar than others The following of lines and circles is certainly the basis for later reading habits.

It might be supposed that large numbers of scientists are at present trying to probe the tantalizing subject of the brain. Actually, not more than a hundred or so top specialists are at work in this field. Some have given up, feeling that the brain's activity is forever beyond human grasp.

It is known that the human brain contains some twelve to fifteen billion cells. By contrast, the largest electronic brain now in existence numbers its components in no more than thousands.

The nerve fibers which conduct the messages in the brain are about 1/1000 inch in diameter. Pulsations may follow each other at the rate of ten a second or more. But it is not known how the brain handles these messages. No one has so far answered the question of how the brain unifies, records and facilitates patterns of activity. Yet the answer, when found, may be quite simple.

A few machines can do just about every job a man can do and a great many things better than a man. But it still takes men to design and construct the machines and turn the switch to get them started. Men with brains, that is.

Time in seconds_____

Directions: Answer each question by selecting the best answer and placing the appropriate letter in the parentheses.

1. This article states that man best understands the workings of the brain of (a) an octopus; (b) a human being; (c) a robot; (d) a dogfish. ( )
2. Professor J. Z. Young makes the point that a step toward comprehending the living human brain may be made by noting resemblances between (a) the octopus and the robot; (b) the octopus and the dogfish; (c) the octopus and the crab; (d) the octopus and the scientist. ( )
3. A man falling in love with a beautiful girl is mentioned as an example of (a) automation; (b) feedback; (c) evolution; (d) focusing. ( )
4. The author says that the basis for reading habits is formed by (a) focusing the eyes; (b) exercising the brain; (c) evolutionary achievement; (d) following lines and circles. ( )
5. The ability of the brain to select and react to various shapes and sounds (a) has never been explained by anyone; (b) is acquired through early schooling; (c) is thoroughly understood through electronic research; (d) is a remarkable evolutionary achievement which will never be explained. ( )

6. The Falcon, developed by the USAF, is a/an (a) electronic computer; (b) guided missile; (c) jet plane; (d) target controlled by radio. ( )
7. The octopus is comparable to the robot, says the author, because (a) their actions are controlled by the results of previous actions; (b) their behavior is similar when confronted by enemies; (c) their brains both have tens of thousands of cells; (d) their nervous structures are both like a telephone exchange. ( )
8. Research on the human living brain (a) is being carried on by thousands of scientists; (b) has been given up completely as beyond human grasp; (c) is being carried on by a hundred or so top specialists; (d) is being conducted by the USAF. ( )
9. The article is intended by the author to show that (a) man's brain is far superior to an electronic brain; (b) man's brain is inferior to an electronic brain; (c) man's brain will remain a mystery forever; (d) the brain of the robot was modelled after the brain of an octopus. ( )
10. It may be inferred that the author is impressed with (a) the number of scientists working on brain research; (b) the Falcon; (c) devil fish as a table delicacy; (d) the living human brain. ( )

DIRECTIONS FOR SCORING

Reading Rate. If you completed the selection within the three-minute time limit by your hourglass, enter your score in the PERSONAL PROGRESS CHART as 330 words per minute. If you failed to complete the selection in the time allowed, try again.

If you timed yourself in seconds, follow directions as in other timed selections.

Answers to Questions. Check the answers to the multiple-choice questions in the CORRECTION KEY TO TESTS.

Progress Chart. Enter all reading rate and comprehension scores in the PERSONAL PROGRESS CHART.

EYE-SPAN EXERCISES

Instructions: On a 3 x 5 card (preferably with a rectangular cut-out as described in CHAPTER THREE) pencil in an arrow which will point directly down the center when the Eye-Span Card is placed on a column of this book.

As you move the card down the page from asterisk to asterisk, you are asked to focus your eyes directly below the pointing arrow.

Thus, when a single word is exposed your fixation will be approximately in the center of the word, as follows:

↓

think

When two words are exposed, your single fixation will also be somewhere near the center, as follows:

↓

think fast

As more and more words are exposed, combined into phrases or short sentences, your fixation will be as follows:

↓

think fast when you read

First try this exercise of five-letter words. Think the words. Do not say them aloud.

Begin

*

dress

*

plumb

*

quirt

*

agony

dross

*

crass

*

amuse

*

ripen

*

stomp

*

navel

*

twist

*

molar

*

waist

*

plump

*

eager

*

mouse

*

cross

*

venal

*

spore

*

wrist

*

Now an exercise of two words, each with four or five letters.

Begin

*

wild grass

*

even rows

*

fast dogs

*

moist lawn

*

upper rock

ebony trunk
*
tired steel
*
torn town
*
third trill
*
rusty pail
*
high solo
*
other thing
*
moral sign
*
sits light
*
never even
*
candy cart
*
tenth item
*
slow burn
*
loud tale
*
wily catch
*

STUDY ASSIGNMENTS

An Eye-Span Card may be prepared for use with any digest-type magazine printed with double columns on the page.

Follow these directions:

On a 3 x 5 index card cut out a rectangular opening measuring 2¼" x ⅛". The opening should be near the edge of the card.

Select an article from one of these magazines and read it as you expose a single line at a time. Try to keep your fixations to a minimum. Move down the page as rapidly as possible.

When you complete a page or two, test your comprehension by writing down as many main points and supporting details as you can remember.

Accelerate your reading as much as possible, although your comprehension may drop off considerably. Keep practicing with unfamiliar material. Eventually your comprehension will begin to improve.

Continue adding to your reading autobiography.

Study your vocabulary flash cards.

As an additional assignment in vocabulary-building, make a list of the words which are connected with your day-to-day activities. Try to think of every word that makes up the specialized language of your business, profession, trade, vocation or, if you wish, avocation.

For example, an individual who made a hobby of breeding tropical fish would need a great number of special words to describe his activities to a novice. Doctors, lawyers, accountants, insurance and real estate men all have languages of their special fields.

Transfer to your flash cards those words you may recognize, but which you hesitate to use in writing or speaking.

In the reading exercise for this chapter were several words which might be added to your cards. Do you know the meaning of the following?

dusky
mottled
analogies
centrifugal
components
facilitates

Look back at the article once again to find these words in context.

Study your vocabulary flash cards frequently. Discard the flash cards of those words you learn. Add new words constantly.

CHAPTER EIGHT

UNDERSTANDING AN ARTICLE

Magazine articles as well as newspaper feature articles cover such a wide range of topics that they are almost impossible to put into categories.

The kind of writing used in these articles is labeled **exposition.** This may be defined as writing which informs and instructs the reader.

Familiar examples of the short forms of expository writing may be listed under such headings as educational, religious, political, financial, scientific, homemaking, travel, sports, pets, crime, hobbies, and literary, dramatic or art criticism, etc., etc.

You may extend the list according to the sort of articles you read.

One entire category of expository writing might come under the heading of "How-to-do-it." Detailed instructions in such pieces may range from **how to bake a cake** to **how to build a house.**

Another way in which material may be presented is by **narration.** In this type of writing, real events are presented in chronological order as in autobiographical sketches, profiles, or personal experiences. Short stories and novels are also examples of narrative writing, using imagined events.

Description is a type of writing which may be compared to painting a picture. An accomplished writer may present a scene in any number of ways. The accomplished reader has the ability to recreate the scene in his own mind's eye.

Still another way to present material is through **argumentation.** In this instance, the writer is trying to convince or persuade the reader. He attempts to communicate certain facts and certain inferences, then hopes the reader will draw certain inevitable conclusions.

The general public, turning to articles not only for enjoyment but also for information, may have little interest in knowing how various pieces are planned and written.

The highly efficient reader is vitally interested in knowing. Or if he isn't he should be. An alert reader may discover almost from the opening paragraph of a feature article the direction toward which the writer is headed.

You soon learn how to take apart an article quickly by understanding how it is put together.

THE STRUCTURE OF ARTICLES

The structure of articles may well be compared to the structure of certain kinds of advertising copy.

First, the writer offers something to attract the reader's attention. This may be a provocative headline or title, an anecdote or a startling statement, or, in the case of many advertisements, a compelling illustration.

The attention-getting opening is followed immediately by a brief and well-reasoned direct statement to the reader telling him why this particular piece of writing is of interest to him.

This approach has been called "the YOU attitude," since the writer often addresses it to YOU.

The main body of the article (or advertisement) comes next. This contains the principal idea the writer wishes to communicate. The principal idea may be supported by details of one kind or another, statistics, comparisons, testimonials, or photographs and charts and other kinds of graphic material.

Finally, a brief climactic ending pulls the entire piece together.

Sometimes in a magazine or newspaper article, and almost always in an advertisement, the ending will ask for some kind of action on the part of the reader.

This method of presentation, with various modifications, is used again and again as the underlying structure of the article.

One highly experienced teacher of writing courses, in reducing this four-part structure to its bare bones, has described it in the following dramatic and humorous manner:

HEY!
YOU!
SEE?
SO!

To attain more speed as well as greater comprehension in reading, you might take a closer look at these four parts of an article.

To begin with, the attention-getting opening may vary considerably. At least five different openings are popular with writers and may be used on occasion.

They may be described as follows:

Summary Opening. In this case the main ideas in the article are summed up at the very beginning. Or, if the article has a single principal point to make, it may be stated forcefully at the outset. In a feature article about education, the summary opening might be something like this: "America's future engineers may one day regret that their college studies don't include literature."

Shock Opening. To make a reader sit up and take notice, the writer may open up immediately with a startling statement. Sometimes it may be exaggerated for effect. For example: "The nation's future engineers will be literary ignoramuses."

Mood Opening. Through the use of words which may heighten the reader's emotional interest in the subject, the writer in this case sets the stage for his factual material. "Lights shine out in thousands of college dormitory windows throughout the nation. The 'midnight oil' burns while engineering students ponder on abstract problems in mathematics. Meanwhile the works of the great poets and philosophers lie dusty in the library stacks."

Delayed Opening. In this case the writer backs the reader gently into the main idea of the article, following the inductive path of the particular to the general. "The most brilliant mathematical minds of the country have entered the classrooms to help young men achieve engineering degrees. Each year thousands of students are being prepared for professional careers. But although they may be highly trained specialists in their own fields, they are likely to be literary illiterates."

Anecdotal Opening. Perhaps the most popular of all, the anecdotal opening is a brief (and usually true) story which leads the reader directly to the body of the article. "In the ten years since he left engineering school, Dr. Amos K. Lacklander has risen to become one of the nation's top research engineers. But last week he turned up back at his alma mater. Asked why he was enrolling for an adult studies course in comparative literature, he replied, 'I want to learn how to read. I missed this part of my education the first time around.'"

It might be noted at this point that some magazine articles are built on a series of anecdotes loosely strung together. The central theme of the story acts as the thread. For example, in writing of a new medical discovery, the writer may describe in anecdotal form the separate events which led up to the discovery.

Another point to note in reading the openings of articles is that the writer usually sets the *tone* for the entire piece with his first words.

Thus, you know almost immediately whether the article is intended to be humorous, satirical, tragic, educational, or whatever.

THE "YOU" ATTITUDE

Immediately following the opening, which may be quite brief, the reader is often addressed directly.

Another form this opening may take in order to bring the reader into the article might be called the "we" attitude. In this case the writer attempts to team up with his reader to form a mutual partnership on the reading journey.

In other cases the writer, after a brief opening, plunges immediately into the substance of his article.

You can readily see that an efficient reader may move rapidly over the opening and proceed directly to the main body of an article. **Nothing of significance is missed by so doing.**

THE MAIN BODY

The main body of an article often has an underlying structure of its own.

You will improve your reading skill by learning how to find this structure as you move ahead rapidly on the page.

What are the possibilities? What are you to look for?

Four ways of presenting expository material come to mind at once, as follows:

Time sequence. The writer begins at a certain point in chronological time and as he moves ahead with the article, he moves ahead in time. Although such an order of arrangement can be dull, the writer may capture your interest by building up to a climax. In any case, the reader is expected to continue on to the end if he is to learn what finally happens.

Space sequence. The writer begins at a certain point in geographical space and as he moves ahead with the article, he moves ahead in space. Incidentally, this sequence need not take readers from country to country, nor even from city to city. It may instead take you from floor to floor of a building, or room to room, or even from left to right. Time and space, of course, are inextricably bound together. As you move in one you move in the other.

Cause and effect sequence. First, the writer sets up the cause for a situation. Then he describes the effects which follow.

Problem-solution sequence. A problem is stated and several solutions may be offered. One solution appears the most likely to solve the problem. Sometimes the reader is expected to choose the correct solution, and then act upon his choice.

Other possibilities exist, both for the openings and for the main body of the article, but the few described briefly here will help you analyze quickly most of the short nonfiction pieces you read.

Specialized forms of nonfiction may be based on other patterns.

For example, book reviewers usually begin by announcing the news of a recently published work. They may then tell you something about the author, give you a notion of the flavor of the book itself, and conclude by pronouncing judgment.

Sports columnists have various approaches to their daily or weekly stints. They often tie in their column with current events in sports, building it up with anecdotes, past and present, or statistics, past and present.

THE SUMMING UP

Sometimes a writer begins an article by stating what he intends to say. Then, in the main body of the article, he says what he has to say.

Finally, a brief **summing up** tells the reader what he has just said.

This is the final step in the four-part structure.

To improve your speed and comprehension, try to get behind the structure of the various forms of writing which you read most often.

HOW TO READ A NEWSPAPER

Readers become so accustomed to the make-up of their favorite daily newspaper that they often feel lost when confronted with a strange one.

News stories, editorials, business and financial news, sports and homemaking pages, radio and television programs, columns (both political and gossip), letters to the editor, comic strips—all have definite places in a newspaper and generally are in their proper places. Regular newspaper readers know just where to look for the things in print they wish to read.

Some persons familiarize themselves with newspaper makeup still more.

They know where to turn for local, national, or international news. They know the approximate place on the page where important news appears. If a news story is being continued from day to day, experienced readers know where to look.

This all leads to efficient reading.

Carry this a step further. If you understand something about how a news story is written, then your reading of a newspaper can be even more efficient.

Although the variety of a journalist's writing may be limited only by his imagination and skill, an underlying pattern does exist.

NEWS STORIES

The opening paragraph or paragraphs of the newspaper story still answer the questions of the five w's—**who, what, when, where,** and **why**—as they have for generations of news writers. The **how** of the story is also usually told, plus whatever **authority** there may be for the information.

Succeeding paragraphs may fill in the story in more detail. And the longer the story, the more detail and background.

All that the reader needs to know to keep abreast of the news, however, is the material contained in these opening paragraphs.

A headline is not enough to keep you informed.

On the other hand, a complete story may contain much more detail than what you want or need to know about a particular event.

Again, the idea of **purpose** enters into the reading picture.

You try to acquire exactly the amount of information you wish to acquire in order to be a well-informed person.

Further analysis of newspaper reading will be found in the exercise which follows.

READING EXERCISE

Instructions: "Say it all in the first paragraph." This might be the advice of a veteran news writer to a cub. Knowing how many news stories are usually written may help in knowing how news stores should be read—rapidly. Read this selection in **three minutes or less.** Answer the questions immediately.

Time Yourself and Begin

THE INVERTED PYRAMID

One of the first things cub reporters are usually taught by newspaper editors is to write news stories by "spilling the beans in the first paragraph." If the reader's interest can be sustained throughout the rest of the story so much the better. But the important thing is to put the climax at the beginning.

This upside-down structure is called "the inverted pyramid." No other form of written composition is quite like it.

Although the method is some hundred years old and not at all a secret formula, many readers have apparently not yet caught on to it. Otherwise they wouldn't complain that they "haven't any time to read the paper."

Many readers never get past the first page.

Others get bogged down on the sports pages. Still others settle for the comic strips.

Imagining a diagram of an inverted pyramid may help you to grasp the structure of what you read in the papers. There is a practical reason for using this form. When lack of space demands it, news stories can be chopped off from the bottom, paragraph by paragraph, and still stand up under the ordeal. Since the heart of the story is in the opening paragraphs, as long as they remain the story is very much alive.

If you don't believe it, pick a news story from a front page and find out for yourself. Try leaving out the last two paragraphs or so. You will see at once that little of importance is lost.

The opening paragraphs, called the lead, and pronounced **leed,** will give you a clear idea of the significant facts of a story in a matter of seconds. They will present the nature of the event being reported, the persons or things concerned, the time, the place, the cause, the result. Most leads, in fact, answer the stock questions of who, what, when, where, why, and how, with the authority for the information either stated or implied.

These questions may be answered in the very first paragraph. Sometimes it may take an additional paragraph or two. Professional news writing requires that the questions be answered as early in the story as possible.

Several types of leads may be used. As an efficient newspaper reader, you would do well to recognize some of them.

The type most frequently seen is the "straight" or "digest" lead. This lead may summarize the whole story in a paragraph made up of one short sentence. If the people in a news story are well known, they will usually be named in this first paragraph; if not, they may be named in the second. Further details are filled in later in the story if at all.

Another type of lead popular with beginning writers, perhaps because it is easy to formulate, is expressed as a question. This is often effective because readers are accustomed to responding to questions. But if the question is a foolish one, the well-known foolish answer might be the result.

When you are addressed as "you" (as you are now), the lead is called the direct appeal. This technique should be thoroughly familiar to all readers through its wide use in advertising copy. Extremely popular at present because of the informal way it takes the reader into the writer's confidence, the "you" lead may eventually wear out from being overworked.

The statement or quotation lead is also in high favor at present. In this case words are taken right out of a speaker's mouth and sometimes placed in quotation marks, sometimes not. Or the writer may open a sentence or a paragraph with an indirect quotation and conclude with a direct quotation.

This type of lead is especially appropriate for reporting meetings or gatherings of all kinds. The quotation may be taken from a political speech, a lecture, a sermon, a learned paper, a prognostication by an authority on anything from the weather to the national economy, or the final words of a condemned man. It is up to the reporter or rewrite person to find the high spot in a mass of words to give a reader the gist of what was said.

In complicated stories with a great deal of interrelated action involving a great many people, the tabulated lead will help you to grasp the story quickly. In this case, the writer either numbers the significant items (1-2-3-4-5 and so on), or heads each separate item with a distinguishing symbol such as a paragraph sign or a black dot.

Opening leads of the inverted pyramid structure and arrangement usually fit one or another of the above descriptions. Journalists are known for their ingenuity, however, and you may find upon occasion original leads that are appropriate to a particular story. Editors are often known to encourage such originality on the part of their writing staff.

Turn the pyramid upside down and the structure becomes the familiar one used in typical feature articles, with the climax at or near the end.

Is a knowledge of leads any real help to the hard-pressed-for-time newspaper reader? Yes, beyond the slightest doubt. Merely becoming aware of some of the various patterns of structure and arrangement will make your daily reading habits more efficient.

Two other aids to efficiency might be noted.

Headlines can be thought of as guideposts to news stories. They give you a strong hint of what may be expected. The efficient reader will rapidly decide to follow whichever guideposts promise to take him where he wants to go, and ignore those that do not.

Jump lines tell you on what page a story is continued. Make a mental note of them, but don't jump immediately to the inside page. Instead, pick up the continuations when you reach them as you go through the paper page by page.

With these techniques a newspaper of even 100,000 words or more (such as the daily *New York Times*) can be covered fruitfully in a half hour or so. A Sunday newspaper which may run to 400,000 words or more can be covered in about an hour and a half. You can become better informed in a shorter time, and you will enjoy your newspaper reading much more besides.

Time in seconds——

Directions: Select the best answer and place the appropriate letter in the parentheses.

1. The principal thought contained in "The Inverted Pyramid" is that (a) writing newspaper stories will make anyone a more efficient reader; (b) awareness of the structure of newspaper stories may lead to more efficient reading; (c) newspapers should be read carefully word by word; (d) headlines and opening paragraphs are enough to keep readers well-informed.   ( )

2. The structure of news stories called the "inverted pyramid" is about (a) 200 years old; (b) 150 years old; (c) 100 years old; (d) 50 years old.   ( )

3. According to the article, news stories are often chopped off at the bottom because of (a) censorship of the press; (b) lack of skill of the writer in holding the reader's interest; (c) reader's complaints of lack of time to read the paper; (d) lack of space.   ( )

4. Professional news writing requires that the questions of who, what, when, where, why and how he answered (a) in the headline; (b) in the opening paragraph; (c) in the opening paragraphs; (d) as early in the story as possible.   ( )

5. The most frequent type of lead, according to the article, is (a) the question; (b) the direct appeal; (c) the digest; (d) the statement.   ( )

6. The direct appeal or "you" lead is often found in (a) advertising copy; (b) learned papers; (c) weather reports; (d) *The New York Times*.   ( )

7. A statement lead would be considered especially appropriate for reporting (a) a fire; (b) an accident; (c) a sports event; (d) a meeting.   ( )

8. Tabulated leads help the reader to grasp (a) stories with a great deal of interrelated action; (b) stories about the weather; (c) stories of executions; (d) political speeches.   ( )

9. It may be inferred that efficient readers of newspapers (a) read only the headlines; (b) read only the leads; (c) follow jump-line directions immediately by continuing stories on inside pages; (d) note jump lines but continue stories later if so inclined.   ( )

10. It might be concluded that an application of speed reading techniques will keep a newspaper reader well-informed in a matter of (a) 15 minutes a day; (b) 30 minutes a day; (c) 60 minutes a day; (d) 90 minutes a day.   ( )

DIRECTIONS FOR SCORING

Reading Rate. If you completed the selection within the three-minute time limit by your hourglass, enter your score in the PERSONAL PROGRESS CHART as 350 words per minute. If you failed to complete the selection in the time allowed, **try again.**

If you timed yourself **in seconds,** follow directions as in other timed selections.

Answers to Questions. Check the answers to the multiple-choice questions in the CORRECTION KEY TO EXERCISES.

Progress Chart. Enter all reading rates and comprehension scores in the PERSONAL PROGRESS CHART.

PLANNING YOUR OWN EXERCISES

"The Inverted Pyramid" is the last of a series of exercises planned for timing with an hourglass. You are urged to go back to CHAPTER FOUR and repeat the entire series.

Either time yourself in seconds or match your speed against the running grains of sand.

You are also urged to plan your own exercises for regular speed practice sessions.

Material for practice may be organized as follows:

Word counts. Choose a reading selection and count the words in ten consecutive lines. Then determine the average number of words per line through dividing by ten.

Next, count the total number of lines on a page.

Multiply by the number of words per line.

This will give you an approximate total count of words per page.

A shorter method, but not quite as accurate, is to estimate the number of words on a page.

To find the total count in a selection, multiply by the number of pages.

Self-timing. Use the sweep hand of a watch, or better yet use a stopwatch. Record the elapsed reading time of a selection **in seconds.**

To convert to words per minute, multiply the total word count by 60.

Then divide this number by the time **in seconds.**

The result is reading speed in words per minute.

Comprehension checks. After completing a selection, jot down immediately the principal ideas in as few words as possible. Then reread to check accuracy of retention and recall.

If the author presented ten main ideas and you accurately noted seven of them, this would give you a comprehension score of 70 percent.

STUDY ASSIGNMENTS

Several study activities are recommended to continue over several weeks.

Your daily newspaper may be used as your textbook for some of the assignments. Select a story on the front page and, as quickly as you can, underline with a pencil the **actor, action,** and **goal** words in some of the sentences.

Select another story and analyze the lead or the opening paragraphs to see if the answers are there to the questions of **who, what, when, where, why,** and **how.**

Then go through the paper to seek out examples of at least three types of leads described in the reading exercise.

Further excellent practice for your reading skill would be to try to **write** a lead for a news story. Choose any happening you wish and try to describe it on paper the way a reporter would.

Apply the test of the 5 W's.

Have they all been answered?

EYE-SPAN EXERCISE—I

Directions: The narrow column of a newspaper provides an excellent means for eye-span practice. Below you will find a brief news story set in conventional newspaper type. Try to read this selection by permitting yourself to take one look at each line. Don't go down the column in a vertical line, however. Move in a zig-zag fashion, attempting all the while to pick up key ideas. When you complete your reading, write down all you can remember about what you read.

Try to complete your reading in 20 seconds or less.

Time Yourself and Begin

FRAUD JURY SPLIT
Oyster County Trial
Ends With No Verdict

Oceantown, Md. November 16—After deliberating for nine hours today, an Oyster County jury informed Judge Josiah Clarke, of Superior Court, that it could not reach a verdict in the case of Mrs. Melanie O. Spirgeon, an unemployed woman. Mrs. Spirgeon had been on trial since November 9 on a charge of obtaining money on false pretenses.

She had been indicted as a result of disclosures made by Dr. George Karn, County Health Officer, after an inquiry into Oyster County finances. Mrs. Spirgeon was charged with collecting $13,980 from the County Health Board, which carried her on the payroll as a nurse.

Time in seconds_____

Directions: Answer these questions in a few words.

1. Who? _____
2. What? _____
3. When? _____
4. Where? _____
5. Why? _____

EYE-SPAN EXERCISE—II

Directions: Many readers have the capacity to perceive at a single fixation three, four or five short words. Using your Eye-Span Card, see how well you do with three short words, some of them totaling 12 to 15 letters and spaces. Move your Eye-Span Card as rapidly as possible from asterisk to asterisk down the page. **Think the words. Do not say them.**

Begin

*

do our door

seek one ear
*
mend a dam
*
rare to order
*
fast by day
*
fort can hold
*
calm on lake
*
state the taste
*
mark in time
*
buy that bag
*
cost is set
*
set a pin
*
wait for walk
*
this fine alley
*
corn is easy
*
last in salt
*
bran to barn
*
why that dray
*
for my roof
*
fault on line

Further instructions: Select from your own newspaper brief items for practice in increasing your span of recognition. **Don't dawdle!** Move your eyes down the column quickly, picking up all the meaning you can. At first, your comprehension may drop off at an alarming rate. Don't let this discourage you. Keep up with your practice until you can read a news story with speed and comprehension.

CHAPTER NINE

HOW TO BATTLE A BOOK—AND WIN

An eminent educator once said in all seriousness: "You can read a book in 30 seconds."

Thirty seconds!

Is it possible?

The answer is, YES. It is possible to "read" a book in that brief time. But you will notice that the word "read" has been put in quotation marks. This indicates certain reservations.

During the discussion which follows, consider the entire reading process as arbitrarily divided into four parts:

1. Selecting
2. Skipping
3. Skimming
4. Scanning

Each one of these parts will now be explained briefly. If you accept any **one** of them as a way of "reading," you will readily agree that a book might take **30 seconds,** or **30 minutes,** or even **30 hours.**

SELECTING A BOOK

Open the covers of a book you have never read before, but written on a subject quite familiar to you.

Note the title and the author's name. Take a rapid glance at the chapter headings. Sample a small part of the preface.

An experienced reader will know that although the preface appears at the beginning, it is the last thing the author writes after he completes the rest of the book. In it he may take the opportunity to give the reader some notion of what is to follow. He may sometimes provide valuable clues to not only the work itself but also his feelings and attitudes toward the work.

In half a minute or less, you may reach a decision on whether or not you intend to spend more time with this particular book.

If you decide **not** to spend further time, then, for all practical purposes, you have completed your reading of the work.

As an illustration of this procedure, imagine yourself an accomplished fresh-water bass fisherman. You've fished for many seasons in various lakes around your part of the state. You confidently believe you know just about all there is to know about catching (and losing!) bass.

Then along comes a new book entitled: **New Ways in Bass Fishing.**

You may be almost certain that once you got your hands on that book, you would be able to determine in a matter of minutes whether or not the author had anything new to say to you.

Once you opened the pages, you might continue looking over the book anyway. But you might also put it aside as something which could not possibly add to your present knowledge.

You might well "read" this book in 30 seconds.

CLASSIFYING A WORK OF NONFICTION

The highly competent reader is aware that he is faced by countless volumes in many areas of knowledge. Even if he were to read eight hours a day, seven days a week, week in and week out for years, he realizes that he would never catch up even in a limited area.

He therefore makes it a point to learn some of the boundaries of the areas, so that before he opens the covers of a book he will have some idea of the contents within.

How does the accomplished reader come by this information?

Various ways may be suggested to increase your ability to size up a book quickly. As a minimum, you should discover the following information almost immediately:

Author's name
Title
Place of publication
Publisher's name
Date of publication

Other helpful information might be as follows:

Further identification of the author, previous works, present or past occupation

Blurb found on the dust jacket about the author and the contents

Reviews of the book in newspapers and magazines

Mention of the book on television or radio programs

Comments of friends about the book

No one finds it easy to bring the wide range and variety of forms of factual prose found within book covers into some manageable classification. Certain forms are fairly obvious. Others may be recognized if you are an experienced reader.

A general list of various forms of writing would include:

Scientific
Technological
Legal
Political
Religious
Historical
Biographical and autobiographical
Critical
Medical
Mathematical

Two additional forms of writing, **fiction** and **poetry**, merit discussion on a separate chapter.

(Textbooks, or books planned and written as study material for classroom use, may range over all of the broad topics listed above. CHAPTER FOURTEEN will be devoted to a discussion of some of the techniques especially applicable to reading for study.)

Within the larger classifications of factual prose, many subclassifications may exist. The overlapping of these sub-classifications in many books may make them almost impossible to put into a rigid category.

To consider just one example:

Under the heading of technological writing you might list the myriad works which have been popularly designated as "How-to-do-it" or "self-help." Since the purpose of such books is to assist readers in achieving goals in any number of activities, from **how to dig a ditch** to **how to know the stars**, the subject matter crosses lines of classification at every turn.

SKIPPING AND SKIMMING

Skipping and **skimming** are not haphazard methods of reading done without either attention or thought. On the contrary, they are both products of continuing practice and developed skill.

Individuals who **skip** skillfully don't necessarily read a book from first page to last to find the information they seek. Instead, they may plunge into the ending, or the middle, or any other part which seems promising.

If you are in search of particular information, with practice you may learn to take a quick glance at the index or table of contents, grab a fist-full of pages, and **skip** over whole sections of the book to get the exact item you need.

Even in works totally unfamiliar to you, you are likely to develop a sixth sense for reaching the place you want in a few seconds, picking out a word here and there and skipping all the rest.

Closely related to the ability to skip directly to the heart of selected reading material is the ability to **skim.**

With your attention alerted and with pertinent questions in mind, you let your eyes race down a printed page so that you may gather a general impression of the contents.

Perhaps you are seeking the principal thoughts of the author. Or perhaps you wish to pick up significant details.

You may be looking for the over-all structure of the materials, or trying to gain an idea of the author's point of view.

You may be comparing or contrasting your own or someone else's viewpoint with the author's, using the peaks and not the valleys of the material.

Without genuinely digging deeply into a book, you may nevertheless become quite familiar with it through artful **skimming.**

A valuable result of using this technique is that you come to see a book as a whole without close reading. In fact, you see it better from this skimming bird's-eye view than you would if you began to plod doggedly through a book from first word to last.

With practice in skimming, you begin to build confidence in your ability to judge a work from rapid inspection.

As a result, you do not hesitate to make decisions about how much time to spend on various books. To some, you will plan to return for a closer look; others you will discard, temporarily at least, without a qualm of doubt.

SCANNING

Webster's **New Collegiate Dictionary** defines the word **scan** as "to examine point by point; scrutinize." The word is also used colloquially to mean something quite the opposite: hasty reading.

The process of **scanning** discussed here will follow the original definition of **close reading.** Thus, when you look at the fine print on an insurance policy or a business contract or a bill of sale, you are seriously engaged in scanning. Not only are you reading the lines themselves but you are also attempting to read between the lines.

Not only do you examine each word closely but you also try to get behind the word to discover what may be some hidden meaning.

Psychological, or philosophical, or religious works are often read in this careful way. The implications may be so weighty that after **selecting, skipping** and **skimming**, the technique of **scanning** is found necessary for adequate comprehension.

Through the initial survey you make of a work, you may learn that the author compresses his principal thoughts into single paragraphs. Instead of ideas standing out clearly in the light of comparisons, contrasts, illustrations, and various details of other kinds, you discover that each principal idea is surrounded by other principal ideas.

Skimming of such material is out of the question. If the material is to be read at all, it must be read closely and perhaps slowly as well.

This discussion inevitably raises a significant question which must be answered at this time It may be asked as follows:

HOW FAST IS FAST READING?

What is the correct speed for reading?
How fast should you read?
When do you read rapidly?
When do you read slowly?
It all depends.
Depends on what?

Perhaps you can answer this by taking a casual look around you.

Harassed office workers, from junior assistants right up to top management, are engaged in a constant battle against a flood of paperwork. Trying desperately to keep themselves afloat in a sea of printer's ink, they find themselves literally swamped. Correspondence, memoranda, technical reports, newspapers, magazines, and books, all contribute to the rising tide.

Students in both undergraduate and graduate schools are faced with stacks of textbooks and stagger under reams of library reports and research papers. Some of them approach examination time with most of the books on their required reading lists still unopened.

Other adults, tempted by best-seller advertisements, subscribe to book clubs, only to watch volume after volume gather dust on the living-room table. In spite of mechanized homes, they "just can't seem to find the time for reading any more."

It all depends.

The publishers of a national weekly magazine evidently believe that most of their readers have a rate of about 270 words a minute, on the basis of their statement that "if you read every word (81,000) in an average issue . . . it would take more than five hours."

But, as you are aware, a skillful reader might read one entire piece in this magazine at a rate three or four times as fast as 270 wpm. On the other hand, the same reader might find another piece in the same issue quite difficult to comprehend and his rate would drop even below the 270 mark.

Now consider the United States Army corporal who gained fame by reading forty-two books in two weeks on his way to a foreign post, and who continued to "devour" books while he was overseas.

The corporal himself figured that he averaged 440 words per minute.

Since his reading covered a wide range, from westerns to mysteries to anthologies to nonfiction, this rate is perhaps misleading.

Slow for some of his fiction reading, the rate of 440 wpm would be moderately fast for some nonfiction.

What, then, is the correct speed?

It all depends.

The answer is simply that there is no one correct speed of reading.

There is instead only an appropriate speed, adjusted to each different type of reading material and to the purpose for which the material is being read.

It's up to you to learn when and how to shift from low into medium gear and back again.

And this is not the entire picture by any means.

It wouldn't do you much good to learn how to make your eyes race across the printed page of a book unless you could take in what you were seeing.

So it's not speed alone that you're trying to achieve but, instead, **Speed and Comprehension.**

You want to *know* what you're reading.

Now you have the balanced formula—**appropriate reading rate with maximum understanding.**

HOW TO TREAT A BOOK

Almost everyone may feel inclined to stand in awe before the rows upon rows of books in the stacks of a large library. But some people are intimidated by a single book.

They often approach their reading in such an apologetic way that, between fear and timidity, the joys of reading are lost to them.

Sometimes this attitude of servility is expressed in the way books are handled. Instead of a masterful, confident turning of pages, the book is treated tentatively as though it were some object too delicate to stand rough treatment.

The timid soul may also constantly regress—looking back and back again at the material covered—fearful of plunging ahead into the unknown.

In some parts of the world this attitude may be understood. Books are so rare and held in such reverence that hardly anyone reads them.

In our own society, however, printed words tumble off giant presses night and day. Every means for securing wide distribution for these words is used.

Books are here, there, and everywhere waiting for an alert, aggressive reader to pick them up, thumb through their pages, and begin to read them.

At home, in the school, in the library, in public conveyances, in private clubs, men and women and children read for a purpose—for enjoyment, for enlightenment.

They also *should* read with determination, with questions, with answers, with anger, with sorrow, with joy.

Books are not abstract pieces of matter, but instead the thoughts and feelings of flesh-and-blood people intended to be read by other flesh-and-blood people.

Treat books well. But don't be afraid to manhandle them upon occasion. Treat them thoughtfully, but treat them firmly.

Sometimes you might even have to battle a book—and win the battle, of course—before you feel satisfied that you have mastered it.

But this will give you added respect both for the book and for yourself.

The Four S's

The reading processes of **selecting, skipping, skimming,** and **scanning** may perhaps best be illustrated by the simple act of looking up a number in a telephone directory. First you must **select** the appropriate book. Then you **skip** over a number of pages until the approximate page is reached. Next you **skim** down the column of names until the desired one is found. Finally, the name, address, and number are **scanned** carefully for accuracy, and the number is kept in mind as long as it fulfills the purpose of dialing (or giving it to the operator, as the case may be).

READING EXERCISE

Instructions: Much has been said of purpose in reading as applied to the reader. But what about the writer's purpose, and how can the reader perceive that purpose to improve his own comprehension and understanding? In this article a successful teacher discusses how you as a reader should strive to share the experiences of the writer. Time yourself as you read. Jot down your time **in seconds** in the space provided. Then answer the questions.

Time Yourself and Begin

A TEACHER LOOKS AT READING
By A. B. Herr

"What's he driving at?"

"Why did anyone bother to write this?"

"What's somebody trying to do to me?"

Such questions in our minds can make us *want* to read almost anything. Trying to find the answers will make us readers.

But why read? Aren't teachers and writers and parents, who tell us we should read more, all a lot of preachers trying to "improve" us and make us "good?" Being "good" is for many reasons not very attractive; we'd all rather be at least a little bit "bad" and go on meeting new people, gaining new experiences, learning about life, and generally having a "good time."

Now the fact is that people who urge us to read, and to become better readers, usually are not much concerned whether we are "good" or not; they are much more worried lest we be small, immature, inexperienced, innocent, ignorant, insensitive, unappreciative, and generally failing to find in life the "good time" we so eagerly want.

They have discovered that through reading we can have all sorts of experiences, good and bad: experiences so "real" that we forget all about our actual surroundings; experiences that we could never otherwise crowd into one lifetime; experiences for which we would not have the money, energy, or capacity in real life; experiences that can cover all the years and ages past, and even range into unexplored outer space, and future time.

Reading can never be a substitute for living; but reading can enormously enlarge the range of our living by bringing us into contact with people, real and imaginary, we never could meet, by awakening and deepening our emotions, lending new meaning to our own experiences, and by giving us most of the facts and ideas without which we could not work or talk or think.

Why doesn't reading mean this to all of us? And do authors *really* write to give us new experiences and enlarge our life? Actually, the reward that writers, like actors on the stage, really work for is the applause, the response that proves they have done something to and for their audience. And we of the audience, do we not laugh and cry and clap—just as when we were little children listening to our first stories—because we have had new experiences, felt new sensations, been given ideas that never occurred to us in just that way before? Didn't our first contacts with reading mean exactly that to all of us? Reading, or listening to reading, was first a marvelously "good time," and we felt that some magician had shared with us his wondrous world.

What happened then—why had reading since childhood become such a bore, such a chore? Well, what about life as a whole? Do we face it and accept it with the same open eagerness we did in childhood? Usually not. Personal attitudes have a great deal to do with what we get out of life—and personal attitudes determine whether we read or do not read. Poor, unrewarding attitudes often have reason enough behind them in some of the disappointments and hard knocks life has dealt us. But to be governed by unfortunate attitudes is to let the dead past rule the living present and future. Would we learn how to "win friends and influence people," *we* must change: wrong habits and approaches must be replaced with more rewarding successful ones. So in reading.

How to do this? Remember our opening words. Have questions in mind. Make reading a search, a challenge, an adventure. Try to get through to the purpose and thought of the author. Behind the words and symbols of any piece of writing there is the mood of the author, a human being, trying to make contact with our mind. If he were standing talking before us, we would scarcely turn our backs and close our ears, at least not without giving him half a chance to say what he was talking about. On the printed page our responsibility is greater. Here the only possible activity is ours: across the gaps of space and time a man is silently trying to reach us; we must extend ourselves and help him get through.

Sharing is a two-way process. "The gift without the giver is bare?" Well, giving without receiving also is meaningless and useless. Reading is an activity, of the mind or of the "heart," opening and moving out to grasp the full meaning of another's offered thoughts. Sometimes reading must become an aggressive attack, to "break the code" of print on paper and guarantee complete communication.

Granted, then, the desire, the will to read—granted the realization that reading is an active seeking to communicate and share: What may we do to change our poor habits, to ensure our thorough understanding and appreciation?

First of all, *read*. That is, if we would improve in reading we must consciously set ourselves a program that includes *more* reading—not impossibly large amounts but something like fifteen minutes more a day, faithfully accomplished—and not, at first, more difficult, advanced material but a wider range of reading at our present level. Let us explore our newspaper more fully: reading some of the news, features, and special sections we have been skipping; really read the magazines we have been only glancing through; read a few of the books that our acquaintances, no older or educationally more advanced, have enjoyed; make sure that we are not just riding a narrow single hobby but tracking a network of expanding interests. (*There is no such thing as an interesting book: there can only be interested readers.*) Gradually we will find ourselves thinking and talking about things we never thought much about before; we will feel "in" on conversations that used to leave us "out"; we will feel sure when we used to feel uncertain; life and the world will seem full where they once seemed empty. As little as fifteen minutes a day of reading what we have been in the habit of skipping and passing, can do that for us in one month. Let us make sure we read.

Then, too, let us make sure we *think*. It is hard not to think at all; but many make the mistake, while reading, of thinking about something else: they think about themselves, about their play or work, about things suggested by *some* of the words they read. The thinking that is effective reading follows carefully along with the writing itself, grasping main ideas, fitting examples and details into their proper positions. The major purpose of the skillful reader is to think with the author, to share the author's purpose and to pursue the same ends which he had in writing. We cannot approach the Psalms and the classified advertisements in the same way: their purposes are different. So, with all forms of reading successful reading begins with sensitive recognition of purpose.

How may we be sure that we have perceived an author's purpose?

First, let us at least be aware of some common purposes and techniques employed by writers. Probably we could make three *major* divisions in a list of purposes for writing: (1) to give information—an intellectual operation; (2) to share experiences, sentiments, and convictions—an operation which includes intellectual comprehension but is not complete without emotion, the feeling of having participated; and (3) to persuade, to change opinions, responses, or habits—an operation whose success depends on emotional acceptance, no matter how intellectual the approach may appear. Frequently the title and first lines or paragraphs give very clear indication of the author's intention; in a full-length book he may even devote a preface or introduction to his purpose. Lacking these, we must keep looking—thinking and feeling—for clues which finally reveal the author's essential purpose in writing. No matter whether the style be formal or intimate, the approach serious or mocking, the content heavy or frothy, in the end it usually appears that any writer worth the reading really hoped to inform, or to share part of his life, or to persuade. And some of our most *entertaining* writers are the most subtly effective in accomplishing their purposes.

Then too, for detecting purposes, we have at hand a few facts and classifications usually taught in "English" classes. A well-written composition is made up of separate paragraphs, each of which has a relatively clear and single purpose. The skillful reader, as well as the skillful writer, must be master of paragraph patterns. As readers bent on finding the author's intention we would do well to brush up on the distinctions among *narration*, *description*, *exposition*, and *argumentation*. Practically all paragraphs can be accurately classified under these four headings; but, more importantly, these four can be very useful in describing the total main trend of a whole composition, article, essay, chapter, or book. We will feel that we know a great deal about the purpose of a piece of writing when we have thought about it far enough to confidently apply to it one specific classification.

But will not such thinking make reading only a slow labor of dissection and analysis? We must use all available energy against just that. Main ideas and purposes are best perceived if we go through a work once, rapidly, to "get the lay of the land." That "once-over-lightly" may give us all we want to know or need to know. If certain parts seem worth rereading, we will read them again with increased comprehension because we see just how they fit into the development of the main outline. Even if we are reading something which finally must be almost memorized, we will master it with fuller understanding and greater ease, if we make our first reading of it as rapid as our minds can move from one main event or idea to the next and until we have the *general* shape and structure of the whole. Many successful readers and careful students bear witness that slow reading is *careless* reading unless we are already familiar with the material as a whole; unless we have first made certain where the author is heading; what his important points are: and, therefore, which details and illustrations are worthy of painstaking attention. Let us make sure that we read with attention, thinking and feeling, to the exclusion of all outside distractions—but that we *keep moving*.

If we read the questions in mind, seeking to get into sympathetic communication with a writer, bearing with him and sticking with him to an end that we reach as quickly as our minds will allow, we will want to read, we will read, and we will be better readers.

Time in seconds____

Directions: Select the best answer and place the appropriate letter in the parentheses.

1. People who urge us to read, according to the author, are worried lest we fail to (a) "improve" ourselves; (b) be "bad"; (c) have a "good time"; (d) be "good."   ( )

2. It is only through books that most people can (a) earn money; (b) explore outer space; (c) meet people; (d) travel.   ( )

3. Authors *really* write to (a) earn money; (b) give us new experiences; (c) enlarge our life; (d) gain our applause.   ( )

4. The author suggests that we consciously set ourselves a goal of reading more each day of (a) 5 minutes; (b) 15 minutes; (c) 50 minutes; (d) 150 minutes.   ( )

5. He counsels us to read (a) newspapers; (b) magazines; (c) books; (d) all of the above. ( )

6. When we read, thinking should be (a) along the path of the writing itself; (b) about something else; (c) stimulated by *some* of the words; (d) repressed as much as possible.   ( )

7. Any writer worth the reading hopes always to (a) entertain; (b) share part of his life; (c) change opinions; (d) arouse emotions.   ( )

8. One of the following lines best states the main idea of the selection: (a) win friends and influence people; (b) sharing is a two-way process; (c) there is no such thing as an interesting book: there can only be interested readers; (d) "once-over-lightly."   ( )

9. You might imply from this selection that (a) writers should do the thinking for readers; (b) reading is a chore; (c) the reader has a responsibility toward the writer; (d) readers should not ask questions.   ( )

10. Another implication is that (a) rapid reading is efficient reading; (b) slow reading is a technique of scholars; (c) perfect communication between reader and writer is always possible; (d) analysis of material in print is necessarily laborious.   ( )

DIRECTIONS FOR SCORING

Reading Rate. Find your reading rate in words per minute by turning to the TABLE FOR DETERMINING READING RATE IN WORDS PER MINUTE.

Answers to Questions. Check the answers to the multiple-choice questions in the CORRECTION KEY TO EXERCISES.

Progress Chart. Enter all reading rate and comprehension scores in the PERSONAL PROGRESS CHART.

REVIEW

Before continuing on to the next chapter, in which you will test yourself again, you are asked to review some of your work up to the present time.

Word recognition. Go back and look at some of the exercises which were planned to help you with recognizing words. Select a passage to read aloud to determine whether or not you have confidence in attacking all the words you meet along the way.

Reading rate and comprehension. Turn back to CHAPTER TWO and try once again the first reading selection, "Thomas Wolfe." Although you may have already filled in the answers to this test, review them anyway.

Vocabulary. Continue your review by looking over carefully the first vocabulary test. Remember that you have but **10 seconds** to complete each item in this test if you wish to finish within the set time limit. Speed is therefore essential for a high score.

Reading autobiography. Continue to add to your personal journal.

Finally, review and study any section of this book you have covered so far which you feel might help you with your next test.

CHAPTER TEN

TEST YOURSELF AGAIN

You are now going to give yourself the second test to determine your reading rate and comprehension level, your vocabulary strength, and your ability to analyze paragraphs.

A comparison with your first test scores will help you to judge your progress since you began this book.

Before taking the test, however, you are urged to follow the directions under the section headed "Review" in the preceding chapter, if you have not already done so.

When you are ready to go ahead with the tests, make sure that you are in a comfortable spot for working with book and pencil, and won't be interrupted for at least the next half hour.

A timing device of some kind, either a watch with a sweep hand or a stop-watch, will be needed. **Accurate Timing Is Important.**

The general directions are as follows:

Note the exact time, then begin to read the article at the rate you ordinarily use for a non-fiction piece in a magazine. **Remember that you are to answer questions about it.**

When you finish, note the number of **seconds** it has taken you. Write this information down **immediately** in the space provided.

Continue then to answer the questions **without looking back at the article.**

When you have completed the questions, go on to the vocabulary section, timing yourself again as directed.

After you have completed the vocabulary section, continue with the paragraph analysis.

At the completion of the entire set of test exercises, you will find further instructions. Follow them carefully.

Are you ready?

Warning: If you are not ready, stop right here and postpone taking the test until you are prepared and consider the test-taking conditions favorable.

Time Yourself and Begin

MARGARET FULLER

A bluestocking, as defined by Webster, is a literary or pedantic woman. The term seems to have been first applied in the 18th century to the females who gathered in English drawing-rooms to meet and talk with the literary figures of the day.

A number of American women of the 19th century, especially in the New England states, were well qualified to receive the bluestocking label, even to their fondness for literary conversations. Heading the list might be the name of Margaret Fuller. Although much of her life story has been handed down more as myth than as fact, her own description of a typical day at fifteen years old is enlightening.

"I rise at five," she said, "walk an hour, and then practice the piano until seven . . ." All of this activity before breakfast! After the morning meal, she continued, she would read French and a little philosophy. At nine-thirty the young Yankee miss went to school to study Greek until noon. In the afternoon, she practiced the piano again, read for two hours in Italian, then went for another walk. After the evening meal, she either played, or sang, or wrote in her journal.

This was indeed before the age of the automobile, the comic book, and the television set.

Born on May 23, 1810 in Cambridgeport, Massachusetts, Margaret was the first child of Timothy and Margaret Crane Fuller. Her father was a lawyer and a politician of sorts who had worked his way through Harvard College. His wife bore him nine children, and one of Margaret's earliest recollections was the death of one of them, a girl two years younger than herself.

Timothy had wanted a son as his first child, and almost from the time Margaret could walk he took over complete charge of her life. He had fixed ideas about how a son and heir should be raised, and although his firstborn was a daughter he still intended to carry out these ideas. Even though sons were born later, he still sternly pursued his plan of a highly disciplined education for Margaret.

Fortunately, Margaret had the capacity for this rigorous intellectual training, though the harsh discipline nearly brought her at one point to a stage of nervous collapse.

She was taught both Latin and English grammar before the age of six, and she was reading Virgil, Horace, and Ovid by the time she was seven.

When Margaret was fourteen years old she was sent to a private school in Groton, forty miles from her home. There she soon made more enemies than friends because of her eccentric behavior. When her classmates turned against her, Margaret began to spread malicious rumors which soon got her into trouble with her teachers.

Summoned before the headmistress, the wildly unhappy girl in a dramatic scene dashed her head against the hearthstone and lay for a time unconscious. Soon afterward she was back again with her family, meek and penitent. Her severe existence at the age of fifteen has been described above.

Eight years later, Margaret was to return to Groton, but this time with her family. Her father, a failure at politics, bought a farm there. The eldest daughter saw herself at this time condemned forever to a lonely, rural life.

Within the next few years her father died and the struggle to keep the farm going became more and more difficult. She finally decided that she might earn her living and help to support her mother by teaching. Thus it was that Margaret Fuller became a teacher of languages at Bronson Alcott's Temple School in Boston.

Far from beautiful, Margaret was nonetheless striking looking, with her blond hair pulled back severely in a spinster's knot and her eyes aglow. A lorgnette was frequently in evidence. Painfully aware that men were not especially attracted to her for her looks but instead for her intellect, she often felt herself alone and unloved.

Once she took up her duties in Boston, however, she was far too busy to brood over her loneliness. Her sound knowledge of the classics in four languages now stood her in good stead. She was an excellent teacher.

A more lucrative post was soon offered her in Providence, Rhode Island. Her salary was set at a thousand dollars a year, an almost unheard of sum for a woman teacher of that day. She took the new position and stayed there for two years.

During these months of teaching, Margaret kept in constant touch with her friends in both Boston and Cambridge. The names of some of these friends sound like a roster of the greatest writers and thinkers of the day: Ralph Waldo Emerson, Nathaniel Hawthorne, William Ellery Channing, Henry David Thoreau, among others.

Margaret edited a famous, but short-lived, literary magazine, the *Dial*; she was often a guest at Brook Farm, the experimental colony for intellectuals; and she held forth in literary and philosophical discussions, one of the popular pastimes of the day. In fact, it was through a series of discussion meetings called "Conversations" that Margaret gained her livelihood during this period.

She became tired of this ceaseless activity, however, and longed for a change. Her longing was soon gratified. Close friends of hers, a brother and sister, invited her to accompany them on a tour of the West.

Her travels took her first to Chicago, and then to a town named Oregon, Illinois, where an uncle resided. She then visited Milwaukee, a genuine frontier town in the 1840's. To experience still more the wilderness of the West she went to the island of Mackinaw to observe the American Indian in his native setting. Margaret spent ten days alone in the Indian village, making trips to the surrounding countryside accompanied by native guides. One of her biographers has stated that she "endured the hazards of shooting rapids in a canoe with a calm not to be expected in one who had led so sheltered a life."

Margaret began to write an account of her journeys after she was back in Boston. This occasioned a search for background material, which she found in the Harvard College library. She was the first woman ever permitted to use the research facilities of the library.

The result was a book published under the title of *Summer on the Lakes*. Although not especially a success, the book did serve to bring her writing and her enthusiasm for the West to the attention of Horace Greeley, the famous editor of *The New York Daily Tribune*. Greeley had already met Margaret at Brook Farm; now he wanted her on his newspaper.

She accepted his offer and moved to New York to live with the Greeleys and to become the literary critic and special correspondent of the *Tribune*. Many of her judgments on the writers and poets of that time are still considered valid, and her articles on prisons, gained after first-hand visits, were in the best tradition of American reporting. She also struck hard blows in the cause of the emancipation of her own sex.

Following an unhappy love affair, Margaret was invited to join some friends in a grand tour of Europe. Greeley willingly agreed to her going and promptly made her a foreign correspondent. On August 1, 1846 she sailed for Liverpool on the steamer *Cambria*.

Her travels took her to England and Scotland and then to France and Italy. Meetings with famous personages of the day were faithfully recorded in dispatches to the *Tribune*. It was upon her arrival in Rome, however, late in 1847 that the events which dominated the final three tragic years of her life began.

Caught up in the revolutionary struggle for an Italian Republic through both her own feelings and her friendship with one of the principals, Guiseppe Mazzini; involved in a love affair with a man ten years her junior, the Marchese Ossoli; married to him and bearing him a son, fleeing into a rural village upon the fall of the Republic; Margaret could still pause and survey her life calmly in 1850.

She wrote: "My life proceeds as regularly as the fates of a Greek tragedy, and I can but accept the pages as they turn.

Through the assistance of friends, passage back to America was arranged for Margaret and Ossoli and their little infant, Angelo. In a gale on the last night out, the ship grounded off Fire Island, within a few hundred yards of the shore. A sailor tried to rescue the baby but failed, and they both perished in the waves.

Margaret and her husband were never seen again.

Thus ended the life of one of America's great women, although she is little remembered today. As her friends said, Margaret was "not a great writer, but a great woman writing." Her most brilliant successes were achieved through conversation, but no tape-recorder was at hand to preserve her words for posterity.

A woman with a formidable and brilliant mind, she provided a constant challenge for men of genius.

Time in seconds——

Directions: Select the best answer and place the appropriate letter in the parentheses.

1. Margaret Fuller's life might be described as (a) that of an embittered woman escaping from life into a world of books; (b) that of a genius who, in spite of a sheltered life, disappointments and tragedy, faced the future with courage; (c) that of a genius who was driven by loneliness into desperate situations; (d) that of an adventuress whose life held no real purpose. ( )

2. Margaret Fuller was born in (a) Cambridge; (b) Cambridgeport; (c) Boston; (d) Providence. ( )

3. At the age of fifteen, Margaret arose in the morning regularly at (a) five; (b) six; (c) seven; (d) eight. ( )

4. When she was a small child, her father was (a) a lawyer; (b) a farmer; (c) a writer; (d) a teacher. ( )

5. Margaret's intellectual activity during her childhood might be attributed to the fact that (a) she was always lonely; (b) her father had planned a highly disciplined education for her; (c) she had always loved to study; (d) her education was much the same as other children of the period. ( )

6. At the private school which Margaret attended in Groton, she was described as being (a) ambitious; (b) studious; (c) pedantic; (d) eccentric. ( )

7. This account specifically mentions that while in her teens, Margaret read (a) Greek and Latin poetry; (b) history and biography; (c) philosophy and French; (d) Homer and Dante. ( )

8. She left school at Groton only to return to the town (a) two years later; (b) four years later; (c) six years later; (d) eight years later. ( )

9. She returned to Groton (a) to teach; (b) to write; (c) because Brook Farm was located there; (d) because her family moved there. ( )

10. Margaret became a teacher because (a) she had to make a living and support her mother; (b) she loved teaching; (c) she believed that women should work outside the home; (d) she could not resign herself to a lonely rural life. ( )

11. She is described by the author of this account as (a) red-haired and homely; (b) blonde and beautiful; (c) brunette and plain; (d) blonde and striking. ( )

12. Through a series of discussions called "Conversations" Margaret earned (a) fame but no money; (b) an appointment to *The New York Daily Tribune* staff; (c) a livelihood; (d) a teaching position. ( )

13. One who was not mentioned in her list of friends in this article was (a) Nathaniel Hawthorne; (b) Henry David Thoreau; (c) Herman Melville; (d) William Ellery Channing. ( )

14. On a tour of the West, Margaret (a) visited a brother and sister; (b) travelled as far as the state of Oregon; (c) spent ten days alone in an Indian village; (d) nearly drowned while shooting the rapids in a canoe. ( )

15. Margaret did research in the Harvard College library, something that (a) had been done before by few women; (b) was permitted to women writers; (c) was permitted her because of her fight for the emancipation of women; (d) had never been done by a woman before. ( )

16. Horace Greeley appointed Margaret to the *Tribune* staff as a direct result of (a) his meeting her at Brook Farm; (b) the publication of *Summer on the Lakes;* (c) her editorial work on the *Dial;* (d) the "Conversations." ( )

17. Considered in the best tradition of American reporting were Margaret Fuller's accounts of (a) the revolutionary struggle for an Italian Republic; (b) the struggle for the emancipation of women; (c) prisons in America; (d) meetings abroad with famous personages. ( )

18. The man Margaret married (a) was the principal in the founding of the Italian Republic; (b) was ten years her junior; (c) had been married before; (d) remained in Europe when she sailed for America. ( )

19. Margaret Fuller perished (a) a few hundred yards from the Atlantic coast of the United States; (b) while fleeing with her infant son to a rural village in Italy; (c) on the first night out at sea on her way back to America; (d) when the steamer *Cambria* foundered in a gale. ( )
20. Margaret's friends considered her (a) a great writer; (b) a great critic; (c) a great woman; (d) a great reporter. ( )

VOCABULARY TEST II

Directions: Read each definition and underline the word which fits it most closely. Do not linger on any one item. Try to complete the test within five minutes. Your score will be the number correct within this time limit.

Time Yourself and Begin

1. Happening by chance rather than design
   (a) unbelievable; (b) fortuitous; (c) unprecedented; (d) irrational; (e) concurrent.
2. Doing good to others
   (a) beneficent; (b) sentimental; (c) gracious; (d) opportunistic; (e) prodigal.
3. Study of speech and language development
   (a) morphology; (b) prehistory; (c) linguistics; (d) philanthropy; (e) polemics.
4. Enjoying great fame and glory
   (a) honorable; (b) illustrious; (c) notorious; (d) munificent; (e) bountiful.
5. Act of taking something from its lawful owner
   (a) burglary; (b) deprivations; (c) vandalism; (d) larceny; (e) foreclosure.
6. A motive for action coming from outside influences or events
   (a) motility; (b) incentive; (c) reaction; (d) directive; (e) mobilization.
7. In statistics, the middle point in a series of data
   (a) axis; (b) average; (c) median; (d) vector; (e) factor.
8. Done without interest or enthusiasm
   (a) perfunctory; (b) chaotic; (c) fruitless; (d) formal; (e) functional.
9. Essential core of meaning
   (a) foundation; (b) lode; (c) truism; (d) gist; (e) element.
10. A person who takes care of horses
    (a) jockey; (b) equestrian; (c) huntsman; (d) squire; (e) hostler.
11. To leap or thrust forward
    (a) lurch; (b) lunge; (c) splurge; (d) veer; (e) lope.
12. Wandering about from one place to another
    (a) migratory; (b) aimless; (c) global; (d) aquatic; (e) pioneer.
13. Having a good effect by a good example
    (a) informative; (b) reformatory; (c) edifying; (d) instructive; (e) moralizing.
14. A broad view or prospect
    (a) lookout; (b) vantage; (c) horizon; (d) firmament; (e) vista.
15. Following each other without interruption
    (a) graduated; (b) successive; (c) proceeding; (d) attentive; (e) unchanging.
16. Plane surface of a cut gem or crystal
    (a) facet; (b) hexagon; (c) bevel; (d) slope; (e) refraction.
17. Inscription on a monument or tomb
    (a) epistle; (b) epigram; (c) epitaph; (d) epitome; (e) epithet.
18. False but seeming to be correct
    (a) shallow; (b) specious; (c) oblique; (d) deluded; (e) obvious.
19. Relating to the sense of smell
    (a) olfactory; (b) odoriferous; (c) sensory; (d) ancillary; (e) auditory.
20. Narrow place between hills cut by running water
    (a) furrow; (b) cleft; (c) valley; (d) gully; (e) plateau.
21. Any business deal
    (a) merger; (b) corporation; (3) auction; (d) transaction; (e) investment.
22. Literary work making fun of human folly or weakness
    (a) sonnet; (b) masque; (c) parody; (d) trilogy; (e) satire.
23. Feeling of being outside oneself, usually with joy
    (a) aesthetics; (b) swoon; (c) hysteria; (d) ecstasy; (e) amnesia.
24. Carry out, perform
    (a) execute; (b) attend; (c) adopt; (d) transgress; (e) exert.

25. Being everywhere at once
    (a) swarming; (b) accessible; (c) ubiquitous; (d) available; (e) prevalent.
26. Closely pertaining to the matter at hand
    (a) important; (b) tenacious; (c) sensible; (d) relevant; (e) weighty.
27. Resembling or containing fire
    (a) ferrous; (b) igneous; (c) flamboyant; (d) limpid; (e) flickering.
28. To return to a former state
    (a) revert; (b) recur; (c) secede; (d) lag; (e) sag.
29. To handle roughly
    (a) torture; (b) browbeat; (c) wrangle; (d) intimidate; (e) maul.
30. Any cheap and showy ornament
    (a) paste; (b) bangle; (c) brilliant; (d) bauble; (e) glitter.

Directions: Read this paragraph once and then answer the questions about it. Try to complete the entire exercise within **five minutes.**

THE PASSIVE READER

By HOWARD MUMFORD JONES

In twentieth-century America the decline and fall of the general literary periodical has been a matter of tremendous import for book publishing. This change has almost wiped out serialization. It has delivered the magazine over to the advertising department. It has made circulation, not content, the criterion of success, and reduced letterpress to an accompaniment of advertising. The appeal of the great popular magazines is physical and pictorial, not intellectual—slick paper agreeable to the fingers, large type, immense and obvious illustration, color work, and eye-catching ads. Magazines are, more than ever, "typed." Who does not know *The New Yorker* story, *The Saturday Evening Post* mystery serial, the formula fiction in *McCall's?* Intellectual challenge, except for special articles, has so far declined in American periodicals, it is unthinkable that Henry James could serialize novels today as he once serialized them in the old *Atlantic;* and if a name like that of Faulkner appears in one of these magazines, it is less because of the merit of the contribution than because Faulkner is a personality and has name appeal. Intelligence tends to be shunted into academic quarterlies. When, not long ago, a then popular magazine based its appeal on statements at the bottom of its articles, "Reading time x minutes," complete reader passivity, the goal of this movement, had been achieved.

Directions: Select the best answer for each question.

1. The main idea of this paragraph is that (a) the famous writers of today never submit their work to the popular magazines; (b) the contents of popular magazines no longer provide an intellectual challenge to readers; (c) without advertising popular magazines could not continue to exist; (d) advertising content of popular magazines attract more readers than editorial content.   ( )
2. According to Howard Mumford Jones a magazine well known for mystery serials was (a) *The New Yorker*; (b) *The Atlantic*; (c) *The Saturday Evening Post*; (d) *McCall's*.   ( )
3. The tone of this paragraph might be described as (a) highly critical; (b) mildly approving; (c) bitterly sarcastic; (d) coldly indifferent.   ( )

DIRECTIONS FOR SCORING

Reading Rate. To find your reading rate in words per minute for the reading selection, turn to the TABLE FOR DETERMINING READING IN WORDS PER MINUTE.

Answers to Questions. First, check the answers to the twenty multiple-choice questions for the timed reading selection in the CORRECTION KEY TO TESTS. Multiply the number you have right by **five** to get your comprehension score in percentages. For example, if you had thirteen correct out of twenty, set down your score as 65 percent.

Finally, check the answers to both the vocabulary test and the paragraph analysis test.

Progress Chart. Reading rate and all comprehension, vocabulary, and paragraph analysis scores should be entered in the places provided in your PERSONAL PROGRESS CHART.

CHAPTER ELEVEN

PEP TALK

You have now passed the halfway mark in your systematic program to acquire greater reading efficiency.

Because most people have a considerable amount of ability in the communication arts and skills, the first weeks of extra practice and study may produce excellent results. For example, your words-per-minute reading rate may have already increased noticeably, with losses in comprehension held to a minimum.

At some point in the learning process, however, a slowdown is likely to occur.

This is a period when past gains must be consolidated, and plans made for future gains. A "pep talk" may help. Whether your progress has been slower or faster than you expected, a fresh look at your present status will help provide the impetus for further advancement.

The brief discussion in this chapter is not intended to be solely inspirational, however. You are asked to carry out practical suggestions at every step of the way.

A drive toward self-realization and self-development must always be serious and purposeful, although not without the pleasures and satisfactions which come from performing each assigned task well.

THE LEARNING PLATEAU

In all communication arts and skills activities certain psychological "laws of learning" are in force. Whether you recognize them as laws or not, you will probably obey them.

You need not necessarily understand how these laws operate. Even professional psychologists, who devote their lives to study and experimentation about such matters, don't fully comprehend the various facets of the learning process.

For example, almost every beginner who has tried to become skilled in the art of doing certain things, from playing a trombone to playing a game of chess, has noticed that he seems to make gains in learning up to a certain point and then stops.

He may not lose any of the gains he has made thus far. But neither does he make any further gains.

He has reached what the psychologists call a **learning plateau.**

Fortunately for the learner, this frustrating situation is merely temporary if either one of two courses of action is followed.

1. Continue practicing as before, with confidence that sooner or later the leveling-off period will come to an end;

OR

2. Put even more effort and energy into practice, with the hope that by force and drive you will move off the plateau onto higher learning ground.

Some psychologists hold the theory that where certain skills, including the skill of reading, are concerned you need not get stalled on a plateau at all. Provided the learning conditions and teaching (or self-teaching) methods are ideal, past gains are consolidated at each

102

learning level and provide a strong base for future gains. Progress continues without interruption until you reach your own highest potential.

But since conditions are rarely ideal, you are likely at some point in your present program to find yourself apparently making no progress at all in the specific effort to read faster and better.

Do not despair.

Instead, tell yourself firmly that this is only a temporary halt, and then go ahead and

Practice.

BREAKING THE SOUND BARRIER

Consider now your reading rate and comprehension scores for the first reading test selection, entitled "Thomas Wolfe."

Compare these scores with those of the second selection, entitled "Margaret Fuller."

You may expect some gain in your words-per-minute rate, with no more than a 25 percent loss in comprehension. (Although comprehension losses may be considerable at first, they will not continue so. Try always to hold them to a minimum.)

Next look closely at your PERSONAL PROGRESS CHART to get a picture of your reading rate scores over a period of time.

If you have made little or no gain in rate, with your words-per-minute scores hovering around 200 and rarely going above 250, **you may still be reading word by word.**

You may even be reading syllable by syllable.

You may be a confirmed vocalizer.

Three important questions are now going to be asked you about **vocalizing.** They require either a **yes** or a **no** answer.

No matter what your reading speed is at this point, you are urged to answer these questions as accurately as you can.

The first question:

1. Do you move your lips when you read?

yes   no

(Circle your answer)

Moving lips are the easiest of all the symptoms of word-by-word reading to detect. If you are not sure whether you have this habit, ask a member of your family or a close friend to observe you when you read. This should be done at a time when you are not conscious of observation.

If the answer is **yes,** you must set about correcting yourself immediately.

Use any or all of the expedients suggested before: put your fingers across your lips, a pencil in your mouth, or chewing gum between your teeth.

Another emergency measure is to put your elbows on a table, with the open book between them and one hand covering your mouth. Then, simply, **read.**

Most important in breaking the lip-movement habit is your awareness that it is a habit and also that it is important that you break it.

If you do not move your lips, or if you are certain that you have corrected this habit, you should proceed to the second question.

2. Do you move your throat muscles when you read?

yes   no

(Circle your answer)

This habit is not so obvious as lip-moving, but with a little detective work you can find the answer.

With your fingertips you can feel lightly for vibrations in your throat muscles as you read. Also look for any signs of fatigue or strain in the throat after you have been reading for a long time.

Again, an observer may help you to find the answer to the question.

The significant point for the reader to remember is that throat movement, no matter how slight, is an almost certain indication of word-by-word reading.

Perhaps you have underlined or circled the **no** to both questions. You still have one more question to go.

3. Do you "hear" each individual word in your mind as you read?

yes   no

(*Circle your answer*)

This is the most subtle form of word-by-word reading.

Your lips may be motionless. Your throat shows no signs of vibration.

Nevertheless, each word is being inwardly pronounced, broken up into meaningless segments, as your eye plods haltingly along a line of print.

You can soon learn to stop muttering when you read.

You can also abruptly stop the motion of lips and throat.

But the "silent and invisible" sound barrier is a formidable one. Until you break through this final barrier, your **silent** reading rate will be held down to approximately your **oral** reading rate.

It may not be easy.

First, you must recognize the problem.

Then you must be convinced that you need to change your approach to silent reading.

Finally, you must have confidence that you can break through the barrier on your own, without either special training or special equipment.

MOTIVATION

Fortunately, almost every human being has an inborn drive toward self-improvement. Once an individual becomes aware that personal problems exist, he is likely to start at once seeking possible solutions.

This basic urge toward betterment often acts as a powerful motivating force in developing the attitudes and skills required for faster and better reading.

In an earlier chapter of this book, you were given a description of some of the mechanical equipment which is used as training aids in many classroom reading courses. All the magical properties which primitive man attributed to inanimate objects modern man apparently finds in the various mechanical devices of today.

Machines used for communication seem to weave a particular spell on most people, from telephones to television.

Scarcely anyone would be skeptical, for instance, if told that a push-button gadget had been invented to make everyone read faster without the slightest mental effort.

The fact remains, however, that no machine can read for you. It can only give you a stimulus for exerting yourself a little harder.

In all communication skills improvement, and specifically in the art of reading, the individual makes the real effort. And the strength of this effort depends on the strength of the motivation behind it.

If you are an aggressive, daring personality, you probably don't have to look any further for reasons to improve your reading. Your own ambitious drives will give you all the inner motivation you need.

On the other hand, your personal temperament may be such that you dislike stress and strain, haste and pressure. You'd be far more comfortable reading along at your old, accustomed, plodding rate forever. Yet as a student, or as a man or woman in the business or professional world, you find yourself, perhaps, in a position where efficiency in reading is essential to your success. This gives you a strong outer motivation.

No matter what your occupation, if you live in the world today you are subject to the constant stimulus of a competitive society. You compete with the efficient brains of your colleagues who have attained a high level of communication skill. You also compete more and more with the efficient "brains" of electronic equipment and their automatically high level of communication skill.

The men and women who can read fast and read well are the men and women who will advance confidently in the midst of the dynamic changes now occurring in a world of atomic power and automation. They will face not only their workaday positions with confidence but also their increased leisure time.

Motivation is thus to be found in everything that goes on around you.

But the inner urge toward self-improvement can be the most powerful incentive of all. You can drive yourself from within much more effectively than you can be driven from without. A keen desire to read faster implemented by regular practice serves you best.

Furthermore, the results are likely to be permanent.

Nevertheless, if the idea of machines still appeals to you, you are encouraged to think of this book and all other printed material that you read as "machines," mechanical gadgets composed of ink and paper to help you accomplish a task.

You might also consider as "machines" the following:

—the 3 x 5 card you lower on a page to accelerate your heading

—the flash cards used to help strengthen your vocabulary

—the egg-timer, the stop watch, or the sweep second-hand of your wrist watch.

Perhaps the most valuable "machine" of all is your PERSONAL PROGRESS CHART in the Appendix of this book. Here you will find what many psychologists consider the strongest motivational device of all—*your own record of achievement.*

If you genuinely wish to learn, a low score provides a challenge; a high score an inspiration.

PRIDE OF ACCOMPLISHMENT

• You keep your senses alert as you practice with your Eye-Span Card

• You glance at a word on a flash card and immediately think of the definition

• You race your eyes ahead on a printed page reading as fast as you can think

• You faithfully keep your PERSONAL PROGRESS CHART, striving always to improve

You may never be entirely satisfied as long as your performance does not measure up to your potential—but you will still have the deep feeling of pride which comes with solid accomplishment at each step of the way.

READING EXERCISE

Instructions: "What I have written here is a rough sketch of my personal philosophy." So says this well-known American woman writer and editor. Read rapidly, but carefully. Time yourself as you read. Jot down the time in seconds in the space provided. Then answer the questions.

Time Yourself and Begin

THE ART OF BEGINNING WHERE YOU ARE

By SOPHIE KERR

A good many years ago, when I was younger and brasher than I am now, I went to a dinner party given by a playwright. May Sinclair, a compact and composed figure, was there and talked about her cat Jetty, a great pet, waiting to welcome her when she went back to England. I liked that. There was another woman writer present who knew Algernon Blackwood and had seen ghosts, and she talked about all that. The playwright talked about his paneled room which was the pride of his life; he took it with him whenever he moved his home, and I believe it finally landed in Hollywood. There was another man who said smugly: "I am an advanced Orientalist. I am often taken for an Oriental." So he talked—lengthily—about that.

But the prize of the evening was a man who had decided that Time and Space are the same and was prepared to prove it. He took a long silver serving spoon and laid it straight on the table before him. "Look!" he said, "I move this spoon to the right. Time elapses as I do so. And as I move it I leave an empty space behind it, which is, in time, the past. The space ahead of the spoon into which it moves is, naturally, the future. So you see that Time and Space are the same."

There was a pause and then the playwright said gently: "But if you didn't move the spoon, even if the spoon wasn't there—Time would still be going on. And though you can move the spoon back in Space, you can't, my dear chap, move it back in Time. Time—right now—each instant as it passes—is the future."

The Space and Time man was furious, and a terrific argument arose to which I paid small attention. I had been given a paralyzing thought: that Now is the Future. To a large extent that remark of my host reshaped and reorganized my life. I do not know whether the reorganization made me happier, for any personal evaluation of happiness can only be relative and uncertain—but it contributed to my peace of mind, my working ability, and my physical health. To believe that the Future is Now, this instant in time, forces me to look forward and think forward and work forward to the limit

of my abilities. It forces me to choose from the day-to-day makeup of my life, and since it forces me to select, automatically I am forced to discard. I began to do this under the impulse of that one man's wisdom. I have continued it through the years. Of course, I knew from the first that no one can have everything, no one can do everything, no one can see and hear everything, but spurred by the urgency of today's importance, I learned very soon that even an average life may be arranged to offer, yes, to provide, an infinite variety, an infinite periphery.

Like most young persons born and brought up in a fairly simple and uncomplicated environment, I had never analyzed nor directed my life with clarity. I had walked up more than one blind alley and bumped my head. I had collected this, that, and the other activity and association from momentary attraction until I was so overweighted I had no satisfaction from any of them. The future had always seemed to me a distant nebula, impossible to anticipate or plan for, but agreeable and hopeful, a sort of mild heaven where clutter would melt away and difficulties would solve themselves. But once I had accepted the idea that the one real Future is Now, I found that practical rules could be made to shape it, rules which could evolve into principles, into guides, with no more nebulae anywhere around.

It has always been a fancy of mine that I'd love to live at least six lives simultaneously. One life for the necessary work of earning my living, hard concentrated work without petty interruptions and irrelevancies. One life for reading and study and meditation on what I'd read and what I'd studied. One life for doing things with my hands like sewing and gardening and polishing mirrors and cleaning silver and maybe a craft or so like woodcarving or weaving. One life to see my friends and acquaintances, for travel and hospitality. One life for political and public interest projects where I could be certain that I was doing something, be it ever so small, of value to my country and my times. And among these I would tuck in the pleasure and pain of shopping, the pleasure and pain of housekeeping, and the complete pleasure of aimless, frivolous loafing.

The catch is that I have only one life so far as I know and I must pack into it all these intentions and desires. If the Future is Now, as I believe it is, I must hold to that policy of choice and discard. Believe me, this is not easy. Actually it can never be perfectly done because of the eternal wobble and jolt of the unexpected—the unexpected which is beyond the control of the individual.

The first consideration of my Future-Now was sheer necessity, the work by which I earn my living, which must be done if I am to eat my meals and pay my taxes. I decided that I must work more regularly and fend off interruptions. There's an airy notion floating in many nonwriters' heads that writing is something which may be done in odd moments between telephone calls, having a cold, stirring up a sauce, and getting a dress fitted. All writers, including those of light fiction, know better. They know that writing is not a filler-in for idle hours but a hard, tiring business. You do not hear writing, you do not see it, you sit down with a pad and pencil or a typewriter and you put down the words which come out of your creative—or imitative—ability. It is never successful, this writing; whatever you imagined so beautifully never comes through to paper without strains, cracks, and spots.

Well, this is not a piece about writing but about arranging existence to get the most from the present moment. Having put earning my living as a fixed routine at the top of my agenda, I found it was at once attacked by the minutiae of housekeeping, meals, laundry, ren-ovation—whatever goes with home sweet home. By relaxing standards here and there, by cutting off items of service and indulgence, and by deliberate scamping, housekeeping duties were reduced. I discovered that a house in order always looks clean, and if I didn't mention streaky baseboards and unwaxed floors and rain-dotted windows they were not noticed, or if they were noticed, my friends said nothing about them—although one friend did remark with a consciously superior smile that *she* had spent the morning rubbing up all brass handles on her chests and highboys. (I did something about that, I had all the visible brass handles in my house taken off, polished, lacquered and put back, so they didn't need rubbing up. My Now definitely wasn't going to be frittered in rubbing brass handles.)

My next move had to do with people. Long before I heard about the Now-Future I had resolved that no one should be invited into my house unless I really wanted her or him; that no business or social expediency should name my guests; that any welcome I gave should be sincere. Corra Harris once wrote bitingly: "I am pale at the memory of the things I have been obliged to do in order to preserve my strength and substance and some semblance of dignity from those people who have been too easily drawn to me not by affection or respect but by the desire of more assistance than it is wise or possible to give." I was not in Mrs. Harris' dire state, but I certainly was seeing more people who meant little to me than people of whom I was fond and in whom I was interested. Gradually I moved out of contact with those for whom I could not feel the warmth of real friendship. At the same time or thereabouts I decided never to argue with anyone on any subject save the trivial and comic. An Irish friend tells me that I am missing the greatest fun in life—she loves argument more even than poetry. To me argument seems a scratchy sort of time-wasting. I couldn't include it in my Now.

By the time I had come this far I had moved out of the field of material possessions and human associations into that of mental habits. It is an obvious but neglected cliché that the mind is as trainable as the hands and that the emotions though less tractable than the mind are sensible to control and direction. For my Now, for my Future Today, I chose to train my mind away from all futile dwelling on the past. We say: If I had been kind when I was unfeeling, if I had held my tongue instead of speaking, if I had understood where I was blind, if I had been strong where I was weak—if I had—if I had—if I had—! And this can go on forever in useless regret to paralyze the will, diminish the mind, narrow the heart. It can also make the person who indulges in such remembered failure a most confounded bore.

And there is also that matter of remembering other, happier times—the good old days, they're labeled! That too is a sterile, narrowing pursuit. Most older people have had some good old days, days when we had more friends, more health, more looks, more appreciation, more power to work and play, more money, more opportunity—but if they are gone, they are gone. They may return again, and we keep on hoping because hope is in itself a happiness, but neither memory of the past nor hope for the future should fill the precious possibilities of the Now. Personally I must look with surprise and pleasure on whatever good I have today, and if I do recall that I once had more, it must be with gratitude for those past favors and not with tears that they are gone. Any mind can do as much, and the reward is a balance, an adjustment which is constantly alive and exciting. Today has something more thrilling than yesterday because it is here, it is new, it is Now. Time has struck off yesterday and come along with us. The mind—any mind

—can learn to acknowledge this and move forward with each inevitable step of the hours.

Emotion is not so malleable as the mind. Bereavements, broken affections, cruel disappointments are stubborn; they will stay with us no matter how convincingly our reason says they must be forgotten; they even come back in dreams if they are rejected in waking hours. Perhaps the best way to meet them is with compromise—if they once were great joys, hold to that part of them and refuse to dwell on the pain and sorrow they have caused; always and always remember that they are in the past and cannot, normally, dominate the Now. No one will quite succeed in doing this, but no one should turn away from trying. To concentrate on past pain and past grief, to look backward always into shadows is to deny the daily miracle of the earth's facing the rising sun.

The Categorical Imperative, I am told, is that every action should be capable of becoming a universal rule of action for all men. Believe me, gentle reader, if you have come this far with me, I have no faintest ambition at aiming at anything so high and splendid as a Categorical Imperative. What I have written here is a rough sketch of my personal philosophy and way of life, awkwardly formed, stumblingly pursued; but though I stumble I am ever constant. It is based on my sense of complete ignorance of what tomorrow will be and my conviction that I am sure only of Today and that I must use it as best I can. Today is my future. I *must* begin from here.

Time in seconds——

Directions: Select the best answer and place the appropriate letter in the parentheses.

1. May Sinclair's cat was named (a) Betty; (b) Letty; (c) Jetty; (d) Hetty.   ( )
2. At the playwright's dinner party one woman writer claimed that (a) she had seen ghosts;

(b) she had lived in Hollywood; (c) she was an advanced Orientalist; (d) she lived in a paneled room. ( )

3. The "paralyzing thought" which Sophie Kerr had at the dinner party was that (a) Time is Money; (b) Now is the Future; (c) Time and Space are the same; (d) Time and Space are different. ( )

4. The Time and Space argument was demonstrated with a (a) spoon; (b) knife; (c) fork; (d) plate. ( )

5. It had always been a fancy of Miss Kerr's to live simultaneously at least (a) two lives; (b) four lives; (c) six lives; (d) eight lives. ( )

6. In her effort to look, think and work forward to the limit of her abilities, Miss Kerr decided to give up entirely (a) all close friends; (b) arguing about anything; (c) housekeeping; (d) polishing brass. ( )

7. It is not easy to choose and discard the activities for a planned life because of (a) the jolt of the unexpected; (b) nostalgia for the good old days; (c) the ringing of the telephone; (d) meals and taxes. ( )

8. That every action should be capable of becoming a universal rule of action for all men is called (a) The Now-Future; (b) The Future-Now; (c) The Categorical Imperative; (d) Orientalism. ( )

9. You might gather from this piece that (a) writing careers and keeping house don't mix; (b) keeping a high shine on brass is a waste of time for writers; (c) relaxed housekeeping standards is a sign of laziness; (d) women writers can still keep a house looking reasonably clean. ( )

10. The main idea of the article can be expressed as follows: (a) you have only one life to lead; (b) an incidental remark can change your life; (c) writing is the highest goal in life; (d) you should arrange your existence to get the most from the present moment. ( )

DIRECTIONS FOR SCORING

Reading Rate. Find your reading rate in words per minute by turning to the TABLE FOR DETERMINING READING RATE IN WORDS PER MINUTE.

Answers to Questions. Check the answers to the multiple-choice questions in the CORRECTION KEY EXERCISES.

Progress Chart. Enter all reading rate and comprehension scores in the PERSONAL PROGRESS CHART.

WORD RECOGNITION AND ATTACK EXERCISE

Directions: You are now to resume your practice of recognizing and attacking words. First, look at the single word, preferably through the Eye-Span Card. Then move the card rapidly to the five words directly below, and pick out with your eyes the word that is exactly the same as the single word. **Do Not Say The Word Aloud.** Continue to the next single word and repeat the operation. Do not make any marks on the page, so that you can repeat this exercise daily for a week or two.

Begin

aspect
repect aspect aspic pectin suspect

lively
livery likely vilely lively silvery

marble
marble warble garble maybe ramble

hasten
fasten wasted hated masted hasten

rattle
ratted tattle rattle nettle battle

refer
reefer defer never refer fear

notion

motion   noted   lotion   potion   notion

*

lessen

lesson   lesser   sells   lessen   leased

*

scanty

scanty   shanty   candy   sandy   caste

*

slaughter

laughter   slaughter   daughter   salter   slanter

*

transient

transit   transom   transient   transcend   trams

*

summary

summary   mammary   summery   sugary   mussy

*

printed

printer   pointed   tinted   printed   primed

*

vantage

vintage   vanish   vaunt   vanquish   vantage

*

duly

dully   ruby   bully   duly   daily

*

abuse

abyss   adduce   allude   accuse   abuse

*

dagger

digger   gadder   beggar   dagger   dabber

*

deceit

decent   docent   decease   deceit   diet

*

except

excess   except   excise   excite   excel

*

faculty

faulty   factory   faculty   facility   fatherly

EYE-SPAN EXERCISE

Directions: You are now to resume practice to help you increase the number of letters and spaces you can see at a single fixation. Use your Eye-Span Card for this exercise. Move it from asterisk to asterisk as rapidly as possible. Try to see the entire phrase at a single glance. **Think The Phrase; Do Not Say It Aloud.**

Begin

*

watch my dog

*

match any dot

*

try this tie

*

pitch the hay

*

nail the board

*

send them soon

*

see the moon

*

arm the men

*

crawl out fast

*

come down last

*

find the boy

*

read the line

*

ride one time

*

beat on tin

*

all are heard

*

dry your eyes

eat some meat

*

grow more wheat

*

hide in there

*

it comes last

*

STUDY ASSIGNMENTS

Below is a reminder check-list of study and practice assignments which you should now be carrying out daily:

• Word study with the use of flash cards. **Use Your Dictionary.**

• Practice with Eye-Span Card, using both numbers and words. Original material can be prepared by either hand-printing or typing.

• Practice in finding information quickly by the use of an index in books of your selection.

• Continued practice in spelling improvement, if needed.

• Speeded reading practice **daily** with use of Eye-Span Card, consciously accelerating by lowering the card at increasing rates down the page.

• Speeded reading practice **daily** with use of a brief newspaper story, moving your eyes down the column in a zigzag manner and seeking key ideas as you proceed.

• Writing your reading autobiography is a continuing activity. Also continue to read what other people have written about themselves. (Consult list of suggested readings in CHAPTER FOUR.)

Now try this new assignment.

Plan an imaginary trip for yourself to any place on the globe. Obtain the appropriate bus, train, or plane schedules needed to help get you there and back. Interpret the essential information as rapidly and as accurately as you can.

Pleasant journey!

CHAPTER TWELVE

THE COMMUNICATION OF IDEAS

Some readers when they fail to comprehend printed material are inclined to blame themselves.

Standing in awe of the fact that the words are published ones, they somehow feel that the responsibility for understanding rests completely on their shoulders. It is a frustrating experience, therefore, for readers who improve their skill to discover that many ideas in print still elude them.

If you can recognize yourself in this situation, perhaps a few pointed questions might help you to get some perspective.

Is the receiver of a message in print always at fault when communication fails?

What about the responsibility of the sender? Furthermore, what about "noise"?

You will recall that "noise," or interference with communication, may mean just what the word usually means—loud, distracting sound. But it may also among other things mean visual interference or distraction, such as typographical errors, or faulty arrangement of words on a page.

To exaggerate somewhat, suppose you were faced with words which appeared as follows:

Apagewithnowhitespaceatallbetweenwordsor betweenlinesandalsowithnomarginsnottomen- tionwithnopunctuationwouldbeextremelydiffi- culttoread

After trying to figure out the meaning of the above sentence, you will agree that the "noise" in this case is as effective for blocking communication as loud static would be on an A.M. radio. That is, white space between words, between lines, in the indentation of a paragraph, and around the margins of a page—all con- tribute to the clear **reception** of ideas which have been clearly expressed.

In brief, the actual way in which words are placed on a page may increase or decrease your ease and comfort while you read.

Good punctuation is another aid to clear reception.

When you see one of the following marks, you are guided to take the appropriate action:

, **Comma**

; **Semicolon**

. **Period**

(take a breath)

(take a longer breath)

(rest)

You give ideas in print the appropriate em- phasis when you see the following:

! **Exclamation point**

? **Question mark**

When you see the following, you anticipate what is coming next:

: **Colon**

Several other principal punctuation marks when used effectively also assist in the com- munication of ideas. The examples follow:

( ) **Parentheses** (These marks are often used to enclose explanatory statements not necessarily a part of the sentence.)

[ ] **Brackets** (These marks are often used to enclose a parenthesis within a parenthesis.)

— **Dash** (This mark is used when a sen- tence is broken off, or when some surprising statement will follow.)

" " **Quotation marks** (These are used to set off speeches and conversations, both real and imaginary, from the rest of the text, and also around words having a special meaning. Sometimes they are used for titles of articles.)

... **Ellipsis** (These three periods may be used after an uncompleted statement, or to show that something has been omitted.)

Various other marks of punctuation clearing the way for the effective communication of ideas may sometimes be noted in print.

For example, many newspapers in presenting a round-up of important highlights in a particular news story may head each separate statement with one of the following:

¶ **Paragraph sign**

• **Bullet**

☞ **Index finger**

△ **Special typographical device**

Not all punctuation is good punctuation. Too many marks on a page may confuse the reader by chopping up the ideas. On the other hand, too few marks may confuse by obscuring the meaning.

Certainly an indiscriminate use of commas and semicolons within a sentence may provide the "noise" which often prevents the receiver from "hearing" ideas in print.

The tendency in writing today is toward shorter sentences, and this ordinarily means fewer marks of punctuation. Nevertheless, competent readers should not be afraid of long and complex sentences, if the writer knows both how to think and how to punctuate.

TYPOGRAPHICAL AIDS TO COMMUNICATION

Objective tests show that there is little difference in readability between most of the standard styles of book type used in printing today.

Good readable type in newspapers, magazines and books may be anywhere from 8 to 14 points in size, with 72 points equalling an inch. For purposes of comparison, this paragraph is printed in 11-point type.

Studies have been made to determine the effect of certain styles of type upon reading speed. According to these, a reader will be slowed down somewhat by material set entirely in the heavy, black type called Old English.

𝔗𝔥𝔦𝔰 𝔦𝔰 𝔒𝔩𝔡 𝔈𝔫𝔤𝔩𝔦𝔰𝔥 𝔱𝔶𝔭𝔢.

Surprisingly enough, the more modern type known as *block* or nonserif also may slow down the reader.

This is nonserif type.

Typewriter type, both in manuscripts and in print, is slightly harder to read.

`This is typewriter type.`

MATERIAL SET ENTIRELY IN CAPITAL LETTERS SUCH AS THIS MAY SLOW YOU DOWN TOO.

And so will material set entirely in italics as this is.

No difference in effect, however, has been noted between lightface type such as this, and **boldface type such as this.**

Size of type in relation to length of line may affect readability. Very large type set in a narrow column is hard to read, as is very fine type set in a wide column.

The ink should not be too glossy black and the paper not too shiny white. Dull black on dull white is best.

Most of the readability points discussed so far can be measured in most instances by the individual reader with a fair degree of accuracy. You can tell almost at a glance at a page whether or not the mechanical standards meet your approval, even though you may not know the fine points of typography.

But there is a much more subtle area of readability which you are now asked to consider.

What about the style of writing in any given piece of printed material?

Granted that the mechanical presentation is adequate, is the material easy to read or hard to read?

And if easy, just how easy?

And if hard, just how hard?

READABILITY FORMULAS

Some thirty different formulas for determining the readability level of material in print have been devised. Most of them have been worked out statistically so that they can be used as objective "yardsticks."

Although they are far from perfect instruments of measurement, many of them have proved to be useful tools for those who write and edit business and industrial publications, government and Armed Forces publications, and general periodicals with mass distribution.

Every formula begins with a single factor: **Vocabulary.**

Evidently no one will argue with the fact that the harder the words, the harder the reading.

But a question immediately arises: **What makes a word hard or easy?**

In general, the shorter the word, the easier the word. A one-syllable word is easier, as a rule, than words of two, three, four or more syllables. Nevertheless, many one-syllable words would be considered hard reading.

Look at the following list. Do you know the meaning of all of these words?

croft
doss
draff
duff
gleb
hasp
hob
kern
lour
prink
quirt

They are not known because they are seldom seen. On the other hand, some words with many syllables are perfectly familiar to most readers and would be considered easy reading.

For example, a few five-syllable words are:
accommodation
accompaniment

conscientiously
confidentially
sarcastically

Some six-syllable words are also easy, such as:
humanitarian
irreconcilable
internationally

And everyone knows the following word, yet it has seven syllables!
enthusiastically

So, to the criterion **word length** must be added **frequency of use.**

The more often a word appears in print, the easier it seems to be. Thus a word appearing by count once in every thousand words in a cross-section of available publications in print, ranging from confession magazines to scholarly journals, is for most readers easier than a word appearing once in every million words in print, or once in every ten million words in print.

Another important factor in determining readability is sentence length.

This doesn't necessarily mean that a paragraph made up of a series of short sentences is easier to read than a paragraph made up of a single long sentence.

It does mean, however, that if you select a generous sample of a total piece of writing and calculate the **average** sentence length, the shorter the average the easier the reading. Some sentences may be long; some short. Variety in itself may contribute to the reading ease of printed material.

The structure of a sentence also may have an effect on readability. A simple sentence (expressing one idea) is usually easier to read than a compound sentence (expressing two or more ideas).

Whether material is easy or hard to read may also be partially determined with two more factors often used as an element in readability formulas.

The first is "personal interest."

The second may be called "idea pressure."

Just how does a writer add personal interest to his material to make it easier to read?

One way this may be achieved has already been mentioned earlier in this book in the discussion on feature articles: It is "the YOU attitude."

By addressing himself to YOU, the writer of nonfiction or factual prose hopes to gain your personal interest and sustain it throughout your reading. The writer may also use other pronouns, such as **we, our, ours, us, your, yours; he, his, him; she, her, hers; they, their, theirs, them** (but not **it** or **its**, since these pronouns refer to things and not persons).

Words that indicate groups have personal interest as well. **People, friends, students, colleagues**—all are examples.

Names of individuals are of course high in personal interest. Everyone finds his own name in print extremely readable.

Personal sentences too may contribute to readability. Examples are material in quotation marks, dialogue, conversation, and sentences which ask questions (followed by a question mark) or make startling statements (followed by one, two, or three exclamation points).

When a writer fills his sentences or paragraphs with main ideas, one after the other, with no supporting details, no examples or illustrations, no comparisons, the reader may well find himself being suffocated in "idea pressure."

Some readers determinedly struggle their way out of this situation, like a diver coming up for air.

Other readers simply give up.

One of the ways you can identify this kind of pressurized writing is by the presence of a great number of prepositional phrases. As an illustration, in the following sentence many of the prepositional phrases are signalled by the prepositions **in** and **of.**

Of interest to everyone in the field of improvement in reading is the fact that the development of readability formulas as we know them today probably began with the basic research in word counts of the psychologist Edward L. Thorndike in his efforts to help teachers in the public schools in learning which of the great number of words in the language occurred more frequently in print.

When a great many ideas are compressed into a small space, easy words become hard reading indeed.

RULE-OF-THUMB MEASUREMENT

Readability formulas were originally devised for use by writers and editors to help them reach the reading public more effectively.

Few readers will want to take the time to apply the formulas themselves. For those who are interested, however, a list of some available formulas will follow this discussion.

You can make a rule-of-thumb measurement without applying mathematical formulas. Although it will be a subjective judgment, it may be fairly accurate.

In the first place, even before you size up a printed selection from a periodical or a book, don't let yourself be intimidated, no matter how hard it looks at first.

Then, if you find yourself blocked in your understanding of what you are reading, ask these questions to help you determine the readability level of the material and analyze what makes it hard for you.

Are the words easy or difficult?

If difficult, you should consult your dictionary.

Is the vocabulary of the writer too highly specialized?

Again, use your dictionary.

Are the sentences long and complicated, with little variety?

Try to analyze the main thought of each.

Does the writing completely lack personal interest?

Unless you have a particular reason for continuing a book with a dull and uninteresting style, try to find one on the same subject which contains more personal interest. Then go back to the first book and try again.

Are the sentences under the pressure of too many prepositional phrases?

Again, try to dig out the main thoughts.

Don't stop at this point, however. Perhaps the writer has done his task well, perhaps not, but **you** may need more preparation.

By continuing with the exercises for improving your reading skill and speed, you will eventually become able to tackle material with confidence that you would previously have given up as being too deep for you to grasp.

Bear in mind always that communication is a two-way process. Thus the reader is expected to meet the writer at some point. The receiver of a message cannot shift all responsibility to the sender.

By systematic use of this book you are steadily improving your capacity to receive messages in print, at all levels of readability.

Δ Remember, you are to increase your reading efficiency by mastering the skill of word recognition.

Δ Use the dictionary to add to your word recognition.

Δ Use the dictionary to add to your word store.

Δ Read widely to become familiar with a variety of writing styles.

Δ Learn how to grasp the meaning of a writer even though personal interest may be lacking.

Δ Develop your own techniques for taking the pressure out of overcompressed writing.

Never forget that writers are human beings, too, and not machines for spreading printers' ink on paper. They have their problems of sending just as you may have your problems of receiving.

You may upon occasion try not only to meet them halfway but to put yourself in their place.

SELECTED PAPERBOUND BOOKS ON CLEAR WRITING AND RAPID READING

Double Your Reading Speed, by The Reading Laboratory, Inc. Fawcett Premier.

Effective Writing, United States Government Printing Office.

Lively Art of Writing, by Lucille V. Payne. New American Library.

Speed Reading, by Robert L. Zorn. Barnes & Noble.

Speed Reading Made Easy, by Nila Banton Smith, Ph.D. Popular Library.

The Art of Persuasion: How to Write Effectively About Almost Anything, by Terry Belanger and Stewart Lacasze. Scribners.

READING EXERCISE—I

Instructions: Readability formulas are in for a rough time of it when this well-known American essayist, poet and editor takes up his pen. Time yourself as you read. Jot down your time **in seconds** in the space provided. Then answer the questions.

Time Yourself and Begin

CALCULATING MACHINE
By E. B. White

A publisher in Chicago has sent us a pocket calculating machine by which we may test our writing to see whether it is intelligible. The calculator was developed by General Motors, who not satisfied with giving the world a Cadillac, now dream of bringing perfect understanding to men. The machine (it is simply a celluloid card with a dial) is called the Reading-Ease Calculator and shows four grades of "reading ease"—Very Easy, Easy, Hard, and

Very Hard. You count your words and sylla-bles, set the dial, and an indicator lets you know whether anybody is going to understand what you have written. An instruction book came with it, and after mastering the simple rules we lost no time in running a test on the instruction book itself, to see how *that* writer was doing. The poor fellow! His leading essay, the one on the front cover, tested Very Hard.

Our next step was to study the first phrase on the face of the calculator: "How to test Reading-Ease of written matter." There is, of course, no such thing as reading ease of written matter. There is the ease with which matter can be read, but that is a condition of the reader, not of the matter. Thus the inventors and distributors of this calculator get off to a poor start, with a Very Hard instruction book and a slovenly phrase. Already they have one foot caught in the brier patch of English usage.

Not only did the author of the instruction book score badly on the front cover, but inside the book he used the word "personalize" in an essay on how to improve one's writing. A man who likes the word "personalize" is entitled to his choice, but we wonder whether he should be in the business of giving advice to writers. "Whenever possible," he wrote, "personalize your writing by directing it to the reader." As for us, we would as lief Simonize our grand-mother as personalize our writing.

In the same envelope with the calculator, we received another training aid for writers—a booklet called "How to Write Better," by Ru-dolf Flesch. This, too, we studied, and it quickly demonstrated the broncolike ability of the English language to throw whoever leaps cocksurely into the saddle. The language not only can toss a rider but knows a thousand tricks for tossing him, each more gay than the last. Dr. Flesch stayed in the saddle only a moment or two. Under the heading "Think Be-fore You Write," he wrote, "The main thing to consider is your *purpose* in writing. Why are you sitting down to write?" An echo answered: Because, sir, it is more comfortable than stand-ing up.

Communication by the written word is a subtler (and more beautiful) thing than Dr. Flesch and General Motors imagine. They con-tend that the "average reader" is capable of reading only what tests Easy, and that the writer should write at or below this level. This is a presumptuous and degrading idea. There is no average reader, and to reach down toward this mythical character is to deny that each of us is on the way up, is ascending. ("Ascending," by the way, is a word Dr. Flesch advises writers to stay away from. Too unusual.)

It is our belief that no writer can improve his work until he discards the dulcet notion that the reader is feeble-minded, for writing is an act of faith, not a trick of grammar. Ascent is at the heart of the matter. A country whose writers are following a calculating machine downstairs is not ascending—if you will par-don the expression—and a writer who ques-tions the capacity of the person at the other end of the line is not a writer at all, merely a schemer. The movies long ago decided that a wider communication could be achieved by a deliberate descent to a lower level, and they walked proudly down until they reached the cellar. Now they are groping for the light switch, hoping to find the way out.

We have studied Dr. Flesch's instructions diligently, but we return for guidance in these matters to an earlier American, who wrote with more patience, more confidence. "I fear chiefly," he wrote, "lest my expression may not be *extravagant* enough, may not wander far enough beyond the narrow limits of my daily experience, so as to be adequate to the truth of which I have been convinced. . . . Why level downward to our dullest perception always, and praise that as common sense? The commonest sense is the sense of men asleep, which they express by snoring."

Run that through your calculator! It may come out Hard, it may come out Easy. But it will come out whole, and it will last forever.

Time in seconds——

Directions: Answer each question by selecting the best answer and placing it in the appropriate parentheses.

1. The tone of this selection might be called (a) gay; (b) sarcastic; (c) mellow; (d) grim. ( )
2. E. B. White's attitude toward readability formulas is evidently one of (a) unqualified approval; (b) qualified approval; (c) unqualified disapproval; (d) qualified disapproval. ( )
3. The pocket calculating machine referred to was developed by (a) General Foods; (b) Ford Motor Company; (c) General Electric; (d) General Motors. ( )
4. The author insists that the ease with which matter can be read is a condition of (a) the written matter itself; (b) the writer; (c) the calculator; (d) the reader. ( )
5. He also reports that Dr. Flesch and General Motors contend that the "average reader" is capable of reading only what tests as (a) Very Easy; (b) Easy; (c) Hard; (d) Very Hard. ( )
6. The English language is compared to a (a) cannon cracker; (b) buzz saw; (c) bucking bronco; (d) racing car. ( )
7. "How to Write Better," a training aid for writers, was written by (a) Flesch; (b) McElroy; (c) Dale-Chall; (d) Gunning. ( )
8. According to the author, the average reader is (a) caught in the brier patch of English usage; (b) a mythical character; (c) uneducated; (d) capable of reading only what tests as Easy. ( )
9. The best expression of the main idea of this selection is that (a) writers should approach readers as if they were feeble-minded; (b) writers should reach down to their readers; (c) writers should respect their readers and not be afraid of asking them to reach up to understand; (d) writers should be schemers. ( )
10. According to the author, the ideas expressed in the quotation from Thoreau at the end of the selection will (a) last forever; (b) soon be forgotten; (c) come out Easy on the calculator; (d) come out Hard on the calculator. ( )

READING EXERCISE—II

Instructions: In the reading selection which follows, the reader can tell almost from the opening line or two that here is a well-written piece with every indication of being easy to read. Applying the factors which are used in readability formulas, you will find easy words, short sentences, personal references, and a sparing use of prepositional phrases. In short, this chapter from a popular and successful book is made to order for fast and enjoyable reading.

Furthermore, the selection illustrates a point made in the discussion. Here is what happened on one occasion when "noise" came between the "senders" and the "receivers."

Time yourself as you read at a rapid rate. Jot down the time **in seconds** in the space provided. If you wish, you may reread to pick up some of the details you may have missed on the first rapid reading. Then answer the questions.

HOW THE MEN FROM MARS RUINED A QUIET EVENING
By BEN GROSS

It was a pleasant little dinner with a few friends in a Tudor City apartment on a Sunday evening in October, 1938. "How about turning on Charlie McCarthy?" one of the guests said.

"Okay," I answered, "but do you mind if we first hear what Orson Welles is doing?"

Just a few days before, at CBS headquarters, I had asked one of the actors of Welles' "Mercury Theatre of the Air" about Sunday's show.

"Just between us," he had said, "it's lousy. Orson couldn't get ready the script he wanted, so he's run in a dramatization of that H. G. Wells chestnut, *The War of the Worlds.*"

"Oh, that," I said.

"Yeah, good old Sunday-supplement fantasy, but he's dressed it up. Anyway, don't bother to listen. Probably bore you to death."

His words had made me happy. There would not be too many programs worthy of comment on the radio the following Sunday, and instead of having to do an entirely new column of comment for the late editions, I should be able to get by merely with the rewriting of two or three brief paragraphs. It would be a quiet and restful Sabbath evening.

But Welles had staged some of the best experimental dramatic productions on the air during that period, and a sense of duty impelled me to eavesdrop on him for at least a few minutes. Even though he might be merely coasting along during this broadcast, if he displayed some ingenuity in dressing up the familiar fantasy, it might be worth a line or two for the Three Star.

The show began conventionally enough, with the announcer saying quite distinctly that the Columbia Broadcasting System and its affiliated stations were presenting Orson Welles and the "Mercury Theatre of the Air" in *The War of the Worlds* by H. G. Wells. Soon we heard a "news flash" which informed us that a tremendous explosion had taken place on the planet Mars.

Now came a veritable cascade of sensational "bulletins." A meteor had crashed near Grover's Mills, New Jersey. More than a thousand persons had been killed. Finally, an "on-the-spot" remote broadcast from the New Jersey countryside. The meteor was no meteor at all; it was a silver cylinder, a miraculous ship from outer space, and from it were streaming horrendous creatures, the like of which had not been seen on this globe before, men from Mars armed with disintegrating and incinerating death-ray guns. There was no defense against these; thousands who had rushed to the field where the craft had landed were being burned to cinders.

The Martians had invaded the earth to exterminate its inhabitants!

We had not yet heard of flying saucers, artificial satellites and other such phenomena; but what came over the air was overwhelmingly terrifying. And the staccato "news reports" and pronouncements by "officials" which followed made it seem even more so. For the National Guard had been called out . . . the Secretary of War was issuing orders to the Army . . . a state of national emergency had been proclaimed . . . the State Department and even the White House were urging the people to keep calm. But what did these appeals matter? By now the Martians, with flame and terror, were marching on New York!

"You know," I remarked, arising from a half-consumed steak, "I think I'd better be getting back to the office. Some listeners might really believe this."

"How could they?" asked one of the guests. "They announced it was by H. G. Wells. That means it's fiction."

"But those who tuned in late didn't hear the announcement," another said.

It was lucky for me that I had returned to the nearby office. Passing through the city room an assistant at the city desk yelled, "Hey! What the hell's going on?"

The switchboard was blazing; lines were jammed and phones rang all over the place. Rewrite men in booths tried desperately to reach CBS, but none of their calls got through; photographers with full equipment scurried toward the elevators.

"No, madam . . . no, sir . . . we don't know anything about an explosion in Jersey," the man at the switchboard was saying. "Men from Mars? . . . Yeah, I know it's on the radio . . . but it didn't happen . . . Nothing's going on, I tell you . . . No, madam . . . no, sir . . . there ain't no men from Mars."

A police official's call reached the city desk.

"It's just a phony, a radio play," the harassed assistant told him.

Then, shouting at me: "*You* try to get CBS. If you can't, go up there."

The two phones in the radio room were clanging wildly and I grabbed both receivers.

"Are they abandoning New York?" a hysterical woman asked over one.

"No, lady, it's just a play," I said.

"Oh, no!" she screamed and hung up.

A Red Cross man was on the other wire.

"I hear they're broadcasting about a terrible catastrophe in New Jersey," the man said. "Do you know where it is?"

"It's only Orson Welles," I explained. "He's on with a fantasy."

"But my wife just called me and said thousands have been killed," he said.

My assistant rushed in breathless with proofs from the composing room. The phones again. "My God! Those calls have been driving me crazy!" she said.

I made for the door. "You're not going to leave me all alone with these phones?" the distraught girl pleaded. I gave her no heed.

Downstairs, in the cab, the radio was tuned to WEAF. "Get WABC" (the CBS station), I said. The cabbie did, and we heard the calm voice of an announcer saying that this was merely an Orson Welles presentation of a story by H. G. Wells. A few seconds later the Martians were marching again. They had just destroyed Trenton and were, in fact, already on the Palisades, rushing with fiery death on to our metropolis . . . Refugees were scurrying from the city in wild flight . . . but that wasn't all . . . some of the invaders, who had followed in other ships from outer space, had detoured to Midwest and the South.

"God Almighty!" the cab driver exclaimed.

"It's just fiction," I assured him. "Didn't you hear the announcer?"

"No, I didn't hear no announcer," the chauffeur said. "You're sure?"

"You don't see any panic-stricken people running about the streets, do you?" I asked.

But just at that moment we passed a movie theatre on Third Avenue. A half-dozen women and children scurried from it as from nearby bars men dashed out to gaze at the sky. On Lexington Avenue and 51st Street a wailing woman sat on the curb and a policeman stood in the middle of the roadway surrounded by a crowd.

"There sure is something going on," my driver said.

And, indeed, there was, although one wouldn't have known it by the lack of turmoil in front of CBS. There was no more than the usual number of pedestrians going by and, showing my pass, I had no difficulty in gaining access to the seat of the hysteria which at that moment was sweeping most of the United States.

The broadcast had ended and the studio and corridors vibrated with chatter, as perturbed executives, attaches, officious page boys and annoyed cops rushed about. I was informed that during the latter portion of the program the policemen, in response to the complaints, had marched into the glass-encased control room, and watched in disbelief as Orson and others of his Mercury troupe, in business and sports clothes, stood stoically before the microphones reading their scripts, ignorant of the havoc they were creating throughout the land.

When the executives and the law burst through the studio doors to confront him after the broadcast had come to its crashing finale, Welles was astounded to hear that listeners had taken his fantasy literally.

"How could they?" he said. "They were told several times it wasn't real."

"Have you any statement to make?" the newspapermen demanded.

"None whatsoever," he said, and ran with his cast from the studio down the corridor. The press followed, but before they could be intercepted, the Mercury troupe was downstairs and in the cabs that had been awaiting them. The reporters in other taxis pursued the fleeing performers, only to lose track of them in the maze of Times Square traffic. There, under the glow of sparkling lights, jittery thousands watched the *Times* electric sign for assurance that the "Martian invasion" had at least been repelled. The outwitted journalists then backtracked to CBS, where a "network spokesman" solemnly promised that "such a thing will not happen again." At the *News* office the phones were still ringing, although the radio was making repeated announcements (until midnight) that Americans positively were in no peril from the spacemen.

So, on this Sunday evening of October 30, 1938, which was anything but "quiet," I not only had to do a complete rewrite of the column but also give a hand in assembling items pouring in via telephones and teletypes. As these flooded the city and the telegraph desks, it became apparent that this was a startling story, with national and even international repercussions.

It had touched the movie theatre just around the corner, where scores had stampeded after a fear-crazed mother had pushed past the doorman to summon her husband and her child. "Get out! Get out!" she screamed. "The city's on fire!" It had touched Harlem, where men and women had fallen to their knees in prayer . . . the Village, where crowds had converged on Washington Square . . . police stations throughout the city, besieged by frantic ones seeking refuge . . . upstate, Connecticut and, above all, New Jersey, where the "Martians" had landed. In that state's Trenton, Union City and other communities, thousands of fearful ones had taken to the streets and highways, and other foolhardy, curiosity-consumed hundreds in motor cars were still driving toward the spot where the "meteor" had crashed.

As the AP, UP and the Chicago *Tribune* News Service wires in our office gave evidence, the panic's coils had also clutched most of the cities, towns and hamlets from coast to coast and down south to the Mexican border. The people of the United States had succumbed to an unprecedented mass hysteria.

Immediately after the country had calmed its collective nerves, there were demands for government censorship of radio, but Washington wisely decided against such an un-American measure. After all, not only CBS but other networks had already decreed that thereafter no dramatic works should be broadcast which employed such realistic devices as news bulletins, flashes, or impersonations of public officials when these were of a kind to create uneasiness or panic.

It was said that this misstep would "ruin" Orson Welles; but instead, it won him a profitable national sponsor, and lifted him from a theatrical "wonder boy," admired only by a narrow circle, to the status of a national celebrity. Even today, despite his many other achievements, his name is synonymous to millions with the great "Martian invasion."

Political pundits, psychologists, psychiatrists and other readers of the mass mind had a glorious time during the months that followed. The newspapers and the broadcasters of Hitler and Mussolini hailed the exhibition of hysteria as a sign of the decadence and cowardice of American democracy. Most of the native commentators attributed the incident to the climate of the times, which were truly hectic. That autumn of 1938 had witnessed one international crisis after another, and the world seemed to be on the verge of a mighty catastrophe.

"Is it surprising that this should have happened?" one analyst of public opinion asked.

"Are not our imaginations so inflamed today that anything seems believable—no matter how fantastic?"

Those who gave serious thought to the episode also pointed out that broadcasting, improperly used by demagogues or dictators, could be one of the most dangerous weapons ever invented. And they called attention to the fact long recognized by the "trade": that a high percentage of those who tune in either do not listen attentively or do not hear accurately. Therefore, they said, major points must be repeated or emphasized several times. In other words, some of those obnoxious commercials which spell out each word and pound in their slogans are psychologically justifiable.

Three years after the Martians had made their foray against our planet, Pearl Harbor was bombed, but the excitement on that day did not approach the hysteria induced by Orson Welles. Observers explained that we had become so inured to tragedy it would be no longer possible to panic the American public. And, certainly, the stoical behavior of the British under the blitz gave them ground for such belief.

For a while, I agreed with them—but now I am not so sure. Just a few years ago, the Welles adaptation of *The War of the Worlds* was translated into Spanish and, with a few local touches added, broadcast over a Latin-American station. The reaction south of the border was even more violent than it had been in this country. The listeners not only gave way to hysteria but, in an outburst of fury over having been "hoaxed," burned down the radio station and killed some of the actors!

And what of the United States? Suppose today we heard over the radio a bulletin that a troop of little men with a death-ray guns had come forth from a flying saucer on some sandy waste in Arizona—just how calm would we be?

Who can give an accurate answer? Frankly, all I know is that back in 1938, Orson Welles and his "Men from Mars" ruined for one radio editor what might have been a quiet Sunday evening.

Time in seconds——

Directions: Select the best answer and place the appropriate letter in the parentheses.

1. The author tuned in to Orson Welles' *War of the Worlds* broadcast because (a) one of the Mercury actors had told him to be sure to listen; (b) as a columnist, he felt it his duty to listen; (c) there were no other programs that would be worthy of comment in his column; (d) *The War of the Worlds* was one of H. G. Wells' most exciting stories.   ( )
2. According to the broadcast, the Martians had landed (a) on the Palisades; (b) at Lexington Avenue & 51st street; (c) near Trenton; (d) near Grover's Mills.   ( )
3. It was announced that the Martians (a) had an artificial satellite for their base; (b) were heralded by a meteor; (c) landed in a silver cylinder; (d) cascaded to earth.   ( )
4. One result of the broadcast was that (a) the police marched into the studio; (b) the National Guard was called out; (c) a Red Cross disaster unit was dispatched to Trenton; (d) hundreds of persons fell to their knees in prayer on Washington Square.   ( )
5. Another and more lasting result was that it was decreed by (a) the Federal Communications Commission; (b) CBS; (c) CBS and other networks; (d) Washington censorship; that thereafter no dramatic works should be broadcast which used news bulletins, flashes or impersonations of public officials when they might cause panic.   ( )
6. The worst result(s) of the panic was(were) (a) shattered nerves; (b) the killing of several persons in a theater stampede; (c) a fire in the CBS studios; (d) traffic accidents.   ( )
7. When told about the effects of his broadcast, Orson Welles was (a) pleased; (b) distraught; (c) astonished; (d) conscience-stricken.   ( )
8. The broadcast was given on (a) October 3; (b) October 10; (c) October 13; (d) October 30.   ( )

9. The author (a) is convinced that the incident was caused by the climate of the hectic days of 1938; (b) still attributes the incident to the publicity-minded ingenuity of Orson Welles; (c) believes the incident was indicative of deterioration of the American mind; (d) is not so sure that the same thing could not occur in the United States again. ( )

10. One explanation for the incident that was offered by some was that (a) people believed it to be a trick of Hitler and Mussolini; (b) people do not listen attentively or hear accurately; (c) Orson Welles was a clever showman; (d) reports of flying saucers were first heard around the time of the broadcast. ( )

DIRECTIONS FOR SCORING

Reading Rate. Find your reading rates in words per minute by turning to the TABLE FOR DETERMINING READING RATE IN WORDS PER MINUTE.

Answers to Questions. Check the answers to the multiple-choice questions in the CORRECTION KEY TO EXERCISES.

Progress Chart. Enter all reading rate and comprehension scores in the PERSONAL PROGRESS CHART.

WORD RECOGNITION AND ATTACK EXERCISE

Directions: Look at the single word, preferably through the Eye-Span Card. Then move the card rapidly to the five words directly below, and pick out with your eyes the word that is exactly the same as the single word. **Do Not Say The Word Aloud.** Continue to the next single word and repeat the operation. Do not make any marks on the page, so that you can repeat this exercise daily for a week or two.

Begin

version
verse venison version service evasion

fractious
fraction fractious factitious factual fragile

assess
assert ascend assist assess abscess

belike
bilked belled killed delight belike

witless
witless vittles witness whiteness littlest

bicker
dicker ticker sicker kicker bicker

bizarre
bizarre blizzard bazaar blazer dizzier

whitish
whitefish whither whitish whitest whist

virile
vile virtue revile virile vilify

tussle
tassle thistle tunnel trestle tussle

traction
fraction attraction caution traction reaction

radiate
radio ration ratio radiate radiant

signature
signaler denature signify ligature signature

emigrant
emigrate immigrate immigrant emigrant migrant

meditate
mediate mendicant hesitate medicate meditate

opium
opium opiate odium opinion pinion

alteration
altercation ablution alteration alternation attrition

strategic
tragedies strategic strategies stratifies tragic

command
commend command remain remand demand

consulate
consulted consoled insulted consulate insulate

EYE-SPAN EXERCISE

Directions: Use your Eye-Span Card for this exercise. Move it from asterisk to asterisk as rapidly as possible. Try to see the entire phrase at a single glance. **Think The Phrase; Do Not Say It Aloud.**

Begin

*

water each plant

*

allow a margin

*

corner the kitten

*

fodder will store

*

sample my cake

*

darken the room

*

brighten the pan

*

easy for everyone

*

garnish a salad

*

prevent a stall

*

lobby is full

*

hurdle will fall

*

model one dress

*

hoist the crane

*

inch along slowly

neither will tell

*

largely on land

*

shallow at dusk

*

many can hear

*

donate on time

STUDY ASSIGNMENTS

Articles found in typical digest magazines are considered moderately easy reading material. Most formulas support this statement. The characteristics of the articles are as follows:

A total of about 150 syllables can be counted in each one hundred words.

Average sentence length is around 15 words.

An estimated 10 percent of the words are personal ones.

Personal sentences amount to about 15 percent.

Your assignment is to count the syllables and words and sentences in a passage of at least one hundred words in **Reading Exercise—II** in this chapter.

Then compute the averages to determine whether or not the piece is easier or more difficult to read than a typical digest magazine article.

You may also make your own selection of any material and compare it to the typical digest magazine pattern.

Vocabulary-building: The following words are taken from the two reading selections in this chapter. Do you know them?

dulcet	cascade	pundit
impelled	horrendous	inured

CHAPTER THIRTEEN

HOW ALWAYS TO FEEL CONFIDENT

Up to this point you have been asked to concentrate principally upon the *techniques* which will help you to improve your reading. If the various techniques are applied during regularly planned practice sessions, your skill in the art of reading is expected to increase.

Learning does not usually go forward in a straight line, however. The discussion in CHAPTER ELEVEN noted that the learning process itself may provide certain obstacles, so that you find yourself at a standstill, on a "plateau."

But these obstacles can be overcome with continued practice and perseverance.

Now suppose you have applied yourself to the assigned learning tasks and your skill apparently does not increase.

You have followed directions.

You have set aside regular practice periods.

You have consciously and conscientiously tried to read both faster and better.

Nevertheless, your PERSONAL PROGRESS CHART tells you that you have not achieved any sustained success at all.

If this is the case, then you may have to look for certain tendencies in yourself which make reading improvement for you more than just a matter of acquiring skill.

RESISTANCE TO CHANGE

Individuals who have limited goals or no goals at all for helping themselves in learning something new may not only fail to do anything well, but also are apt to feel guilty about it.

Life for them is often composed of unfinished business. Few tasks begun are even completed. Many tasks are postponed for a later day that never arrives.

Those tasks which are completed are far from being completed well.

You might read over your written **reading autobiography** at this point and see if it reflects some of these characteristics in your own personality.

Logically, you might expect that people who ask only a little would manage to achieve at least something. But a lack of initiative is often accompanied by a resistance to change.

These same people feel that the **status quo** must be maintained at all costs.

Everyone has this feeling of resistance to change to some extent. It is one of the most common defenses against anxiety. If you are not yet aware of it in yourself, think back a little.

Can you recall the first day you began school, or the day you got married, or the day you began a new job?

Then you must also recall the feelings that accompanied these experiences. You were leaving behind the familiar pattern of a former existence and going into a strange new pattern. Of course you felt a natural anxiety, and with it a degree of resistance to the inevitable changes you faced.

But if this anxiety is too great, it can actually prevent a person from acting.

The way in which such strong feelings of resistance to change can affect your reading rate becomes evident.

Word-by-word reading may be a familiar, beaten path along which you plod. As one slow reader expressed this aversion to change from the slow to the rapid pace: "I feel safer when I fondle each word in turn."

A snail-like reading rate is often cherished and defended. The excuse given is not infrequently the convenient rationalization of "laziness" or "inborn slowness."

Other arguments for resisting change come easily to stubborn slow readers.

They will insist that if they increase their rate even slightly their comprehension will drop. This may in fact happen. But it happens more from lack of confidence than from the increase in reading rate.

Accompanying all of these arguments is likely to be the vague but insistent feeling of guilt.

THE PERFECTIONIST

Now consider the individuals who do not set their goals too low but at the other extreme set them too high. These people are sometimes called **perfectionists.** Everything for them must be just right if it is to be anything at all. Nothing less than perfection will do.

A compulsion to read word by word follows almost inevitably.

Perfectionists also can rationalize this pattern of slow reading.

They will argue as follows: "If a writer didn't intend all his words to be read, then why did he write them?"

Or: "If a single word is omitted in a sentence this may destroy the entire meaning."

These arguments have the appearance of being logical, since in some instances every word really does require careful scanning.

Good poetry, for example, needs to be read slowly to get the full effect of every single word the poet set down on paper. And in other cases, as for example in a legal contract, every "if," "and," and "but" may be exceedingly important.

Actually, of course, your **purpose** determines how much attention should be given to each word.

But no amount of persuasion can get perfectionists to risk the slightest loss of comprehension for the sake of reading faster. Even if assured that in many kinds of reading their comprehension is improved through rapid skimming, they are not impressed.

Every word of every piece of written material, they feel, must be thoroughly chewed and digested.

As a result, even reading the daily newspaper becomes a forbidding task. A short story can take up an entire evening. Longer works of either fiction or nonfiction are rarely begun.

Also typical of the perfectionists' attitude is the feeling that a task once begun must be completed. Consequently, they often find themselves involved in senseless "trash."

You might expect the perfectionists to be willing to do anything to improve. But they too resist change. They will continue to read word by word even when convinced that this is not efficient reading, and their feeling of guilt persists. This seeming stubbornness can be explained to some extent by a lack of confidence.

Slow reading is safe, they feel. A sudden burst of speed might plunge a reader into the unknown. Individuals who skip and skim confidently over the printed page searching for ideas are daring adventurers who live dangerously.

A fear of missing something of significance may also be present. The perfectionist's argument goes this way: If you dare to move ahead faster than your usual comfortable rate allows, some important point might be overlooked. This is sure to be the point you might be held responsible for knowing at some crucial moment. If you do not know it you will fail to get a reward. In fact, you may even be punished for your ignorance. Better play it safe. Plod on at the old word-by-word rate, "fondling" each syllable in turn.

The fallacy of this reasoning can be easily pointed out. No system of rewards and punishments exists. Even if it did, word-by-word or syllable-by-syllable reading wouldn't help you achieve the rewards or avoid the punishments.

If you are a perfectionist you may as well face the refreshing fact that you will not win any prizes for being perfect, if by perfection is meant having a slow reading rate. The prize, if there were one, would go to the adaptable reader who adjusts according to his purpose and the difficulty of the material.

You will also not be rewarded for finishing every word of everything you begin to read. The reward, if any, would go to the reader who is selective and can skip or skim as he wishes.

If on the other hand you feel that you are naturally slow or lazy, you might take a careful look inward. Often you will discover that this is a convenient excuse to cover up supposed inadequacies and a sense of failure. Keep firmly in mind that the art of reading is a communication skill and that anyone who can learn to read can learn to read well.

No matter what your temperament (and great differences do exist among people in the rate at which they think, and move, and respond) you can still read faster than you are reading now. Perhaps you can turn a feeling of guilt to some account and use it to spur you on to sustained practice. Improvement is bound to follow.

High goal, low goal or no goal, perfectionism or laziness, the symptoms are the same—a feeling of guilt and a habit of word-by-word reading. Direct action is called for. Don't attempt to analyze yourself too deeply. Instead, spend your energies on improving the techniques which help to improve reading skill.

Be aggressive about tackling new words; build your vocabulary; analyze sentences, paragraphs and longer writing forms.

Act outwardly with confidence and this confidence will grow inwardly.

Skip, skim, scan, depending on your reading needs.

If you find your reading comprehension goes into a sharp decline at first, don't get panicky. Force yourself to read faster than your comfortable rate. You will eventually find your comprehension returning and very likely improved.

Also be alert to use all the other communication skills. Listen and observe. Try your hand at writing. Engage in conversation at every opportunity. Above all, try to let everything you see, hear, and read provide you with food for thought.

Another inner barrier to progress when you are trying to improve your communication skills will probably sound familiar to you. It may be expressed in various ways, depending on the circumstances. Perhaps you can recognize your own plaintive cry of protest in one of the following quotations drawn from reading autobiographies:

"My mind wanders . . ."
"I can't concentrate . . ."
"I start daydreaming . . ."
"I can't keep awake . . ."
"I begin to worry . . ."

All these expressions are variations on the same theme, the inability to **attend** to the printed material at hand.

Forcing yourself to read with comprehension under these circumstances is at best a struggle. If you finally toss your book aside in despair or drop off to sleep in the middle of a sentence, the struggle is lost.

Obviously something else is more important to you than the reading at hand. It might be a good idea to find out what that something is. You can usually find out if you try, by simply letting your mind wander and doggedly following along its own path, no matter how winding that path may be.

UNSOLVED PERSONAL PROBLEMS

Perhaps the trail will lead you to a problem which is urgent and pressing. Worry and anxiety thrive on unsolved problems. If you can't concentrate on your reading because you really want to concentrate on something else, say a problem of personal finances, by all means lay your book aside.

For everyone some problems do arise which cry out for attention: health, personal relationships, status in your work or your community, and the inevitable finances. Find a way to solve these or any other problems now if you can. If you can't do so because more time is needed, plan realistically to solve them at some point in the future.

Then go back to your reading.

Sometimes problems cannot be solved by the individual concerned. Assistance is needed. The question now arises, where can you take your problems and your troubles?

The first place to look is close by. A member of your immediate family, a relative, a friend, your minister, rabbi or priest, or family physician, or legal adviser, any or all of them may be called upon to help you.

If your problems are connected with your work, perhaps a discussion with the personnel manager will lead to a solution. Many large companies have trained psychologists on their executive staffs to assist employees who need information, advice or counseling. Colleges have guidance departments for students desiring similar help.

In many communities organized groups can be found to help individuals solve a wide range of problems involving vocations, finances, health, marriage and children. Their services range all the way from simple information-giving and reassurance to psychiatric and medical treatment. The complexity of the conflicts of modern times has resulted in the statistical fact that at least every other person in the nation does require such services during a lifetime.

Whether mild or severe, real or imaginary, troubles inevitably hinder successful communication. The troubles may be either mental or physical, or quite possibly both.

The symptoms may include a partial or a total reading disability affecting the entire personality of the individual and his relationship to the society in which he lives.

To function well in these times man must be able both to cooperate and to compete, and for both he must be able to communicate.

A healthy mind in a healthy body is an important concept in American culture. Superior men and women are expected to be physically strong, mentally alert and ready to meet all emergencies. They are expected to either carry on by themselves or work readily with a group.

They are also expected to be responsible citizens at home, in the local community, and in the larger community of the state and nation.

They are expected furthermore to have at least a nodding acquaintance with just about everything going on in the world today.

Since print is still the major medium for spreading information and knowledge, all of these great expectations for superior men and women in our society are based on the ability to read, to write, to speak and to listen, and to do them all well.

THE WORRY HABIT

Troubles, problems and worry all cause interference with successful communication and must be dealt with forcefully.

Worry is perhaps the most difficult habit to deal with. Some people seem to acquire a pessimistic outlook on life at a very early age. They are likely to become the so-called chronic worriers.

This state of mind often builds a genuine

block to self-improvement of any kind, especially as the affected persons get older. They take the glum view that it is impossible for them to learn new skills or improve present ones. They refuse to consider the evidence that the communication skills, especially the art of reading, can be improved at any age.

Their attitude is one of being licked before starting to fight. The chronic worrier is sure that he can't do it, so he doesn't. In this way he proves to himself that he is right, and actually gets considerable satisfaction from failure.

The fact is that although your *capacity* to learn doesn't increase after you leave your teens behind you, *learning* still goes on throughout life as long as drive and motivation exist.

Vocabulary, indeed, can increase as you get older, the rate of increase depending on your willingness to keep on learning.

Reading ability can also improve from day to day, week to week and year to year.

To keep on learning, however, means more than passively sitting back and nodding agreement with improved reading methods without constant application of techniques. It means more than just doing the exercises in this book. It means more than doing the reading which has satisfied you in the past.

It means moving out aggressively into the world of the printed word, seeking always to widen your acquaintance with all the worthwhile things which have already appeared, and are now appearing, in print.

An active, positive approach to the printed page will help you to **pay attention** more readily. Personal problems, troubles, worries may have to wait. You may not feel that the battle is entirely won for a long time, but it is not lost, either.

Remember, if your mind wanders, let it wander. Then follow along immediately to find out where it goes. Finally, do something about it— and then return to your reading.

READING EXERCISE—I

Instructions: A clinical psychologist who is also a successful classroom teacher considers some of the emotional difficulties in reading. Read rapidly, but carefully. Time yourself accurately. Jot down your time **in seconds** in the space provided. Then answer the questions.

Time Yourself and Begin

IT'S NEVER GOOD ENOUGH
By Beulah Kanter Ephron

When the little child in school spells "cat" with a "k," he does not get two-thirds credit for the "a" and the "t." He is either *all* right or *all* wrong. When the mother says to the little child, "You were bad today," the little child feels he has been *all* bad, that goodness is entirely excluded. He is one or the other, right or wrong, good or bad. He feels he cannot be both good and bad, both right and wrong at the same time. Absolutism and perfectionism rule the day.

A college student said, "I feel I have to read every word of every page of every book on every bibliography. It's slavery! If I don't do it that way, I feel I'm doing something wrong, almost as if I am doing something bad." To counteract this slavery, he decided that he would not read a word again until he felt like it. He stopped reading altogether for quite a long time, because it had to be all or nothing, and to give up the nothing meant taking on the tremendous burden of the all, which created unbearable anxiety.

Another student with the same conditioning reported the same feelings. He quickly saw how his pattern of reading mirrored his pattern of meeting other life challenges. He reported that when he has to buy a pair of new shoes, he searches all the stores for the best possible pair of shoes, the one best pair for him. Buying a pair of shoes becomes a test situation, as does his every life experience, and all pleasure is missing.

The phenomenon of "cramming" . . . is understandable as a time mechanism for relieving the pressures of perfectionism and absolutism. When one has all semester to read a textbook in history, or economics, or accounting, or whatever the subject may be, he feels there is no excuse for not learning *perfectly*. With oceans of time ahead of one, what reason can one have for not living up to one's standards of absolute perfection? "If, however," the student says, "I have only these eight hours remaining in which to cover this big book, then I must be practical and realize I can hope to do only so much in those eight hours. I'll be satisfied just to pass the course. I'll give up the wish for an A-plus and settle for a B-plus, since it will be remarkable for me to pass at all in the short time left for study."

In other words, when there is no longer a time freedom-of-choice, one is somewhat freed from the crushing burden of having-to-do-the-work-perfectly. One pressure is traded for another, and that should convey an idea of how dreadful the pressure of perfectionism is. The anguish of last-minute study imposed by the clock is preferred to the anguish of the self-imposed pressure of perfectionism. It is such a familiar picture: Midnight, and a big book on the desk out of which one must get at least the main ideas. The fatal moment is eight hours away. "With so little time left, all I can be expected to do is pass this test. If I just pass it, okay." That is the bargain with destiny.

Having thus negotiated with the gods, the student sometimes experiences, to his surprise, a felling of exhilaration during this last-minute studying, provided he is not too exhausted, and if his supply of benzedrine does not run out. (It used to be coffee and caffeine tablets; now it seems to be benzedrine for last-minute magic.) Why this unexpected upsurge of exhilaration at this harrowing time? This feeling frequently has been misunderstood and has been described as the beneficial effect of anxiety; that is, "some people do better under conditions of anxiety." The writer believes that it is not anxiety that helps the student to study well at the eleventh hour; on the contrary, anxiety itself interferes with integrated activity. What seems to happen is that there is a momentary freeing from the pressure of perfectionism, an excitement at being liberated from one's own harsh standards, and thus a more intensive application of one's energies to the challenge at hand.

Regard our student: A whiff of freedom, like a breath of springtime, stirs his soul. The possibility of happier days ahead gently kindles his imagination. It is now that he makes resolutions for the next semester. He says to himself, "Why did I think this text was so much to do! There's nothing to it! Here I am, quickly covering the main ideas in only eight hours. With a *whole semester* to deal with it, what I *could* have done!" Here he begins to fall into grievous error, for instead of asking himself, "Then why didn't I? What stopped me? What *really* got in my way?" he turns his eyes towards new resolutions without new understanding, thus doomed to repeat old mistakes. "Boy, *next* semester things are going to be different! I'll tackle the text the first night I get it, not the last night I need it. I'll be all ready for finals by the end of the first week, so far as the book goes. I'll know it cold."

Thus, in the midst of the joy of newly glimpsed freedom, in a moment of relief from perfectionistic standards, shackling resolutions are made that close the door to freedom. The student promises himself he will do much better next time—He will do perfectly next time. As ever, the over-disciplined person seeks salvation in more discipline. Then, bewildered and unhappy during the middle of the following semester, he finds himself not able to concentrate. Naturally, he is in reaction against the crushing standards he has set up for himself. When cramming time rolls around again, he curses himself for having all semester failed to live up to his resolutions. Then the clock, on the eve of the examination, gives him a brief respite from his self-imposed burden of perfectionism.

Many students are puzzled by their own pattern of starting a task with high enthusiasm and soon losing interest. This pattern is another manifestation of the perfectionistic, absolutist conditioning. The individual begins with a dream of what he would like to do and be; the first time he fails, or thinks he has failed, in any little step on the path to the dream, he feels the dream is totally spoiled. Excitement dies and boredom arises. He loses interest in the task, or in the vocation, because it no longer holds the magic promise of making him a perfectly wonderful, or wonderfully perfect, person.

Why does he need to be this wonderful? Why does he cling to grandiose dreams of perfection? He dreams the dream of perfection because he needs it to save him from his own cruel self-criticism. He was conditioned to feel that one had to be perfectly good and perfectly perfect in order to be lovable, in order to be considered a worthwhile person, in order to "count!" Since his conception of perfection is impossible in reality terms, he is repeatedly facing the self-concept of being a failure.

Finally, his only escape from constant feelings of failure is to try nothing, risk nothing, want nothing. He feels bored with life, because he has not the courage to be his real self. His real self does not seem to him to be good enough to make him acceptable. Perhaps he will just stay in his room and do nothing at all, to avoid the whole painful prospect of meeting nothing but his own self-criticism, cruel, constricting, unrelenting. One young woman said, "I stayed in bed almost the whole week-end. At least for two days I felt I would avoid any chance of making mistakes."

The perfectionist is defeated before he begins, because to succeed on his terms is hopeless. His teachers, parents and friends may call him "lazy," when the opposite is true. He is excessively ambitious, and his inertia is filled with desperation. His self-criticism and his compensatory strivings must be understood and their irrationality ameliorated before he can mobilize the courage to make mistakes and the resulting energy to be productive. If a student's eggs are all in one basket, that is, if his feeling of worthwhileness depends on his perfect success academically, then he must have a guarantee of success before making any efforts. He cannot afford to take chances, because too much is at stake. Writing a term paper may seem to hold the promise of magic, complete fulfillment (unreal because measured by perfectionistic standards) or the danger of complete nullification. The risk is too great, and he prefers to choose failure than to chance it. He holds onto his dream of perfection, and his activity in reality terms is paralyzed.

The word-by-word reader, making sure he is missing nothing, suffers from these fears of being nothing if he is not perfect. He shares the too prevalent misconception that it is noble to have irrationally high standards, even though they are so high that no one could possibly achieve them, and even though the constant measuring of what one really is against the vision of what one "ought" to be leaves one too heartsick and hopeless to do what one is able to do.

Despite the fact that this way of life is inefficient, the person caught in it makes a virtue of his irrational necessity in order to maintain it, since he has the illusion that in this way lies safety. Thus, a student coming for help to overcome his word-by-word reading may gradually become aware that he wants the practical advantages of giving up his crippling perfectionism, and, at the same time, wants to cling to the unreal "safety" of his perfectionism.

On the surface, this pattern gives rise to what looks like paradoxical behavior. The word-by-word reader asks for help to overcome his habit; he claims he wants to read faster, with more fluency. However, when encouraged to be less "sticky" and more selective in his reading, to skip words that are not essential to the meaning, he becomes ruffled and a little resentful, petulant and defensive. The suggestion that he try to do just an adequate job, that he strive towards being average rather than remarkable, gives rise to considerable strong feeling.

Sometimes the instructor is accused of promoting carelessness, inefficiency, mediocrity, even dishonesty—as though skipping a word were immoral. The instructor is reaping the results of exposing a weakness which has been exalted into a virtue as part of a safety system. The student's lack of self-confidence makes it impossible for him to be selective, to decide what words to read and what words to skim over; he sees this fear-ridden performance rather as evidence of his being an extraordinarily good child, perfectly "clean," conscientious and thorough.

The excessive carefulness, despite all the trouble it causes, has become a source of pride, and the possessor of the perfectionistic attitude would like to be praised for it. When no special rewards are forthcoming for being so good— in fact, when it is intimated that one is foolish and ineffectual when one is *that* good—there is, quite naturally, a rage reaction. One young woman, proceeding from a discussion of her word-by-word reading to a discussion of her similarly cautious mode of activity in other life areas, said, "When I think of all the years I've wasted, never expressing my real feeling, never really living, always waiting for someone to reward me someday for my goodness, I could explode, I'm so angry!"

Thus, when an instructor or remedial-reading specialist tries to change reading habits, he is trying to change a great deal more than that. All kinds of feelings are stirred up, and safety systems erected to forestall anxiety are threatened. "Help me to read fast," the students request. "But," they add, in effect, "don't take away my perfectionistic standards."

Time in seconds——

Directions: Select the best answer and place the appropriate letter in the parentheses.

1. According to Dr. Beulah Kanter Ephron, the overdisciplined person ever seeks salvation in (a) more discipline; (b) benzedrine; (c) less discipline; (d) magic promises. ( )
2. The phenomenon of "cramming" for an examination is said to be understandable because the student (a) always works more efficiently with this method of study; (b) has more time for social activities; (c) gains relief from the pressure of perfectionism; (d) doesn't need to plan in advance. ( )
3. It might be argued from this selection that "cramming" (a) generally results in failing grades; (b) inevitably causes nervous exhaustion; (c) often leads to habitual drug-taking; (d) may help some students to study well. ( )
4. According to the selection, people often lose interest in a task because they (a) generate too much enthusiasm; (b) master the techniques too quickly; (c) have an unreasonable fear of failure; (d) start things without considering the results. ( )
5. Dreaming dreams of perfection is said to be needed as protection from (a) self-criticism; (b) boredom; (c) anxiety; (d) failure. ( )
6. In discussing perfectionists Dr. Ephron uses quotation marks around "lazy" because she feels the word has (a) no meaning; (b) an opposite meaning; (c) a special meaning for students; (d) a special meaning for psychologists. ( )

7. According to Dr. Ephron, resentment may arise from a reader who is asked by an instructor to (a) read word by word; (b) avoid all mistakes; (c) hold onto a dream of perfection; (d) skip non-essential words.   ( )

8. Deciding what words to read and what words to skim over requires (a) carefulness; (b) pride; (c) experience; (d) confidence.   ( )

9. It may be inferred from the article that people should have the courage to (a) maintain perfectionistic standards; (b) study by "cramming"; (c) make mistakes; (d) read word by word.   ( )

10. The author evidently believes that a person's skill in reading well (a) gives rise to paradoxical behavior; (b) ties in closely with personality; (c) develops solely from regular practice; (d) depends upon perfectionistic standards.   ( )

DIRECTIONS FOR SCORING

Reading Rate. Find your reading rate in words per minute by turning to the TABLE FOR DETERMINING READING RATE IN WORDS PER MINUTE.

Answers to Questions. Check the answers to the multiple-choice questions in the CORRECTION KEY TO EXERCISES.

Progress Chart. Enter all reading rate and comprehension scores in the PERSONAL PROGRESS CHART.

SELECTED PAPERBOUND BOOKS ON PSYCHOLOGY

A Primer of Freudian Psychology, by Calvin S. Hall. New American Library.

A Primer of Jungian Psychology, by Calvin S. Hall and Vernon J. Nordby. New American Library.

About Behaviorism, by B. F. Skinner, Vintage.

How to Avoid a Nervous Breakdown, by Frank S. Caprio, M.D., and Frances S. Leighton. Hawthorn.

The Individual and His Dream, by Calvin S. Hall. New American Library.

Psychology Is About People, by H. J. Eysenck. Penguin.

Psychology Made Simple, by Abraham P. Sperling, Ph.D. Made Simple Book, Doubleday.

Toward a Psychology of Being, by Abraham H. Maslow. Van Nostrand Reinhold.

READING EXERCISE—II

Instructions: Read the following selection, taken from a current textbook on reading for college students, at the rate you ordinarily use for brief, informative material. Do not push yourself too hard, but also do not dawdle. The moment you finish reading, following the directions. **You do not need to time yourself for this exercise.**

Begin

DEVELOP ADEQUATE HABITS OF CONCENTRATION

By HOMER L. J. CARTER *and* DOROTHY J. McGINNIS

Students, business men, and professional people frequently report that they have not been taught to concentrate and that they need practical and specific suggestions. Several brief recommendations are provided.

Read with a definite purpose. Determine what you want and then go after it. Develop the habit of asking questions of your book.

Work with pencil, paper, and the necessary reference materials. Keep in mind that study is an activity which involves more than just looking at a book. Study is an active process, not a passive one.

If possible, plan to do all studying in one place. All of us are creatures of habit. We have places for worship, amusement, sleeping, eating, and even for taking a bath, so why not have a place for study? Students having one habitual place for their work report gratifying results.

Begin studying the very minute you sit down at your desk. Do not dilly-dally, for frequently this is an unconscious attempt to put off an unhappy task. Delay for a time such activities as combing your hair, filing your fingernails, and renewing the lead in your pencil. Assume your responsibilities of doing a good job immediately.

Develop an interest in each subject you are studying. Try to see the relationship between the subject upon which you are trying to concentrate and the ultimate goal you have set for yourself.

Keep in mind that your ability to concentrate upon a subject is in proportion to your knowledge of the subject. Other students find the topic or text to be of interest to them. Are you curious as to why they find it so?

Avoid overstimulation and an excessive press of activity. Plan a well-balanced work-study schedule and if possible adhere to it. If you must depart from it, at least you will have something definite and well-planned to which you can return.

Keep all distractions such as pictures and unnecessary equipment off the desk. Pin-up girls and trophies of various sorts can be distracting. This is especially true if the student consciously or unconsciously wants to delay a task assumed to be unpleasant.

Alternate periods of concentration and relaxation. Work when you work, however, and play when you play. Short periods of rest make it possible to renew the attack upon difficulties, real or assumed, with increased vigor.

Determine, as the result of your experience, how long you can concentrate and then make yourself do it. Individual differences are apparent in ability to concentrate. Concentration varies in duration and intensity. You must determine your own limits.

Reward yourself for not breaking a set period of concentration. Do the job first. Successful students report that they set up for themselves units of work to be accomplished before they take time off to indulge in more satisfying activities. Read the chapter and work those problems before you eat a candy bar.

See that such physical factors as heat, lighting, and ventilation are satisfactory. In order to do effective reading and study, the student must be comfortable and ready for work. All physical factors which contribute to this readiness must be satisfactorily adjusted.

Directions: In this selection were twelve paragraphs of recommendations on how to concentrate as you read. **How Well Were You Concentrating?** To test yourself, write in the spaces provided below (without looking back at the selection) the principal ideas in eight of the paragraphs. Set them down briefly **and in your own words.** If you wish to try this exercise again at a later time, write your answers on a separate sheet. When you complete the assignment, look back to find out how well you concentrated.

1.

2.

3.

4.

5.

6.

7.

8.

EYE-SPAN EXERCISE

Directions: Use your Eye-Span Card for this exercise. Move it from asterisk to asterisk as rapidly as possible. Try to see the entire phrase at a single glance. **Think The Phrase; Do Not Say It Aloud.**

Begin

*

take up the slack

*

one at a time

*

say what you mean

*

forty cars can run

*

easy for the young

*

see our nice vase

*

as we were before

*

when you can sail

*

force met by night

*

send him next Tuesday

*

halt with the crowd

*

dry on a rack

*

look back to December

*

caught on a look

*

bound to each other

*

grasped at one trial

*

deeper for the fish

tenth in the line

*

cowed by a bat

*

zoo in the dark

*

STUDY ASSIGNMENT

You might stop adding to your reading autobiography at this time and carefully evaluate what you have already set down about yourself.

First, review your **Personal Data Sheet** in CHAPTER FOUR.

Have you any additions or corrections to make?

Do you feel that if you were to answer the questions again various changes would have to be made?

For example, do you now say words aloud as you read, or do you move your lips, or subvocalize?

Are you now able to keep both your hands and your jaw under perfect control, avoiding such mannerisms as finger-pointing along a line of print, or nail-biting, or hands to face?

Consider again the image of yourself as a reader, your posture, your expression, your attitude, both outwardly and inwardly.

Reread this entire chapter again after you have looked through your reading autobiography. See if any of the psychological problems which are discussed can be applied to your own reading pattern.

In the next chapter, reading for study will be taken up in more detail.

CHAPTER FOURTEEN

READING FOR STUDY

RTP
PQRST
SURVEY Q 3R
PERU

These are not magical formulas. Nevertheless, all of them contain certain ingredients which if applied properly may well produce magical results.

They are formulas for helping you with study type of reading material.

The first one, **RTP**, is a favorite of some training instructors in the Armed Forces. The letters stand for

Read The Problem

Look at these three words carefully. Think about them in relation to reading for problem solving. They should convey a great deal of meaning to you.

One of the frequent complaints of teachers everywhere is that a student may have the right answers—but to the wrong questions!

Why is this so?

Simply because the student has failed to "get" the question. He has apparently read the relevant material. He has turned to the correct page in the textbook. The words are in front of his eyes.

Nevertheless, the student is not **reading** at all. He merely thinks he is reading.

To explain further this paradox of "reading without reading," consider the other three reading formulas.

PQRST[1] stands for

Preview
Question
Read
State
Test

In the next formula, **SURVEY Q 3R**,[2] the **Q** also means *Question*.

The symbol **3R** stands for **Read, Recite,** and **Review.**

Finally, **PERU** simply means to

Preview
Enquire
Read
Use

Each of these formulas, you will note, says very much the same thing in a slightly different way. A serious application of any one of them will help the reader to attack a study type of reading material with confidence.

Note especially the position of the word **Read** in these formulas. Even the brief **RTP** implies that a certain amount of thoughtful attention must precede the actual **reading for study.**

All of them suggest that reading for study is reading for a **purpose.**

The purpose usually is to answer questions and to solve problems, thus adding to the sum total of your knowledge.

But it is impossible to accomplish your purpose unless you have first formulated the questions or stated the problems in your own mind, or in the margins, or in a notebook.

---

[1] From *How to Study*, by Thomas F. Staton, McQuiddy Printing Company, Nashville, Tennessee.

[2] From *Effective Study*, by Francis P. Robinson, Harper & Brothers Publishers, New York.

Before considering the essential procedures for study you should first consider the matter of study habits.

PREPARING FOR STUDY

Under what circumstances do you study best?

Perhaps you can answer this question immediately. For example, some people know that they prefer the evening hours, when the daytime distractions have ended. Others choose the early morning. Still others the middle of the day.

Some people must have almost complete quiet when they study. Others are actually stimulated to do better work when they have a certain amount of activity and noise around them.

These are elementary illustrations of basic differences and preferences. In specific details individual patterns of reading for study probably vary as widely as do individual students.

If this is the case, how can you tell correct study habits from incorrect?

A brief generalization may help to clarify things.

The best work habits for study are those which are best For You.

Two general rules, however, apply to almost everyone:

1. Study in the **same place** daily. (Or if this is impossible, try to stick to the same two or three places when you have a choice.)

2. Study at approximately the **same time** daily.

When you study at a regular time, in a regular place, you soon become conditioned to the fact that **at this time, in this place** (whenever or wherever it may be), you will not idle away the hours but instead will apply yourself to serious, concentrated work.

Once you've settled on the time and place, then it is up to you to support your decision in every way possible. See to it that you have a comfortable place to sit. See to it that the light is adequate.

Arrange to have the tools of your occupation at hand—pencils, erasers, notebooks, and perhaps a typewriter.

Within easy reach should also be your reference works, including a dictionary.

Some students will add a radio or a stereo to their requirements for study. Perhaps fortunately, no one has as yet found out how to concentrate on a textbook with a television set turned on.

Objective studies have shown that some people actually do work better with a musical accompaniment. Others do not.

Some people require frequent rest periods, say five minutes out of every half hour or ten minutes out of every hour of study. Others work well for long periods without a break.

Some people work at their best before breakfast. Others do better after meals. Some prefer daytime hours; others, evening hours.

It is up to you to discover your own best conditions, and then follow your own individual pattern.

But whatever your pattern, get the place-habit and the time-habit working for you.

BIRD'S-EYE VIEW

Now return once again to the formulas for study.

The first step is that of the **survey** or **preview**.

To get a grasp of the reading material you are going to cover for study, you are first asked to see it as a whole. Try to get a comprehensive, bird's-eye view.

In an earlier chapter, you will recall that in reading any book of nonfiction you were advised to get as much information about the work as possible by taking a rapid glance at the chapter headings, and also by sampling the preface.

This procedure can be extended in preparing to read a textbook. Not only the table of contents in the front but also the **index** in the back should be quickly skimmed.

Careful attention should be paid to the **preface,** or **foreword,** or **introduction,** as the case may be. In these sections the textbook author often states the purpose of his work, gives the reader some idea of his method of presenting the material, and outlines the contents to follow.

Textbooks also may have graphic aids to understanding which should be examined briefly during the initial run-through. Charts, graphs, tables, maps, photographs and similar types of illustrations, as well as any other supplementary material, need to be surveyed and previewed before they are studied in detail.

An assigned (or self-assigned) piece of reading for study need not necessarily be an entire textbook. You may wish to cover only part of a book, or even part of a chapter.

In this case, also, you should skim rapidly to first get the total impression.

On the other hand, as many graduate students are aware, an assignment may cover a number of books on a certain subject or a variety of subjects. Sometimes a prepared bibliographical listing of such works is furnished.

Knowing what books to select, what books to skip, what books to skim or scan out of such a listing requires a special facility on the part of the reader. For working near the peak of efficiency, the student needs to have **in advance** some familiarity with the published works in a given field.

To acquire this familiarity often means preparing your own listing or **bibliography.**

Even before you open the cover of a textbook, you may wish to know certain facts about the work. A bibliographical listing would include the *author's name*
title
city of publication
publisher
date of publication or revision
a brief annotation telling you in a sentence or two something about the book, usually drawn from reviews or abstracts.

To keep your listing up to date, the best system is to use file cards. Make a separate card for each reference.

Reading a file card is not intended to be a substitute for reading the book itself. Nevertheless, in an age when even specialized areas of knowledge have produced literally thousands of separate volumes, it may be impossible to permit yourself the luxury of a leisurely reading of everything on the subject.

A bibliographical listing, whether prepared by you or by someone else, helps you to select what is essential for whatever your study purpose may be.

STUDYING FOR A PURPOSE

When you make your survey or complete a preview, you need to keep constantly in mind the next step you are going to take in reading for study.

This step is to formulate questions you wish to answer or state problems you wish to solve.

Since your approach to study-type material depends almost completely on your purpose, this step is highly important to study success.

For example, if you are preparing for an essay-type examination where a broad knowledge of principal ideas is required, you approach your reading material with this goal in mind.

Seek out the main ideas.

Turn them into questions, or state them as problems.

Note these questions or problems in your mind, or in the margin of the book in your mind, or in the margin of the book you are previewing, or in a separate notebook.

Follow this procedure without fail!

As discussed in CHAPTER TWELVE, various typographical arrangements on the page may give you considerable assistance. This is especially the case with textbooks.

Chapter headings are invariably printed in CAPITALS.

Sections within chapters are usually headed by subheadings in CAPITALS OF BOTH LIGHTFACE AND **BOLDFACE** TYPE.

Divisions of the material within the sections may be headed by *italics*.

Many textbooks have marginal subheadings which highlight separate sections.

To illustrate the way type selection may be used to help the student, the following is a sample of headings from a psychology textbook:

PART THREE
THE EMOTIONS
CHAPTER 11
EXPERIMENTAL STUDIES IN EMOTIONAL DEVELOPMENT

How Emotions Are Studied In Clinic and Laboratory
Differences in clinical and laboratory psychology
Different origins
Different goals
Different procedures

Headings and subheadings very often have a twofold value to the reader.

1. They announce the main topic or the principal idea of the material to follow.

2. They provide a statement which can easily be rephrased as a question or stated as a problem.

Many textbook authors also supply a summary at the end of each chapter. Here is another rich source of material for formulating questions and stating problems.

In some instances, the textbook writer will supply the questions and problems himself. The reader can then supplement this ready-made material with his own.

Important points are often listed in textbooks by numerals or letters.

For example:

1.
2.
3.

or

I.
II.
III.

or

A.
B.
C.

etc., etc.

Certain signal words or phrases, some of them already mentioned in an earlier chapter, point the way for the alert reader to pursue and discover key concepts and ideas.

as follows
for example
include the following
at the same time
by a comparison
usually
in most instances
on the contrary
to enumerate
obviously
in addition
of course
thus
in the first place
actually
in consequence
as you know
first of all
in like manner
etc., etc.

During the preview or survey of a textbook, or any work you wish to read for study, a pencil is almost an indispensable tool. Comments, notes and questions should be jotted down in the margin of every page covered.

If the book is not your property, then use a notebook for the information, with accurate page references so that you may consult it later.

Key ideas should be underlined or otherwise noted for future reference.

Some students work out their own systems which involve the use of a series of checkmarks, or various kinds of underlining or circling of works, or even marking with colored crayons.

Few people have photographic memories for recalling the main ideas of material in print they skip or skim over rapidly. A few well-placed pencil marks may help to make up for this lack.

If you are preparing for an objective type of examination, with multiple-choice questions or **true** and **false** questions to be answered, you must also note carefully many of the details which support the main ideas.

In any case, during your survey or preview of the material at hand, when questions are being formulated and problems stated you should proceed as follows:

Underline important ideas and details
Make notations in the margin
Keep a notebook

At long last you begin to **Read.**

READING AND RECITING

You have obtained the bird's-eye view of the material you wish to study.

You have formulated your questions and stated your problems.

Now you read with the clear purpose of either answering questions or solving problems.

Your reading should be fairly rapid if you intend only to look for broad, general answers and solutions. Seek out topic sentences, look for key phrases, identify principal thoughts.

Relatively long periods of time are best for this kind of thoughtful study-reading.

If you intend to pick up and remember many supporting details in the material, then you may have to pause upon occasion to fix them in your mind.

Short, high-powered bursts of study-reading are best for grasping and holding details. If you wish to memorize anything in print, you will do better to work intensively for brief periods. Repeat at frequent intervals.

Reciting or stating the material is the next step in reading for study. This step, although described separately, is actually an integral part of the reading process.

As you read, you organize the answers to questions and advance your solutions to problems. This may be done entirely by thinking to yourself. **Compare what you read with what you already know about the subject.**

Or you may wish to stop occasionally and either write or say aloud the answers or solutions.

Most important, you should carry out this step in exactly the way you expect to be tested or examined.

If you will have to write an essay or theme, then practice by writing an essay or theme.

If you will have to make an oral presentation, then practice by thinking to yourself may be sufficient.

But however you prepare, give your complete attention to the task. Weigh ideas, compare, criticize, CONCENTRATE.

REMEMBERING AND FORGETTING

Although not all psychologists subscribe to the theory of the **learning plateau,** discussed in an earlier chapter, nearly all of them agree on the **curve of forgetting.**

Picture to yourself a steep hill. Imagine then as you study that you are arduously climbing up this hill. As time passes you absorb more and more from your reading and thus continue toward the theoretical top of your learning capacity.

Then you stop reading.

Immediately you begin to slide downward.

But unlike sliding down a real hill, slowly at first and then gathering momentum, in this downward slide of forgetting **you go with extreme rapidity the moment you stop your learning.**

Only one thing can stop this immediate and rapid descent and that is reviewing what you have already learned.

If you review the material within a short period of time—say in an hour or so and definitely within twelve hours—you will abruptly halt the unceremonious descent and begin your climb upward once again. The next time you stop, your descent won't be quite as rapid. With each review session you stabilize your learning at a higher level.

Another activity can help keep you near the peak of a learning period and that is **use.**

Moreover, the material you have learned through study should be used as soon as possible after the learning has taken place.

THE PRÉCIS AND THE OUTLINE

Two learning devices which are likely to prove valuable to students are the **précis** (pronounced pray-see) and the **outline.**

Both are ways of getting ideas from your reading down on paper so that both comprehension and retention are increased.

A précis may be defined as a brief but exact statement of the essential material contained in a longer selection. The rules for preparing a précis are as follows:

1. Hold the length to no more than one-third the number of words of the original material, and shorter if possible.

2. Present the essential thoughts in the order in which they are presented in the original.

3. Use your own words.

4. Be both concise and accurate, but set down your ideas with a smooth continuity.

5. **Don't omit any important points.**

Two types of outlines will be considered here. One is the **Topic Outline,** the other the **Sentence Outline.** Both are constructed in exactly the same way except that the topic outline consists of **phrases** and the sentence outline of **complete sentences.**

Either one may be used to help you with reading for study.

Since a textbook author often plans a work from an outline, if you can discover this plan it may help you in your understanding of the work. Ideas are often presented in some order of time, or space, or cause and effect, or problem and solution, or various combinations of these.

Look for the relationships.

The conventional structure of an outline is as follows:

I. (First main idea)
  A. (Supporting detail)
  B. (Supporting detail)
  C. (Etc.)
II. (Second main idea)
  A. (Supporting detail)
    1. (Sources leading to A.)
    2. (Important item relating to A.)
      a. (Subordinate relating to 2.)
      b. (Another subordinate item relating to 2.)
III. (*And so on and so forth*)

A final word about reading for study.

Occasionally the student finds himself bogged down because the textbook material is too difficult for him. The fault is not always the reader's. Specialists in a subject sometimes write their textbooks as though they were addressing fellow specialists.

Preparing a précis or an outline from the material may help the reader. Or the work may be divided into small sections and attacked in that manner, with frequent use of reference works and a dictionary.

Another solution is for the student to turn to an easier work on the same subject.

Simply written but excellent popularizations of quite difficult material are often available.

After you have read the easier work, however, you should always attempt once again to read the source material.

In pursuing reading for study, the competent readers will have little difficulty in finding their way around. Experienced travelers in the vast realm of study-type reading material, they know exactly where they are at all times.

They also know where they are going and at what speed they are moving.

With patience and practice, you can achieve this facility.

READING EXERCISE—I

Instructions: People are always people in America, states this author, because they are members of a group and are thus respected as individuals. In this selection of a study type of reading material, you are asked first to make a survey. Note main ideas on the way and time yourself **in seconds.** Then answer the multiple-choice questions in Column A. Next, reread the selection to grasp the supporting details, **without timing yourself.** Then answer the same multiple-choice questions, using Column B. Compare your answers.

Time Yourself and Begin

SOCIALITY
By JURGEN RUESCH

Sociality, or the tendency to form social groups, has its roots in the herd instinct of the individual. In America foremost recognition is given to this group need; as a matter of fact it has resulted in a culture of living which vividly contrasts with certain foreign civilizations, which cater to the development of object systems. At first this statement sounds paradoxical, inasmuch as America is known for its technical genius and the use of machinery in every walk of life. On second thought, however, one can understand this contradiction. Consider, for ex-

ample, the way machinery is treated in America: A car is unsparinglyly used until it has to be replaced. Typewriters, horses, and cars are lent to neighbors and friends, and no property feelings are attached to any object. In America the object is truly subservient to life. Europeans, by contrast, have less respect for an individual's need for action and expansion, but great interest in protecting inanimate objects; the guarding of works of art, furniture, books, houses, and churches is really put ahead of the needs of the individual. These facts are clearly brought out when American families with children visit their European relatives. The American youngster, when introduced into a European home, is considered ill-mannered when he subjects the home furnishings to wear and tear and, while doing so exhibits the boastful exuberance of youth, which is accepted with tolerance on this side of the Atlantic.

In America the process of living and of interacting with others is sought as a goal in itself. Americans treat others always as people, while Europeans in many situations will treat other people like objects or as if they did not exist. Regardless of occupation or of the job performed by an individual in America, his superiors or inferiors will always treat him as an individual. Such attitudes indicate that in the minds of the people there exists an awareness that persons have families, want to live, and need a certain environment in order to survive. In brief, in America people are always people; they never become machines or animals. The fact that life is cherished is further borne out by the many excellent provisions for saving lives in emergencies; members of the police and fire departments, lifeguards on public beaches, rangers, members of the Coast Guard and the armed forces are trained to respect and to save lives. During World War II, the medical services of the United States Army were vastly superior to those of any other nation in terms of saving lives of wounded soldiers and rehabilitating them in civilian life. No expense is ever spared if a person is in need of rescue. In addition to these emergency measures there are in the United States all those educational institutions, public health campaigns, insurance companies, and the school health services of the medical and dental profession who do everything in their power to preserve health and promote longevity.

The treatment of persons as individuals seems to be an expression of the fact that every person is a representative and member of a group, and the group assumes the responsibility for the individual. Offense against a person is an insult against a group. The American abides by decisions of the group and recognizes it as the ultimate authority. While in the patriarchal system it is quite sufficient to abide by the rules of the chief in order to be a member of the group, in a system of equals it is necessary to please many. This is the meaning of conformance.

Conformance is encountered as a consideration in practically everyone's mind. One "can't do that," "it isn't done," and "he is impossible" are examples of comments which denotes the preoccupation with conformance. "Keeping up with the Joneses" is an activity of conformance which permeates social life, the purchasing of homes, automobiles, and household appliances and induces people to join clubs, to contribute to welfare organizations, and to donate their time for worthwhile causes. However, adjusting one's own actions to conform to those of others always has a competitive undertone. While the American conforms to the actions of others, he is at the same time concerned with doing things "bigger and better." Hence, in America, conformance, competition, and group membership are always found together.

In order to sustain group membership the American has to be gregarious. The value of gregariousness has its roots to some extent in the circumstances of the first settlers and pioneers, who were forced to share in order to protect themselves against a hostile environment; hence getting along in a group was essential for survival. Furthermore, gregariousness is in some ways a substitute for the extended family, which frequently is not available to the American. Either family members live far apart and spread over the continent, or part of the family has remained in Europe. In the course of time, therefore, sociability became a national feature. Today it is associated essentially with middle-class behavior, which is closely identified with the national characteristics of Americans. The value which is placed upon smooth functioning and a friendly front, low intensity and avoidance of deep involvement, as well as readiness to disengage from the existing relations and to enter new human relationships, may be termed sociability. In America this personality feature is frequently taken as one of the most important criteria in assessing adjustment.

The American becomes uneasy when he finds himself alone. To be left alone is a situation to be carefully avoided; girls accompany each other to the rest rooms or for coffee in the afternoon, and boys and girls have roommates, rarely live alone, and practice double-dating. Not only do bathroom, eating, and social habits of Americans portray this fact, but it can also be observed in the arrangement of houses, or the structure of resort places. In America houses are built close together even if the owners could well afford much larger lots; in public parks and on the beaches picnickers join one another and one group attracts the other, all avoiding isolation. The foreign traveler who with an open eye inspects the American scene is amazed at the public facilities which have been created for fostering and accommodating gregarious people. From the national parks and picnic grounds to the playgrounds in smaller communities, from the commons in New England towns to the squares of western cities, there are always facilities which enable people to meet. Grange halls and lodge buildings provide meeting places for specific groups which are set aside for social gatherings. Likewise do state and federal government provide for calendar festivals such as Thanksgiving, Fourth of July, Labor Day, Memorial Day, and the like, which provides an opportunity for family gatherings or larger group reunions. In brief, Americans always travel in a group. Lacking associates is a sign of not knowing how to win friends, of not being sociable. In America one associates with others to give the impression of popularity, and if one is popular, one makes more friends. These, of course, disperse when the barometer of popularity declines. This American concept of popularity contrasts with the concept of friendship in Europe; there the test of real friendship comes when hardships and difficult situations make associations survive. . . .

The American's basic need to move in a group and his concern with sociability have led to a far-reaching organization and differentiation within the group. From earliest childhood, the child is trained to become a member of a team; baseball, football, and basketball are training grounds for later industrial research and military teams, while fraternities and lodges in the recreational sphere, or town meetings and other organizations in the political sphere, provide the necessary training for teamwork. Every American knows how to behave and how to fit into the organization of a group. Adjusting to the group and engaging in teamwork brings marked advantages to the individual. The group protects its members when they get into trouble with members of other groups, or when disease or disaster strikes. The sort of reliance that an Englishman would derive from the knowledge that the judicial system and the police look out for law and order, the American citizen derives from the knowledge that the group will support him and if necessary exert pressure to protect him. Therefore, no American will shy away from expense or effort to join a team and to subordinate himself to its over-all purpose, and in return, to expect some security from the team for having "played ball."

Time in seconds———

Directions: Select the best answer and place the appropriate letter in the parentheses.

A B

1. According to the author of "Sociality," the tendency to form social groups seems to be accompanied by (a) ill-mannered children; (b) strong property feelings; (c) no strong property feelings; (d) cultured living.   ( ) ( )
2. In America the process of living and interacting with others is sought as (a) a good business policy; (b) a goal in itself; (c) necessary for survival; helpful in protecting inanimate objects   ( ) ( )
3. Conformance, according to the author, is the result of (a) individuals abiding by the rules of a chief; (b) individuals trying to please the many; (c) individuals not concerned with doing things "bigger and better"; (d) individuals with no competitive feelings.   ( ) ( )
4. Americans evidently become uneasy when (a) someone wants to borrow a typewriter, a horse or a car; (b) they visit relatives in Europe; (c) someone induces them to purchase homes, or automobiles or household appliances; (d) they are alone.   ( ) ( )
5. Smooth functioning and a friendly front, low intensity and avoidance of deep involvement as well as a readiness to disengage from existing relations and enter new human relationships is a personality feature

termed (a) aggressiveness; (b) sociality; (c) interaction; (d) sociability. ( ) ( )

6. Foreign travelers in the United States are amazed at the (a) double dating of boys and girls; (b) arrangement of houses; (c) picnics on the beach in summer; (d) the number of public facilities for social gatherings. ( ) ( )

7. It might be gathered from this article that (a) federal and state holidays are especially provided so that people can get together; (b) automobiles are used sparingly by most people in America; (c) many people in the nation are treated like machines or animals; (d) the excellent provisions made for saving lives in emergencies are a sign of technical genius. ( ) ( )

8. The American concept of popularity is (a) the same as the concept of friendship in Europe; (b) universally accepted; (c) associating with a great many people; (d) having friendships survive during periods of hardships and difficult situations. ( ) ( )

9. According to the author, every American knows how to (a) play baseball; (b) engage in industrial research; (c) behave in a group; (d) win friends and influence people. ( ) ( )

10. One of the principal ideas of this reading selection is that (a) Americans care more for property than they do for people; (b) Americans dislike being alone under all circumstances; (c) Americans rely on the group for both support and protection; (d) Americans belong to a group for entirely selfish reasons. ( ) ( )

DIRECTIONS FOR SCORING

Reading Rate. Find your reading rate in words per minute by turning to the TABLE FOR DETERMINING READING RATE IN WORDS PER MINUTE.

Answers to Questions. Check the answers to the multiple-choice questions in the CORRECTION KEY TO EXERCISE. Compare carefully your answers in Column A with the answers in Column B.

Progress Chart. Enter all reading rate and comprehension scores in the PERSONAL PROGRESS CHART.

READING EXERCISE—II

Instructions: Write a précis based on the following selection, taken from an educator's popular work on the English language.

THE KING'S ENGLISH IN A DEMOCRATIC WORLD
By CHARLTON LAIRD

Language must not only have flexibility to live and grow, it must have currency to be understood. Like money, it is no fit medium for exchange unless it has sufficient currency so that he who gives the coin values it in roughly the same terms as he who receives it. And like money, it must have sufficient stability so that what is given today has approximately the same value tomorrow. Without stability we might never learn to speak, because the language could be changing faster than we were able to learn it; without currency, even if we learned to speak we could not communicate widely, because our medium of exchange would not be acceptable to enough others to make it usable. We understand each other only because large numbers of people over great areas of the earth have lived in mutual if unconscious agreement that certain words are symbols for certain meanings and not for other meanings; that strictly determined ways of handling these symbols reveal their relationships. We agree that the symbol *table* stands for a flat surface supported from beneath, that it is not a container used to enclose fire for heating purposes. We agree that in the construction *the red table, hot from the red-hot stove,* the table has a permanent color and the stove has a temporary one, and that this distinction is apparent in part through the varying positions of *red* and *hot* in the sentence.

Thus there is a fundamental inconsistency in language and in the way in which we make it and use it which forever prevents the establishment and the upholding of any standards from being entirely logical. Language is a living thing. It must survive in men's minds and on their tongues if it survives at all. In so doing, it changes the minds, lives, and the use of vocal apparatus. But at the same time, language can function only if it has stability in time and place. Change is inevitable in language, and yet all change damages language, although it may at the same time revitalize it. We may be able to minimize the effects of this inconsistency, but we cannot remove it.

VOCABULARY EXERCISE

Directions: The exercise below is patterned exactly after the 30-item vocabulary tests which measure your reading improvement progress at regular intervals.

You are to read each definition and underline the word which fits it most closely. Do not linger on any one item. Try to complete the exercise within **five minutes.** Your score will be based on the number correct within this time limit.

Time Yourself and Begin

1. Fortress commanding a city
   (a) parapet; (b) barricade; (c) turret; (d) rampart; (e) citadel.
2. Poetic work telling of heroic deeds
   (a) romance; (b) novella; (c) epic; (d) adventure; (e) tale.
3. Healthy and plump
   (a) buxom; (b) florid; (c) wholesome; (d) rotund; (e) winsome.
4. To split by a forceful blow
   (a) slug; (b) chip; (c) smash; (d) cleave; (e) hack.
5. Frank and impartial
   (a) candid; (b) breezy; (c) affable; (d) amicable; (e) pliable.
6. Edge at the top of a steep slope
   (a) precipice; (b) vale; (c) brink; (d) abyss; (e) ravine.
7. Make a dull, explosive sound
   (a) rumble; (b) snort; (c) mutter; (d) throb; (e) chug.
8. A solid figure whose sides taper evenly to a point from a circular base
   (a) spheroid; (b) dome; (c) pyramid; (d) cone; (e) pendentive.
9. Home for members of a religious community
   (a) vicarage; (b) sanctuary; (c) retreat; (d) hermitage; (e) cloister.
10. Concerned with agricultural interests
    (a) agrarian; (b) rusticated; (c) horticultural; (d) rural; (e) husbandry.
11. Related on the father's side
    (a) fraternal; (b) paternal; (c) patriarchal; (d) filial; (e) familial.
12. Carrying boats or goods overland between waters
    (a) transport; (b) salvage; (c) export; (d) steerage; (e) portage.
13. According to sound reasoning
    (a) logical; (b) hypothetical; (c) practical; (d) rhetorical; (e) inimical.
14. Guarantee certain expenses
    (a) donate; (b) bequeath; (c) underwrite; (d) defray; (e) grant.
15. To look at someone flirtatiously
    (a) ogle; (b) shimmer; (c) gaze; (d) flout; (e) glower.
16. Produce on the spur of the moment
    (a) surprise; (b) sally; (c) extemporize; (d) promote; (e) compose.
17. No longer fashionable or in use
    (a) inoperable; (b) obsolete; (c) abandoned; (d) forgotten; (e) dilatory.
18. Lacking musical harmony
    (a) tonal; (b) chromatic; (c) dissonant; (d) tempered; (e) stressed.

19. Needed in advance of something else
    (a) prerequisite; (b) prologue; (c) prerogative; (d) proceeds; (e) proviso.
20. An optical instrument for magnifying small objects
    (a) prism; (b) microscope; (c) bifocal; (d) binocular; (e) periscope.
21. Distribute in shares
    (a) equalize; (b) proscribe; (c) consign; (d) allot; (e) devise.
22. Damp, cold, sticky
    (a) tepid; (b) clammy; (c) turbid; (d) muddied; (e) pallid.
23. Set of religiously held beliefs or principles
    (a) maxim; (b) catechism; (c) creed; (d) thesis; (e) commandment.
24. Combine parts into a whole
    (a) formulate; (b) foliate; (c) integrate; (d) create; (e) rejuvenate.
25. A representative sample
    (a) stereotype; (b) census; (c) progeny; (d) specimen; (e) species.
26. Inhale audibly through the nose
    (a) sniff; (b) snore; (c) gape; (d) yawl; (e) snarl.
27. Resembling an eagle's beak
    (a) piercing; (b) aquiline; (c) classical; (d) attenuated; (e) protruding.
28. To spread all over, to soil or defile
    (a) smear; (b) gloss; (c) smelt; (d) swathe; (e) blot.
29. Definite relation between things, quantities or numbers
    (a) portion; (b) agreement; (c) ratio; (d) numeral; (e) calculus.
30. A pointed part of anything
    (a) knob; (b) hub; (c) stud; (d) stub; (e) nib.

DIRECTIONS FOR SCORING

Check the answers to the vocabulary questions in the CORRECTION KEY TO EXERCISES in the Appendix.

If you did not complete the vocabulary items within the five-minute time limit, do this now. All words which you missed should be entered on flash cards for further study.

A score in this vocabulary exercise of 28 or over can be considered excellent; 25-27 items correct, good; and 24 or under correct, an indication that intensive work with flash cards and a dictionary is needed.

EYE-SPAN EXERCISE

Directions: Use your Eye-Span Card for this exercise. Move it from asterisk to asterisk as rapidly as possible. Try to see the entire phrase at a single glance. **Think The Phrase; Do Not Say It Aloud.**

Begin

*

lawn was too dry

*

fill any cup full

*

call when store closed

*

gun had no sight

*

on a sad day

*

kick the new ball

*

worn by the town

*

down on the mall

*

eel had no fight

*

has to say where

*

island in the sea

*

worry has no place

*

fortune of the times

*

certain to be done

villain in the cast

*

matchless for each task

*

nicely to your taste

*

joyous as the day

*

open when you go

*

proper for the place

*

STUDY ASSIGNMENT

Select an extended passage from any text-book or other study-type material. You may use the next chapter of this book if you wish. Count the number of words in a column on a page and divide this amount by 7.

Jot down the result at the bottom of each column or page for several successive pages or for an entire chapter.

This is the time in seconds you will allow yourself in reading each column or page.

For example, if you counted 210 words in a column, divide this by 7 and then put the number 30 at the bottom of the column. You may assume that successive columns will have approximately the same word count. This means that you will have 30 seconds or half a minute to read each column.

Check your watch or clock and start!

The moment the noted number of seconds have elapsed, jump to the next column (or page, as the case may be). If you have to skip material at the bottom of the column do so.

Better results will be obtained if someone else does the timing for you, announcing aloud each time you are to jump ahead.

When you have completed your reading, write a précis based on the material covered. Then check your comprehension.

Even if you have had to skip words or lines your rate for **covering** the material has been 420 words per minute.

This exercise is designed to give you practice in accelerating. If you wish to attempt a rate of 480 words per minute, divide the number of words in a column or page by 8; 540 w.p.m., divide by 9; 600 w.p.m., divide by 10.

As a review, turn back to **READING EXERCISE—II** in CHAPTER THIRTEEN and look over once again the suggestions for developing adequate habits of concentration.

HOW TO FIND INFORMATION IN A LIBRARY

Whether you are a student or not, set yourself an assignment of looking up a piece of information in a school or public library. In most instances, the librarian or an assistant will be eager to assist you.

To help you find your way around on your own in seeking facts and data, learn to use the standard reference works. Below is a selected listing.

Dictionary of American Biography
The Encyclopedia Americana
Encylopaedia Britannica
Familiar Quotations, compiled by John Bartlett
Information Please Almanac
Rand McNally Concise Atlas of the World
Reader's Guide to Periodical Literature
Webster's American Biographies
Webster's Biographical Dictionary
Webster's New Geographical Dictionary
Webster's New Third International Dictionary of the English Language
Webster's New World Companion to English and American Literature
The New Columbia Encyclopedia
The World Almanac and Book of Facts

CHAPTER FIFTEEN

READING FOR BUSINESS

Business and professional men and women as a group have a high potential for fast and accurate reading.

That they don't always realize their potential as individuals may be due to differences in communication skill or psychological attitude —or both.

The fact remains that business executives, lawyers, clergymen, physicians, scientists, engineers, educators, editors, publishers—in short, all those who deal with written words—are faced with tremendous reading demands.

A not unusual pattern is reported by an executive for an engineering firm.

Routine reading for him consists of five or six books and twelve to fifteen technical and professional journals monthly, plus three or four general weekly periodicals. Day-to-day reading includes at least two newspapers and about fifty letters averaging two pages each.

On the desks of most business and professional people at all levels of responsibility you will usually find two trays known as the in-basket and the out-basket, for incoming and outgoing mail of all kinds. Two or three or four times a day in most offices, the in-basket is piled high with letters, circulars, memorandums, reports, and other material, printed, typed, or handwritten. This material must be examined and then acted upon: discarded, initialled, answered briefly or at length.

If each piece were given the same attention, the in-basket would never be emptied, the out-basket never full.

Word-by-word readers find the task hope-less. Even lugging a stuffed briefcase home for after-hours work won't enable them to catch up. All the hours in a day or a week are not enough to handle all the written material they have to face. For they not only have an in-basket to battle; they also have newspapers to read, and periodicals, and countless books on subjects relating to their particular field of specialization.

All of this reading must presumably be covered regularly by conscientious executives before they can even consider taking up a magazine or book outside their work, for relaxation, for pleasure, and for personal development.

A physician in our society is faced annually with over 12,000 medical periodicals from which he must select material appropriate to his professional needs. It has been estimated that in the one area of physiology alone a medical specialist, reading a page a minute for an eight-hour day every day, would need over thirteen months to cover the material published each year!

Top management in business and industry have been practically forced to depend on the digest, the summary, the briefing session, the pictorial presentation, as a basis for policy-making decisions. Nevertheless, somebody has to prepare the data from available material in print. This task often goes to executives at the middle management level.

In spite of these great demands on business and professional people, testing shows that by and large their reading skill is not better than that of the rest of the literate adult population.

They too, as a group, read at a median rate

of 250 words per minute, with approximately 75 percent comprehension. But many of them eventually are forced to face the fact that this rate is simply not fast enough.

Successful as they may be in other respects, as readers they are literally incompetent.

SPEED READING

The competent reader (and you may consider yourself approaching competency if you have consistently improved your reading skill over a period of time through study and practice) may have the capacity to cover some printed material at well over a thousand words a minute.

Good comprehension will accompany this rapid rate.

To achieve such speed in reading, as well as speeds two, three and even ten times this fast, you must accept as integral parts of the reading process the 4-S technique of

Selecting
Skipping
Skimming
Scanning

This technique was originally introduced in CHAPTER NINE in the discussion on reading books, specifically books of nonfiction or factual prose.

Now the same technique will be applied to reading the kinds of printed (or sometimes typewritten or handwritten) materials which face business and professional people almost every day of their workaday lives: journals, memorandums, newsletters, reports, directives, correspondence, and the like.

But first some requirements for speed reading success must be mentioned:

You must have good eyesight, with or without glasses.

You must have a broad background of education and information (either formal or informal) in the general area in which most of your reading needs fall.

You must know the vocabulary of the subject matter of the reading.

With these fundamentals you will almost certainly become a **superior reader**, but you are still not necessarily a **speed reader**.

This may require more than developed skill. It may require a change of psychological attitude toward reading.

Speed reading is **not** reading single words at an accelerated rate. Nor is it necessarily reading either phrases or whole sentences at a faster clip, although this may well be a part of the process.

More significant in speed reading is the ability and willingness to reject material as well as select it.

To the speed reader, the negative act of skipping words on the page may be as important as the positive acts of skimming and scanning.

Consider these concrete illustrations.

An executive has two separate pieces of printed material on the same subject before him. Each piece contains a thousand words. In a glance he sizes up the reading situation.

He makes his decision. One piece goes into the wastepaper basket; the other piece is skimmed through in less than half a minute. Another half minute is spent in scanning slowly a summary at the end of the second piece.

This executive has a specific purpose: to extract from both brochures a certain piece of information he is seeking. He succeeds. Comprehension for his particular purpose is thus 100 percent.

Reading time: 2,000 words per minute!

Another example: A method used by a successful editor for doubling his reading speed on some occasions is to read every other page. He states that **for his purpose** this alternate-page system works perfectly. As far as he is concerned, his comprehension is usually 100 percent for the particular editorial task he has set himself.

Another successful editor has described a method used to cover some 4,000 books each year as one of moving the eyes "diagonally down the page."

These original methods as well as other speed reading techniques and methods are not so easy to carry out as you may suppose.

A high order of reading intelligence and reading skill is required. Also required may be a profound change in psychological attitude.

A NEW LOOK

If you wish to pursue the meteoric path of a speed reader, you must prepare yourself for looking at a printed page—or any other written material—in a new way.

The first step is one of **orientation.**

What is reading?

How do you define the art, the act, the skill of reading?

You must decide once and for all that it is not necessarily looking at every word on a page.

Instead it is a reasoning process.

In reading you relentlessly search for meaning, sort out facts from opinions, compare and contrast ideas, draw inferences and conclusions, evaluate and judge. Then you often apply what you have read to problem-solving.

Reading a paragraph has, in fact, been compared with solving a problem in mathematics.

Thus if you can grasp the meaning of a paragraph by reading a first sentence, or a last sentence, or a key phrase—depending on your purpose and need—you may successfully solve your problem without reading further.

A second consideration for the speed reader is one of **motivation.**

You may have a strong **motive** to read better and faster by skipping and skimming, but nevertheless lack **motivation.**

What is the differentiation here?

When your future behavior is determined by a stated goal—chosen either by you or by someone else—you may call this motive.

For example, suppose the training director of the corporation you work for announces that he is launching a home-study reading program, complete with portable accelerators (mechanical devices which lower a shutter over a printed page at timed rates of speed). He is depending on a single motive to get you to improve your reading at home: fear.

You will either learn to read better on your own—or else!

You may improve rapidly as a result of this motive, since your livelihood may be at stake. However, the improvement may not last long once the outer pressure no longer exists.

Motivation, on the other hand, must come from within. When individuals have a genuine and powerful inner drive toward improving themselves, the results are not only authentic but also lasting.

The ideal combination of motive and motivation is, of course, a planned outer goal and a healthy inner urge.

MENTAL SET

Sometimes you may see only when you want to see on a printed page, not what is actually there.

This leads to a third factor in changing your attitude toward how you read: **Mental set.**

Mental set may be defined as preparation for a mental task. It should be appropriate to the task, however, for speedy and efficient performance.

Experimental psychologists have made a number of objective studies to illustrate this point.

Perhaps the most widely known study involved laboratory rats that mastered jumping at a card bearing a large circle instead of one bearing a small circle.

When a large triangle was substituted for the large circle, they jumped at it instead of at the small circle, **in spite of its being the circles which carried the reward of food.**

In this case, the mental set was not on circles (the correct goal) but on size (the incorrect goal).

It might not be too far-fetched to compare the behavior of a businessman facing a huge pile of correspondence with that of a bewildered laboratory animal facing squares and triangles. When mental set causes inappropriate responses and constant blocks to quick understanding, the morning mail can become a formidable task indeed.

Thus, to realize your potential ability in speed reading, you may have to change a great many things more than your words-per-minute rate. You may have to change habit patterns, attitudes, and quite possibly your personality.

PICTURE READING

A tremendous boost can often be given to speed reading and the speed reader by such visual material as maps, charts, graphs, and other illustrations.

A single drawing may not necessarily take the place of any number of words, but it may give the reader the dramatic insight essential for a quick interpretation and understanding of the words.

In surveying a book or article containing factual prose, you will do well to note if the author has supplied any graphic material to aid you.

Especially note the relationship of the material to the text, and also the type of visual presentation chosen. Different kinds of illustrations serve different purposes.

You should be familiar with all kinds.

Three main types of charts are often used as graphic illustrations, as follows:

1. Table Chart

Useful for presenting complicated statistical information in a compact way, the table chart often provides a quick source of information in easy-to-read tabular form. One example of this type of chart is the *Table for Determining Reading Rate in Words per Minute* found in the Appendix of this book.

2. The Flow Chart

Three subdivisions will help to describe the flow chart.

The organization chart. On a single page, with a minimum of explanation, the organization of a business, an industrial concern, a government, and any other type of institution, can be clearly presented. The flow of authority, responsibility, and communication can be graphically shown, in some detail if desired, from chief executive to office boy.

The process chart. This chart is used to show the flow of a manufacturing process from raw material to finished product.

The distribution chart. This chart is used to show the flow of products from manufacturer to wholesaler, to retailer, to consumer.

Four main types of graphs can be described, as follows:

1. Line graph.

The commonly used **line graph** expresses differences by a continuous curve or line background of horizontal and vertical guide lines. Day-to-day stock market fluctuations, department store sales, and general business productivity are familiar uses of this type of graph.

2. Pictorial graph.

The **pictorial graph** (or pictograph) often makes a dramatic use of tiny silhouetted figures to present statistical information.

3. Bar graph.

The name of this graph indicates how the statistical information is projected on paper. The lengths of the bars, placed either horizontally or vertically in relation to the guide lines, vary according to the amounts being represented.

4. Circle graph.

The **circle graph**, more familiarly known as a pie graph, shows the percentage of statistical parts in relation to a whole. A vivid and easy-to-read statistical picture can be presented if each "wedge" of the pie is given a different color, with the percentage number in each section.

A map is obviously not the territory itself. Nevertheless, map-reading is an invaluable way to obtain information you might not get from either words about the territory or an actual visit.

Maps can show you not only what grows above the ground but also what lies beneath the ground. Graphically representing portions of the earth's surface and its highways and by-ways, hills and streams, mountains and rivers, states and nations, oceans and continents, a map can also represent what goes on in these areas.

Maps of various projections and various scales should not be a mystery to the efficient reader.

BUSINESS CORRESPONDENCE

So intensely competitive is the world of business-letter writing that an executive may "read" some of his mail without opening the envelope. That is, he can sum up what its message value is to him by merely looking at the sender's name and return address, and open or discard it accordingly.

Some letters may be given at least a glance. Others may merit considerable attention.

Perhaps no single operation in a busy day at the desks of business or professional people requires so much reading flexibility.

One reason that a high degree of speed reading skill is required is obvious. Although business letters have the single objective of getting results, they may take on an almost infinite variety of forms to achieve that objective.

From your own experience, you can perhaps add to the following list of business correspondence categories:

sales letters
business promotion letters
order letters
acknowledgment letters
letters requesting information
credit letters
collection letters
adjustment letters
remittance letters
letters of introduction
letters of recommendation
letters of application
etc., etc.

It is almost impossible to find a common denominator for the reader in the great variety of writing forms and styles of **all** business correspondence. Yet, if he is alert, it is possible for him to know what to expect from each one.

Routine correspondence can be dismissed immediately as mail which can be handled routinely but rapidly. The opening paragraph of such letters almost always refers to the date of previous correspondence, if any. The middle paragraph says what the letter has to say. The final paragraph asks for the appropriate action, if any need be taken.

Sales letters, on the other hand, may follow an entirely different pattern.

Often that pattern is similar to that of many feature articles and much advertising copy as discussed earlier in this book. The writer tries first to attract attention, then proceeds to the step which tells you how a product or service may be helpful to **you.**

The third step in the sales letter is the description of the product or service itself. And the final step is an explicit statement of what action you may take to obtain the product or service.

Where can the interested reader find the key to the entire letter? In the third part, of course.

A generalization might be made here about all the kinds of business letters which are written by experienced and competent writers.

The order of arrangement of ideas in general begins with the reader's interest and leads gradually to and ends with the writer's interest.

Thus, if you want to find what a business letter (other than routine daily correspondence) is all about, you look at the section approximately two-thirds of the way through.

Keep always in mind that the letter writer is looking for results. Read with one compelling question in mind: **What action does the writer of this letter want me to take?**

Direct your attention to the heart of the matter as fast as you can.

Apply the 4-S technique of speed reading:
Select (and reject)
Skip
Skim
Scan (if and when necessary)

READING EXERCISE

Instructions: One of the bitter battles of modern times appears to be man's struggle against the mail. Occasionally in the midst of it a rallying cry is heard. Read this article as rapidly as possible. Jot down your reading time in seconds. Answer the questions immediately.

Time Yourself and Begin

HOW TO MASTER AN IN-BASKET

The distinguished British official finally retired "full of honors and of years," according to a recent newspaper account. His former associates were in for a shock, however. A routine housecleaning turned up a batch of important papers stuffed under the office rug!

Perhaps this official shouldn't be judged too harshly. Every executive has undoubtedly been tempted upon occasion to get rid of some of his own business correspondence in just such a fashion.

When an **in**-basket begins to threaten you, any number of desperate measures may be taken.

The cartoonist who portrayed an American businessman "clearing his desk" at four p.m. by sweeping off everything into the wastepaper basket was simply stating in a humorous way what is often not especially funny. A pertinent question: *Is there any solution to this increasingly vexatious problem of the daily mail?*

An obvious and sensible line of action is often overlooked. The way to master an **in**-basket is not through plodding persistence. Instead, it is through increased skill—specifically, increased reading skill.

Correspondence, memorandums, reports, newspapers, trade and professional publications, not to mention direct mail advertising material, can all be dealt with much more efficiently each day if you acquire this skill.

You may go about it in two ways: one, by increasing reading speed; two, by increasing reading flexibility.

Before considering the steps which will lead toward fast and flexible reading one point might be stressed.

Useless printed and written material not only clutters up desks but also clutters up minds.

Some of the material entering an **in**-basket therefore needs to be rejected completely. This process permits no time for dawdling. Useless stuff should be dealt with promptly and without a second thought.

Rejection may not necessarily mean the wastepaper basket. Perhaps somebody else will be interested in seeing the latest statistics on imported cowbells from Ruritania. If so, then that information should by all means be routed on to the person who will appreciate it.

Other material may gain a tentative consideration but be put aside for later perusal. This is a fine idea if used in moderation. Experience shows, however, that if you let deferred material pile up too high, nothing will ever be done about it.

Still other material needs to be read at once, rapidly and with understanding so that intelligent action may be taken. This is the material which demands skill in reading, and skill comes only with practice.

Practice, in this case, means reading a wide selection of printed material systematically, at varying levels of difficulty, accurately timed and with careful checks on comprehension.

Some businessmen have decided to go back to school to find the quick-reading way of battling a basket. Speed reading courses for adults have thus been flourishing on college campuses, in the so-called commercial reading laboratories, and in company in-service training programs.

Happily, these courses for the most part produce fruitful results.

Group work has certain advantages. Individuals are stimulated to compete with others, in spite of the fact that they are competing against their own scores and not with the scores of anybody else.

A disadvantage of the formal classroom is that the businessman as student often expects too much. He may literally lean back in his chair facing the instructor with a belligerent attitude of: "All right, now teach me!"

The despair of reading specialists is the businessman-student who practically demands to be taught to read at up to 10,000 words a minute. And with perfect comprehension to boot. He may have a friend named Jones who can actually read this fast (or claims as much) and if Jones can do it, so can he.

Publicity about reading courses often encourage dreams of supersonic speeds. Median scores are rarely reported in newspapers, radio and television, but instead the sky-high scores of the whiz in the class who can analyze an entire book before anybody else can take the stiffness out of the binding.

Moreover, such reports are likely to be accurate. Some people *can* read certain material at 10,000 words a minute—and double that, upon occasion—with comprehension adequate for the particular task.

But these sensational results are obtained by exceptional individuals, who have the knack and skill of moving down a page of print like a brilliant broken-field runner on a football field.

Although most businessmen exposed to reading training, either on their own or in the classroom, respond well they ordinarily do not reach in ten easy lessons a cherished 10,000 w.p.m., if they ever reach it at all.

Individual reading rates will, however, often double and sometimes triple and quadruple.

For example, executive personnel at the Humble Oil and Refining Company, in Houston, Texas, entered a training program, with a median score of 280 words per minute, and 77.3 percent comprehension.

At the end of a few weeks, they were reading at a median of 554 w.p.m. Comprehension rose to 87.5 percent.

A beginning class of adults at Pace University Reading Laboratory tested initially at a median of 260 w.p.m., with 70 percent comprehension. After a few weeks, they were reading at 460 w.p.m., with a comprehension level of 85 percent.

Available data show that about 50 percent of the gains made in these classes were still held a year after training ended.

These figures are fairly representative. Other groups in classrooms across the nation could match and some could even better these scores.

Individuals working conscientiously on their own in reading can also compare their scores favorably with the classroom groups.

Some executives begin their reading speed-up campaign by having their secretaries screen out useless material. The secretaries also high-light important ideas in required reading matter by using a red pencil to underline main points and principal passages.

An efficient reader, however, can do both these tasks for himself, employing both his eyes and his brain.

Now for a rapid run-down on the steps to follow for better and faster handling of printed, typed, or handwritten material.

1. **Discriminate.** Select the material which requires attention, and reject firmly the useless. Route information to others if it is appropriate to do so.

2. **Practice.** Learn to speed up in reading by timing your performance and keeping a record.

3. **Adjust.** Be flexible in your approach to various kinds of reading material found in your **in**-basket as well as to various levels of difficulty.

A conscious application of these three plans for action will soon demonstrate who is the master in your office, the **in**-basket—or you.

Time in seconds——

Directions: Select the best answer and place the appropriate letter in the parentheses.

1. A sensible solution for the incoming mail problem in a business office is to (a) stuff important papers under the rug; (b) sweep off everything into the wastepaper basket at 4 P.M.; (c) speed up your reading; (d) all of these.   ( )

2. Another possibility for efficient handling of daily mail is to (a) let printed material pile up for later perusal; (b) route certain material on to people who will appreciate it; (c) take time to mull over the correct action; (d) use a sharp letter opener.   ( )

3. The mythical country of Ruritania, mentioned by the writer, supposedly exports (a) wood-blocks; (b) triangles; (c) cymbals; (d) cowbells.   ( )

4. Improving reading skill through classroom work has the advantage, according to the writer, of (a) stimulating progress through apparent com-petition with the group; (b) direct competition with the reading speed of others in the group; (c) shifting the burden of learning to an instructor; (d) shifting the burden of learning to a machine.   ( )

5. You might infer from reading this article that a reading speed of up to ten thousand words per minute is (a) easy; (b) not possible; (c) possible, but not probable; (d) harmful to the eyes.   ( )

6. The name of the oil company mentioned as having a reading program for executives is (a) Humble; (b) Texas; (c) Shell; (d) Standard.   ( )

7. According to the article, after a period of training individual reading rates will often (a) double; (b) triple; (c) quadruple; (d) any one of these.   ( )

8. Secretaries are likely to be helpful to the executive in his reading speed-up campaign by (a) throwing away all mail; (b) reading all mail; (c) underlining important passages; (d) taking a course in speed reading.   ( )

9. One plan of action for battling an **in**-basket **not** mentioned in this article is to (a) discriminate; (b) practice; (c) resign; (d) adjust.   ( )

10. The distinguished official described in the opening of this article was (a) American; (b) British; (c) French; (d) Ruritanian.   ( )

DIRECTIONS FOR SCORING

Reading Rate. Find your reading rate in words per minute by turning to the TABLE FOR DETERMINING READING RATE IN WORDS PER MINUTE.

Answers to Questions. Check the answers to the multiple-choice questions in the CORRECTION KEY TO EXERCISES.

Progress Chart. Enter all reading rate and comprehension scores in the PERSONAL PROGRESS CHART.

EYE-SPAN EXERCISE

Directions: Use your Eye-Span Card for this exercise. Move it from asterisk to asterisk as rapidly as possible. Try to see the entire sentence at a single glance. **Think The Sentence; Do Not Say It Aloud.**

Begin

*

Take this plan to school.

❖

These roses can grow now.

❖

Next Tuesday is the day.

❖

Will the light die down?

❖

Ask them for the task.

❖

Make a pie right now.

❖

You see a doctor first.

❖

Hurry with that chipped ice!

❖

I cannot see the raft.

❖

She will not go back.

❖

Can the dog go far?

❖

Dye the wool bright green.

❖

Fix the faucet this instant!

❖

Grass will not grow here.

❖

School will soon let out.

❖

Make a fire to last!

Prepare a meal for all.

❖

Question him at some length.

❖

What is the next problem?

❖

Wishing won't make it go.

STUDY ASSIGNMENT

Can you read a book in thirty minutes? Try it. If you like, set an alarm clock to ring half an hour after you start.

Select a work of nonfiction, preferably on some subject in which you have a fair background of knowledge. Approach your task with confidence and determination. This is no time for timidity.

Look at the preface, foreword, or introduction, skimming over the material to get a general idea of what the book is about. The table of contents and the index may also help to give you a quick leafing through the pages to see how the book has been put together.

Illustrations will often point up the text, as will also maps, charts, and graphs. Every typographical signalling device should be noted, such as boldface type, italics, indentations, marginal information and the like.

Select, skip, skim, scan.

When your thirty minutes are up, consider whether or not you have gotten enough information out of the work to fulfill your practical needs.

If so, you have read the book.

Are you ready? **Set your clock.**

Go!

CHAPTER SIXTEEN

READING FOR PLEASURE—AND PROFIT

When you read nonfiction or factual prose you usually have a definite reason for doing so: to keep informed, to learn a new skill, to advance in a career, to seek further knowledge.

No such explanations seem to be expected of you when you read fiction or imaginative prose.

Although almost *all* reading for the skilled reader is reading for pleasure, the reading of novels and short stories is often thought of as especially enjoyable.

Yet many people admit that they derive little satisfaction from reading fiction, either popular or classical. They make an occasional effort, but soon lose interest. This lack of appreciation is more likely than not due to a lack of skill.

Skills techniques and methods of approaching the printed page are just as important in the art of reading fiction as in the art of reading fact.

What is fiction?

Simply, fiction is narrative—a story told by a story-teller. The better the story-teller, the better the fiction.

The narration may be based on true events or it may not be. Most significant is the fact that even if the things in the story really happened in real life, **they did not happen in precisely the same way.**

Fiction, then, is not a mere chronicle of actual events in time.

A precious ingredient has been added. This ingredient is the author's special flavor, the product of his unique imagination and artistry.

Thus, though you might make a tape-recording of actual dialogue as it took place and set it down as part of a short story, it would read neither impressively nor convincingly.

Even historical fiction, supposedly a record of true events, is successful only when imaginary events are artistically interwoven in the entire fabric of the story.

BEHIND THE WRITING SCENES

Three separate forms of fiction will be discussed in this chapter: short stories, novels, and plays. Some attention will also be given to reading poetry.

The discussion will have an intermediate and a final goal, as follows:

1. To arouse your interest in reading fiction (if you are not already a fiction reader).

2. To increase your reading efficiency so that you will become highly selective in your choice of fiction.

The way toward achieving the final goal may be arduous. But once you do achieve it, you will find spread out before you greater riches than you ever suspected existed on this earth.

You may then wonder sadly how it is that some people live their whole lives without ever discovering the exciting world of imaginative prose.

A famous dancer once said of her art: "A dance is like a Persian rug—the audience sees only the design, but the dancers see the threads and threads-ends on the other side." This simile applies equally well to literature, especially fictional literature: the readers see only the story, not how it is constructed.

Yet it is possible to go behind the scenes of both dancing and writing and emerge, not with a loss in the sense of glamor but with increased appreciation of the art and skill involved in their creation. And with this, inevitably, comes increased skill in understanding them.

Many readers will do this kind of exploration willingly in nonfiction. They examine critically a news story or a feature article to see how the writer achieved certain effects.

But they resist looking at fiction in this special way.

Taking apart imaginative prose to see how it is put together is primarily considered a task for a professional critic or a teacher of English literature.

Many creative fictional works are admittedly difficult to figure out. A trite and obvious design in a popular magazine story may be artfully concealed in a serious novel. Nevertheless, structure and form do exist in superior short stories, novels, and plays just as much as in the read-today-and-discarded-tomorrow type of fiction.

It is up to you to discover the various ways you can approach a work of fiction to add to your reading enjoyment.

If you are like most people, you will be influenced by the opinions of others even before you begin the first word. Someone you know has read a book, enjoyed it, and gets pleasure by recommending it. Or you may see a favorable or provocative review in a newspaper or literary magazine.

Other mass media of communication, such as television and the motion picture, may also give you information about certain books before you get around to reading them. In the past, people ordinarily first read a novel or short story before seeing it dramatized on stage or screen. Today, they often see it first and then turn to the original work on which the dramatic version has been based.

Whatever may have stimulated your interest in a book, follow it up eagerly.

Begin anywhere.

Let one work of fiction lead to another. Be completely receptive to suggestions.

A paperback book on a newsstand may attract you. Or an interesting title on a public library shelf. Or the cover of a volume under a friend's arm.

Respond—and see how one book will lead you to another.

Something about story-telling can even be learned from the presentations of popular classics in comic book form. These stories are often told in as highly conventional a way as any news story or feature article.

Constant readers of detective or murder stories, westerns, science-fiction, or romantic or "gothic" novels will testify that they expect those fictional forms to follow certain patterns. In fact, many readers not only are disappointed but also feel cheated if the story-line does not follow a certain course.

Styles in fiction of this type change slowly.

To illustrate, the good guys and the bad guys in western novels and the beautiful but vicious girl in detective novels have been with the reading public for some time now, and would be seriously missed if they suddenly should disappear.

THE READER AS PARTICIPATOR

The search for a pattern becomes more complicated as you venture into more lasting works of fiction. Here no advance set of blueprints exists to help guide you through what may be a labyrinth of human behavior and emotions. Getting behind the scenes of the story or even behind the author's typewriter will not help you much.

You have to try instead to enter the author's mind. Put yourself in his place. **Better yet, put yourself in the place of the fictional characters.**

No longer are you looking for the structure of the writing, but instead you are trying to participate in the narrative action. You do not even attempt to be a critic or a book reviewer, although your attitude may not be entirely uncritical.

Rather, you are a **reader** in the fullest and happiest sense of the word.

This means that you must approach imaginative works of fiction in quite another way than factual material. This approach will not necessarily speed up your reading. It may even slow it down upon occasion.

But it will almost certainly strengthen your understanding, your comprehension, and your critical judgment.

To learn how to become a participating reader, you are now to learn to consider a work of fiction in terms of the following: **plot, characterization, setting, style, symbolism, theme.**

THE PLOT STORY

Conflict is the essence of plot.

The conflict may be man against man, man against woman, man against nature, man against fate, man against himself, man against the machine, but conflict there must be or else the story has no plot.

Another essential in most plot stories is that they must have a **beginning,** a **middle,** and an **end.**

The **beginning** of the story sets the stage, with the cast of characters assembled.

An incident often sets the action going, which leads directly into the **middle** of the story. The action itself is in the nature of a quest by the leading character or characters. Obstacles arise to block the quest. The narrative proceeds, gathering momentum and increasing in intensity and suspense on the way. A climax is reached.

Then the **end** of the story resolves the action in one way or another. If the quest is fulfilled the story may be said to have a happy ending. If unfulfilled, the story may be said to have an unhappy ending.

Sometimes the burden of resolving the action may be placed on the reader himself. But usually everything is explained by the author in an unravelling (or *dénouement*), a method of explanation dating back to the tragedies of the ancient Greeks.

Many short stories are not plotted in this classical sense, but instead contain a so-called "slice of life." The characters are picked up by the author at a certain point in time, often near a crisis of some sort, and left at a later point in time.

During this period, however, something must happen.

Moreover, something must happen to someone. A change must occur. Otherwise, not only is there no plot, but also no story.

An author who plots stories well and writes well besides will usually hold the reader with him to the last word by suspenseful action during the quest. In some instances, he may purposely lead the reader in one direction and apparently resolve the conflict, and then in a sudden turnabout resolve the conflict in another way.

A story may have a straightforward resolution of the conflict, or a double-twist, or even a triple-twist.

The well-plotted story may be likened to a road upon which the reader travels, with signposts directing the way. These signposts have an odd feature, however. The directions are printed on the side **away** from the reader.

It is only when you reach the end of your reading journey that you are allowed to look back and see every twist and turn of the road plainly marked.

Rereading a successful work of fiction is recommended as a way of studying the craftsmanship which goes into the writing of a strongly plotted short story or novel.

A playwright must handle his fictional material differently, of course. He has certain limitations which have to be considered. Action must be divided into scenes. Certain scenes cannot be dramatized because of the requirements of staging.

As a play unfolds, three things are going on at the same time. Both as a reader and as a viewer of plays, you should be aware of them. They are as follows:

1. Through dialogue the playwright has his characters look backward in time to tell you much that has gone before.

2. The present action unfolds before you.

3. Frequent signposts point toward what is going to happen in the future. (But again, these signposts have their directions printed on the side **away** from you.) Even a casual playgoer knows that on the stage nobody ever uses a revolver in the last act unless that revolver has been introduced in some manner in the first act.

Past, present, and future are therefore often performed simultaneously.

Plays are written to be played, of course. The theater is their proper setting. But the competent reader, using his own imagination and skill, can find play-reading a rewarding experience.

This is another situation in which speed in reading is not called for, unless you are engaged in an initial reading to find out quickly what happens.

Try to project yourself into the dramatic action from every angle. Imagine that you are watching the play from a critic's seat on the center aisle in the orchestra. Think of how you would play each part and speak the lines.

Follow stage directions carefully in your mind as if you were indeed the director. Visualize each scene if you can, with appropriate stage sets.

This may sound like a large order, but it can be done—and you will find it highly entertaining.

Some readers of fiction of all kinds concentrate almost exclusively on plot. They race down the printed road, ignoring every carefully placed signpost. All they are interested in is finding out what happens at the end.

To these readers, the outcome is more important than anything else in the story.

This method of approaching fiction is not recommended except for light fiction. Here it has a function which most people will describe as "killing time."

You may be glad to know, however, that this method serves another purpose. It is excellent practice for speed reading.

Furthermore, the reading skill gained from rapidly racing through easy-to-read fiction is actually transferable to nonfiction.

Genuine satisfaction that can be gained from reading a play or a novel with any depth at all is completely missed if you only skim over the surface.

A good plan is to read a work of this sort rapidly on the first reading. Then, if you feel it may have substance and value for you, return to it for a more leisurely reading.

You already know the **outcome.** But now you want to learn why the characters behaved as they did to produce the outcome.

What kind of people were they? And how did the author present them?

This is the element of characterization in fiction.

CHARACTERS MAKE THE STORY

Plunge right in and get acquainted with the people you are going to live with for a time as you read a short story, a novel, or a play. You might even go a step further and identify yourself with someone you meet on the printed pages.

As you get closer and closer to the characters in a story, the more your pleasure will heighten.

How do you come to know these men and women who a short time ago were total strangers?

Your introduction will be effortless if you are aware of how the author has brought them to life. Soon they will come alive for you, too.

The first thing to think about as you enter into the living presence of these fictional but very real people is what professional writers term **P.V.**, or **point of view.**

Most fiction is written from the point of view of a single character. Everything is portrayed as it appears physically, emotionally and psychologically to this one person.

The author apparently is "inside" this character. Often, so is the absorbed reader.

Frequently, the point of view is that of the protagonist, or leading character. You may think of this person as the hero or the heroine. Sometimes he or she may be the villain.

The P.V. may also be that of a minor character. The story then unfolds as seen from this person's mental vantage point.

Another P.V. is that of **author omniscient.** In this case, the writer is here, there, and everywhere. He sees all and knows all. He may even be at several places at one time.

The P.V. may change from one character to another. Or it may change from a character to the author. But the changes are clearly signalled in a variety of ways: by a change of time or place, by a new chapter, by a deliberate statement, by asterisks or other typographical devices.

Whatever the P.V., however, or whatever the shifts made back and forth, you can depend on one thing. The successful author applied himself seriously to the problem before he wrote down the story.

Some authors have in fact rewritten an entire work simply because they were dissatisfied with their original choice of a point of view and decided to change it.

In much of fiction, the author selects his P.V. after careful deliberation and stays with it to the end.

Once you have discovered the point of view, you can begin to enter into the lives of the characters. How well you come to know them depends on your art and skill as well as the art and skill of the author.

As an understanding reader, you need to be aware of how the author makes his characters live and breathe on the printed page.

Here are a few of the ways, and you will notice others in the course of your reading:

how the character thinks
how the character looks
how the character dresses
how the character talks
how the character behaves
how the character reacts to the behavior of others

Sometimes the author tells you these things about a character in so many words. At other times you may learn them from the dialogue, or from what other characters say or think.

You often learn a great deal about people in fiction, just as you do about people in real life, from observing **how they act in a crisis.**

A GAME OF TAG

In a short story, the author obviously can't take too many words to describe his characters. He must give them quick "tags" for rapid reader identification.

For example, the tag for an advertising executive has come to be a grey flannel suit. Other tags may be added for further identification, such as heavy, shell-rimmed glasses, and a fondness for cocktails and wisecracks.

Here is a game for you. Supply the tags which will identify the following characters:

a juvenile delinquent
a private eye
an alcoholic husband
a precocious child
a village half-wit
a young doctor
a poor little rich girl
a jazz musician
a politician
a newspaper reporter
a foreign correspondent
a big-league baseball player

Many of these characters may be so familiar to you they won't even need their tag for identification!

In a longer work of fiction, the author can take more time to develop the personalities of his imaginary people. He builds slowly. The major characters gradually stand out as fully realized individuals.

You can look at them from any angle and see them whole.

Tags may still be used for minor characters. But the conscientious author will make every reasonable effort to avoid stereotypes.

SETTING

Some plot stories with their cast of characters intact could be acted out either on a desert island or in a crowded city. The background would make no difference.

Boy can meet girl, and lose girl, and finally win girl in any country of the world at any time, and in some countries out of this world in the time of the future. The plot is universal, the cast always the same: The setting may be changed at will.

Some stories, however, cannot be told unless they are told in a specific setting.

In certain short stories and novels the setting may even dominate the action of the plot and the characters themselves.

You must have read such works, in which the particular action couldn't happen except in this jungle, or on that battlefield, or on some named street in a named metropolis.

Take note of each scene in the fiction you read. Use your mind's eye to visualize the setting as though you were present at the place described.

You may also have to bring other senses into play. You may not just be asked to see, but also to taste, and to smell, and to hear the sights and sounds and odors of the described scene.

STYLE, TONE AND MOOD

An author has just one medium to work with to achieve what is called his **style** of writing: **words.**

After reading some powerful and enduring works of fiction, many readers feel that they have been moved so deeply that an actual change has taken place in them psychologically.

Serious and dedicated readers are convinced that no other communication medium yet discovered can exert such a profound effect as great imaginative prose.

THEMES AND SYMBOLISM

Must every piece of fiction hold a moral or state a theme?

Most, if not all, of the enduring stories or novels or plays do. The author has something to say, and he says it.

If he were a painter, he would use canvas and oil. If he were a composer, he would use music paper and pen.

The writer expresses himself in words, and his theme can also usually be stated in words by the reader. A single sentence or phrase may be adequate.

Words are not always what they seem, however. They are first of all symbols, representing both ideas and things in the real world.

Words and phrases and sentences may be compared to the graphic material you find on a road map. The straight lines and curved lines, the broken lines and colored areas, as well as the many other signs and symbols are not the territory you travel over in your car.

This hill on your map is not the hill you intend to climb to tomorrow. It is the graphic representation of the hill.

Just so, the words are not the things they represent.

But the author may go still further in his use of symbolism. He may use words which appear to represent certain things or events but actually have significance beyond the surface appearance.

Illustrations of this way of using words date back at least as far as the Bible, with the parables as a classic example. You may go even further back to the tales of Aesop, in which the behavior of animals symbolizes the behavior of human beings.

From the time man first set down words he has evidently used them not only as symbols but as **symbols of symbols**.

Always look for the meaning behind the meaning when you read, to add to both your enjoyment and your understanding.

READING POETRY

This is a prose age.

Few people read poetry. A great many people do get some pleasure out of various verse forms, such as jingles, limericks, and song lyrics. They rarely go on from popular verse to serious poetry.

Yet some of the greatest works in the English language are in poetic form.

Resistance to reading poetry nowadays is commonly blamed upon the poetry itself, as being impossible to understand. Classic verse is presumed to be artificial and stilted, without much meaning for modern readers. Contemporary verse is considered "obscure," with the meaning deliberately hidden under a cloud of unusual words and private allusions.

So, the nonpoetry reader usually argues, if you can't make sense out of a poem, what point is there in reading it?

This argument is best met by several questions.

First, have you really given poetry a "fair chance?"

Have you sampled the works of different poets, at different periods, comparing one style with another to find something to your own taste?

Have you tried to understand some poetry in particular a little better by reading a biography of the poet, or a critical essay on his or her work?

If you haven't, you'll be surprised at how absorbing a study this can be. Poetry is one of the most intensely **personal** forms of human expression. The reader who approaches it with sympathetic awareness of the poet as a person is rewarded with the feeling of actually sharing in the drama of another's life.

It may be a drama of adventure, of philosophical thought, or fulfilled or unfulfilled passion, of religious exaltation or despair.

Whatever the subject, it is a rich human experience given symbolic expression through significant images fused with rhythmical language.

In some respects poetry closely resembles music.

Just as an "ear" for music is sometimes completely lacking, so that the listener really cannot hear the tones, only meaningless sounds, some persons have no ear for the emotional tones of poetry. A sense of rhythm in language, like a sense of rhythm in music, may also be missing.

If, after a sincere, open-minded effort to find interest and value in poetry you still feel that, temperamentally or otherwise, it is not for you, there is no reason why you "should" go on. Obviously, you will get far greater satisfaction from prose.

But do not give up reading poetry as hopeless without first trying it. Perhaps some of your difficulties will turn out to be merely technical ones, easily mastered if they are understood.

It is evident to even the most inexperienced poetry reader that in a poem words are employed in a special way. To fit the pattern of a rhyme scheme or rhythm scheme, sentences are often turned inside out. To get the sense meaning of the poem, you may have to bring a fair amount of concentration to bear.

Paraphrasing—that is, taking each sentence of a poem and rewriting it in your own prose, is an entertaining exercise and a challenge to understanding, although naturally the poetic flavor is lost.

You may also have to seek further for some of the allusions, turning to an encyclopedia, a mythology, or another reference work. You may look for some of the poet's easier works to give you a clue to his way of presenting material.

All of these activities are excellent training for the potentially good reader of both poetry and prose.

FREE READING

Free reading is reading what you like when you like.

You will find, however, that even though at first you roam at will among short stories and novels, plays and poems, gradually your preferences will lead you to organize your reading somewhat.

If your fiction-reading efficiency is improved, so also may your fiction-reading tastes. You may discover then that you are reading not only for pleasure—but also for profit.

The profit cannot be measured in dollars and cents, nor can it be measured in an increase in words per minute.

It is a matter of quality, not quantity, of growth in sensitivity and the consequent enrichment of your whole personality.

Experiment with free and independent reading.

A single work that you find truly exciting may lead you to another, and another, and still another. You may then discover for yourself what treasures are in store for you.

READING EXERCISE—I

Instructions: A distinguished novelist sets down her ideas about the influences on a creative writer's work: **environment, experience,** and **the work of other writers.** Read this selection **twice** before you answer the questions, first rapidly. Jot down your time **in seconds.** Look for details on the second reading.

Time Yourself and Begin

THE SPONGE OF THE PRESENT
By Elizabeth Bowen

In studying the development of an artist, the factor of influences upon him must, I imagine, always be taken into account. Analysis of influence, its general force and its particular workings, devolves in the main on the critic and art-historian: this field is held to require specialized knowledge and an aesthetic discernment possessed by few. By the rest of us painting, sculpture, music, architecture may be enjoyed without being historically comprehended: we react, that is to say, to the masterpiece without thought as to what may have been its complex origin. Where it is a matter of color, form used plastically, or pure sound, we are inclined to leave the genesis of the work of art to the trained mind. But where the medium is language, all is different—words are the general property; they link with *our* experience, so the creative use of them comes within our critical scope. The writer is less at a distance than other artists; one does not require to be a specialist to study him. His technique, the processes of his formation, lie open to any reader who cares enough—in this case, where influence is at work it almost always can be suspected, if not detected. The writer is amongst us; in number writers multiply every day; in our epoch writing, of all the arts, evokes most social interest and most human concern. With regard, then, to writers let us consider influence.

One may classify influences, one may trace them, one may discuss whether, in a particular instance, such-and-such an influence has acted favorably. What one cannot, with any profit, do is attempt to answer that frequent question—whether it is a "good" thing to be influenced, or not? Influence, in one sense if not another, is inevitable. The question as to whether it should or should not be avoided therefore falls to the ground—yet does, not only because it is asked often but because it is asked seriously, deserve respect. The idea of "good," in this context, probably has an ethical no less than aesthetic background—there is a latent notion that the writer subjecting himself to influence (from, presumably, another literary source) is in some way practising a dishonesty, advancing through using a borrowed power, or endangering what should be most sacred, in being most original, in his own talent. This objection to influence may be due to confusion—that is, failure to distinguish—between influence and out-and-out imitation: the latter *is* a malpractice; it is also calculated and voluntary. It might, indeed, not be too much to say that the distinction between influence and imitation demarcates, equally, the imaginatively creative from the merely cerebrally inventive writer. Where writing is a matter of invention, and nothing more, there may well be a temptation to copy the successful inventions of other people. Imagination, though by its nature susceptible and affectable, tends all the time to the *new;* it is bored by the second-hand.

Susceptibility, it should be understood, plays a great part in the makeup of the creative writer. He is susceptible to environment, to experience, and, in the same way and not less, to styles and energies in already-existing art. From all three sources he is attracting influences; all of which will leave their mark on his work. It is the third, the aesthetic-literary, which is most easily recognized by the reader; and for which the writer is most often called to account, and indeed reproached. Style—the actual choice and rhythm of words—most often carries an influence, and most clearly shows it. But with style, vision and outlook are interknit: did not Flaubert call style "a manner of seeing"? As we all know, a strongly directed film or a striking collection of pictures by one artist can so invade the receptive eye that, coming out of the cinema or the gallery, one continues for hours after to see life in terms of So-and-So's film or So-and-So's painting. A creative manner of seeing is infectious—small wonder that writers at the tentative stage find it hard to shake off the magic effect of a master's vision. And this may be true not only of visual but of moral angle. In fiction one senses the power, these days, of affective novelists such as Henry James, Faulkner, and Mauriac (unalike to each other as these may be).

The literary influence on a writer is, of all three, likely to be the most transient, ending with the period of apprenticeship—indeed, being a form of apprenticeship in itself.

Throughout his oscillations from style to style, his experiments in manner after manner, the writer is making his own growth. He will shell off, one by one—he may even react against—the influences which have up to a point fostered him. At the same time, he will have absorbed something; and he will continue to owe something to his place as a link in art's continuity. As he reaches maturity, and himself tends to become influence, he in his turn will be transmitting something—there is an honorable nay, necessary artistic heredity. As to literary influence, we may leave it that only uncertain talent stifles during this phase: the stamp of inherent originality is that sooner or later, and sooner rather than later, it must emerge.

The influence of environment is the most lasting; and, except in the case of "regional" writers, operates deepest down. Sometimes the force of environment may be felt by a writer's conscious, sharp reaction against it. Admittedly, it is the atmosphere of the scenes of youth which is most often decisive—though it has happened that, some way on into life, a writer has stumbled upon a place, perhaps an entire country, which he in some way recognizes, which seems to claim him, and which offers a hitherto lacking inspiration to his art. In that case, there is a sort of psychological adoption: a new phase of freshness of feeling, equivalent to a second childhood, sets in. But the majority are haunted by the shadowy, half-remembered landscape of early days: impressions and feelings formed there and then underlie language, dictate choices of imagery. In writing, what is poetically spontaneous, what is most inimitably individual, has this source—the writer carries about in him an inner environment which is constant; though it also, as time goes on, tends to become more and more subjective.

One must remember that the inner environment has been always, to a degree, selected: as we now know, there is an element of choice, however apparently involuntary, in memory. The writer is influenced by what he retains; and still more, perhaps, by the very fact that he has retained it—and the picture, by continuous dwelling upon, may be so much intensified as to become changed. Thus, though to an extent the environment creates the writer, he also plays a part in creating it—his art, by demanding this kind of sustenance, has reached back past the bounds of actual memory into a phantasmagoric hinterland quite its own.

Experience as an influence needs least comment: this is taken for granted—perhaps too much so. There is a tendency to think that the direct transcription of experience (into novel or poem) and the *action* of experience are synonymous. True action of experience on the creative powers is erratic, indirect and slow—also, insofar as writers do make use of their individual experience as persons, they almost invariably transform it. The experience which really influences art does not consist in drama or incidents; it is a sort of emotional accumulation, or at its best, a slowly acquired deep-down knowledge. Experience is the reaction itself—and in that sense experience is, like environment, to a degree selected. The meaning which is extracted from occurrences varies, and varies in its importance, according to the writer's choice as to feeling: he allows some things to "take" with him more than others.

The catastrophic disaster, the sudden primitive joy, are of course irresistible: they impose themselves. These leave behind in the writer what he has most in common with humanity: it is by its power to co-ordinate what is major with what is small in life that the soundness of his art is to be tested.

Is it true that the writers of our day are too much subject to influence, from whatever source? Do they lack the resilience, the independent hardiness of their predecessors? Literary influence (the first) seems harder now to throw off than once it was: it has been said that we have too many disciples, too few masters. If this be so, it may be found that, as a generation, we writers are in a transitional, learning stage: the task of expression appears a vast one—the old simplicities of the world are gone; the artist is hard-pressed by what is happening round him. Our century, as it takes its frantic course, seems barely inhabitable by humans: we have to learn to live while we learn to write. And to write, we must draw on every resource; to express, we need a widened vocabulary—not only as to words, as to ideas. The apprentice stage, given modern necessities, cannot but be a long one: some of us there may be who will not outlive it. But at least we are keeping going a continuity; we may serve to link the past with the future masters.

Time in seconds———

Directions: Select the best answer and place the appropriate letter in the parentheses.

1. One conclusion which may be drawn from "The Sponge of the Present" is that present-day creative writers (a) rise above all influences; (b) find literary influence harder to throw off than it once was; (c) behave in a frantic way; (d) need a much wider vocabulary.   ( )
2. According to Elizabeth Bowen, technique and the processes of formation of a writer (a) can be understood by everyone creative; (b) lie open to any reader who cares enough to investigate; (c) require a trained mind and specialized knowledge to understand; (d) will always remain incomprehensible.   ( )
3. Influences on a writer of one kind or another are (a) avoidable; (b) bad; (c) good; (d) inevitable.   ( )
4. Being bored by the second-hand and tending all the time to the new is a mark of (a) the cerebrallyinventive writer; (b) the critic and art-historian; (c) the specialist; (d) the imaginativelycreative writer.   ( )

5. Writing style is explained as (a) the actual choice and rhythm of words; (b) the processes of a writer's formation; (c) a borrowed power; (d) a matter of invention.   ( )
6. Another definition of writing style as "a manner of seeing" is quoted from (a) Henry James; (b) Faulkner; (c) Mauriac; (d) Flaubert.   ( )
7. Writers "at the tentative stage," states Elizabeth Bowen, find it hard (a) to copy the successful inventions of other people; (b) to shake off the magic effect of a master's vision; (c) to be susceptible to environment; (d) to be honest.   ( )
8. The most decisive influence on a creative writer is likely to be (a) a college writing course; (b) artistic heredity; (c) his childhood environment; (d) a master's inspiration.   ( )
9. The most transient influence on a creative writer is likely to be (a) criticism; (b) environment; (c) the work of other writers; (d) experience.   ( )
10. According to the article, personal experiences of writers are invariably (a) transformed before made use of; (b) set down exactly as they occur; (c) irresistible as subject matter; (d) of small importance in their creative development.   ( )

DIRECTIONS FOR SCORING

Reading Rate. Find your reading rate in words per minute by turning to the TABLE FOR DETERMINING READING RATE IN WORDS PER MINUTE.

Answers to Questions. Check the answers to the multiple-choice questions in the CORRECTION TO EXERCISES.

Progress Chart. Enter all reading rate and comprehension scores in the PERSONAL PROGRESS CHART.

READING EXERCISE—II

Instructions: Although the following selection is one of the shortest of short stories, it still illustrates beautifully many of the elements of plot, characterization, and setting discussed in this chapter. Read once and follow the directions. **You need not time yourself in this exercise.**

Begin

BIRTHDAY PARTY

By KATHARINE BRUSH

They were a couple in their late thirties, and they looked unmistakably married. They sat on the banquette opposite us in a little narrow restaurant, having dinner. The man had a round, self-satisfied face, with glasses on it; the woman was fadingly pretty, in a big hat. There was nothing conspicuous about them, nothing particularly noticeable, until the end of their meal, when it suddenly became obvious that this was an Occasion—in fact, the husband's birthday, and the wife had planned a little surprise for him.

It arrived, in the form of a small but glossy birthday cake, with one pink candle burning in the center. The headwaiter brought it in and placed it before the husband, and meanwhile the violin-and-piano orchestra played "Happy Birthday to You" and the wife beamed with shy pride over her little surprise, and such few people as there were in the restaurant tried to help out with a pattering of applause. It became clear at once that help was needed, because the husband was not pleased. Instead he was hotly embarrassed, and indignant at his wife for embarrassing him.

You looked at him and you saw this and you thought, "Oh, now, don't *be* like that!" But he was like that, and as soon as the little cake had been deposited on the table, and the orchestra had finished the birthday piece, and the general attention had shifted from the man and the woman, I saw him say something to her under his breath—some punishing thing, quick and curt and unkind. I couldn't bear to look at the woman then, so I stared at my plate and waited for quite a long time. Not long enough, though.

She was still crying when I finally glanced over there again. Crying quietly and heartbrokenly and hopelessly, all to herself, under the gay big brim of her best hat.

Directions: Answer these questions briefly, then reread the story.

What is the conflict?

With what descriptive phrases or words are the characters brought to life?

What phrases or words are used to set the stage?

From what point of view is the story told?

What single word could you use to describe the narrator's tone in the story? (Cheerful; whimsical; sympathetic; tragic.)

What is the theme of the story, if any? (Women are sentimental; good intentions often go amiss; men are often insensitive.)

READING EXERCISE—III

Instructions: Read the following poem at least **twice**, the second time slowly and thoughtfully. **You need not time yourself in this exercise.**

Begin

OZYMANDIAS

By PERCY BYSSHE SHELLEY

I met a traveler from an antique land
Who said: Two vast and trunkless legs of stone
Stand in the desert. Near them, on the sand,
Half sunk, a shattered visage lies, whose frown,
And wrinkled lip, and sneer of cold command,
Tell that its sculptor well those passions read
Which yet survive, stamped on these lifeless
    things,
The hand that mocked them, and the heart that
    fed.
And on the pedestal these words appear:
"My name is Ozymandias, king of kings;
Look on my works, ye Mighty, and despair!"
Nothing beside remains. Round the decay
Of that colossal wreck, boundless and bare,
The lone and level sands stretch far away.

Directions: Write briefly in your own words what you think is the meaning of this poem. Note that it is a **sonnet**, an **iambic pentameter** poem in fourteen lines. If necessary, look up the definition of these words which describe the pattern of the poem in your dictionary. One line in this poem usually poses a problem in interpretation, and that is the following: **The hand that mocked them, and the heart that fed.** The accepted solution is that "the hand" is that of the sculptor; "the heart" that of Ozymandias. After you have completed your writing assignment, turn once again to the poem itself for another reading. You might find it a valuable experience to memorize this immortal sonnet.

SELECTED PAPERBOUND SHORT STORIES, PLAYS, AND POEMS

American Short Stories Since Nineteen Forty-Five, ed. John Hollander. Harper & Row.

The American Short Story, ed. Calvin Skaggs. Dell.

Best Short Stories of the Modern Age, ed. Douglas Angus. Fawcett World.

Concise Treasury of Great Poems, ed. Louis Untermeyer. Pocket Books.

Fifty Great Short Stories, ed. Milton Crane. Bantam.

Great Modern Short Stories, ed. Bennett Cerf. Vintage.

Immortal Poems of the English Language, ed. Oscar Williams. Washington Square Press.

Mentor Book of Short Plays, ed. Richard Goldstone and Abraham Lass. New American Library.

Moderns and Contemporaries: Nine Masters of the Short Story, eds. Jonathon Baumbach and Arthur Edelstein. Knopf.

The Pocket Book of Verse, ed. M. E. Speare. Washington Square Press.

The Pocket Book of Modern Verse, rev. ed. by Oscar Williams, Washington Square Press.

Poems: An Anthology, ed. Raffel Burton. New American Library.

Six Great Modern Plays Incl. Chekhov, Shaw, Ibsen, O'Casey, Williams, and Miller, Laurel Editions Editors. Dell.

30 SELECTED PAPERBOUND GREAT NOVELS

Adam Bede, by George Eliot.

An American Tragedy, by Theodore Dreiser.

Anna Karenina, by Leo Tolstoy.

Brave New World, by Aldous Huxley.

Brothers Karamazov, by Feodor Dostoevski.

The Charterhouse of Parma, by Stendhal.

Crime and Punishment, by Feodor Dostoevski.

Dead Souls, by Nikolay Gogol.

Emma, by Jane Austen.

The Grapes of Wrath, by John Steinbeck.

Great Expectations, by Charles Dickens.

The Heart of Midlothian, by Sir Walter Scott.

Huckleberry Finn, by Mark Twain.

Jane Eyre, by Charlotte Brontë.

Joseph Andrews, by Henry Fielding.

The Last of the Mohicans, by James Fenimore Cooper.

Lord Jim, by Joseph Conrad.

Madame Bovary, by Gustave Flaubert.

The Mayor of Casterbridge, by Thomas Hardy.

Moby Dick, by Herman Melville.

Nana, by Emile Zola.

Of Human Bondage, by W. Somerset Maugham.

Père Goriot, by Honoré de Balzac.

Pride and Prejudice, by Jane Austen.

The Portrait of a Lady, by Henry James.

A Portrait of the Artist as a Young Man, by James Joyce.

Robinson Crusoe, by Daniel Defoe.

The Rise of Silas Lapham, by William Dean Howells.

The Red Badge of Courage, by Stephen Crane.

Return of the Native, by Thomas Hardy.
Sister Carrie, by Theodore Dreiser.
Sons and Lovers, by D. H. Lawrence.
Tom Jones, by Henry Fielding.
Vanity Fair, by William Makepeace Thackeray.
The Way of All Flesh, by Samuel Butler.
War and Peace, by Leo Tolstoy.
Wuthering Heights, by Emily Brontë.

EYE-SPAN EXERCISE

Directions: Use your Eye-Span Card for this exercise. Move it from asterisk to asterisk as rapidly as possible. Try to see the entire sentence at a single glance. **Think The Sentence; Do Not Say It Aloud.**

Begin

*

You can read much faster.

*

Speed up when you can

*

Read always with a purpose.

*

Speed and comprehension go together.

*

Read slowly when you should.

*

Concentrate on the main ideas.

*

Don't read word by word.

*

Remember details as you read.

*

Build your vocabulary each day.

Everyone can learn to spell.

*

Word recognition is a skill.

*

Attack new words with confidence.

*

Don't vocalize at any time.

*

Reading flexibility is your goal.

*

Compete with your own scores.

*

Read as fast as you think.

*

Solve personal problems as they arise.

*

Read with questions in your mind.

*

Try always to improve your skill.

*

You can read better and faster.

STUDY ASSIGNMENT

Plan to read at the first opportunity at least one of the great novels listed in this chapter. Also plan to read at least one play, five short stories, and five poems.

Vocabulary-building: The following words are taken from **Reading Exercise—I** in this chapter. Do you know them?

discernment	evokes	imagery
genesis	latent	phantasmagoric
epoch	demarcates	resilience

CHAPTER SEVENTEEN

THE MATURE READER

Self-improvement in reading demands careful organization of both your time and your mind. You must decide for yourself whether or not the returns are worth the energy devoted to the task.

You have already learned that practice in better and faster reading is competitive. But the competition is with **your own** reading rate, **your own** comprehension level, **your own** development as a mature person.

No one can read for you. This book is intended to help you, but it requires your fullest cooperation.

Regular timed practice with nonfiction material, wide and free reading of all kinds, and a conscious application of all you have learned so far are essential.

7 WAYS TOWARD EFFICIENT READING

Here is a quick summary of all that you have been asked to do:

1. Attack new and unfamiliar words aggressively as you read, seeking clues to meaning in both the form of the word and the context in which it appears.

2. Build your vocabulary by constantly reviewing selected words and defining them in detail. **Use the Dictionary!**

3. Listen actively to good speech in the language. Learn to pronounce words correctly. Learn to spell words correctly.

4. Learn enough about the structure of English sentences and paragraphs so that every "if," "and," and "but" in a passage won't become a stumbling block. Seek ideas on the printed page and not meaningless words in isolation.

5. Study the underlying forms of the various kinds of writing in the language, from a proverb to an instruction manual, from an axiom to a three-act play.

6. Let your purpose determine how you approach a work in print. In general, reading for study is best accomplished by getting the overall picture in your mind with a rapid first reading. Reading for relaxation is best accomplished by using various reading methods and speeds, depending on the type of material. Added enjoyment may come with added speed, however, for the excellent reason that you will have the practical means of making the acquaintance of so many more good things in print.

7. Remove inner psychological barriers to efficient reading. **This is admittedly more easily said than done.** Keep in mind always, however, that no reading problem is wholly insoluble. Insight sometimes comes slowly when the reader is working alone. Some method of outwardly expressing inner feelings helps. The reading autobiography, if faithfully kept, may lead to a measure of self-understanding. Your words about yourself often hold up a mirror to both your strengths and your weaknesses.

DISCOVERING YOURSELF THROUGH OTHERS

No two persons are exactly alike, and no two reading problems are exactly alike, either. Underlying patterns of similarity will often exist with notable differences in details.

Finding out in what ways you are similar or different from someone else in your approach to the printed word is often helpful in understanding your own problems.

After you feel that you know your own pattern of reading behavior through constant and accurate self-evaluation, you might try moving out into the world of people so that you may compare and contrast yourself with others.

What follows is merely a suggestion, but one which should not be difficult to carry out.

Invite a small group of friends and acquaintances to meet in an informal setting and talk about reading.

The meeting should be relaxed and cheerful, although its purpose ought to be stated clearly in advance. Without a definite focus for discussion, such a gathering would soon turn into a small-talk session. Needless to say, the television set will have to be kept turned off.

Some of the material in this book might be used as starting-points for discussion.

In a group of six to ten people, one person will usually emerge as the discussion leader. Some friendly agreements might be arrived at beforehand:

. . . that no one will dominate the conversation;

. . . that all will have an opportunity to air various problems in reading;

. . . that notes will be taken by one person for future reference.

A discussion leader may occasionally remind everyone to observe the rules of mutual give and take.

A tape-recording machine is an excellent device for preserving the discussion. A play-back of the tape could serve to open a succeeding get-together.

If it is impossible for you to arrange such a meeting, then try to discuss reading in general casually with just one or two other people, members of your family, close friends, interested neighbors.

You are not expected in any of these proposed discussion sessions to arrive at any great and final decisions about either yourself or your reading. No problems, if they are real, are so easy to solve.

The goal is to sharpen your critical sense about yourself and your reading by comparing yourself with others.

Talking with other people about reading will, if nothing else, be a pleasant social activity. It is apt to be much more.

You are likely to find, perhaps to your own amazement, that many others are as much interested in the subject as you are and quite eager to exchange information and ideas that will give mutual help and satisfaction.

PATHS TOWARD YOUR GOAL

You may be aware at this point that many paths can be found to help you speed up your reading and improve your comprehension. Some you may use and some you may not even attempt. But the paths are there for you to try if you wish.

In your primary approach to reading as a skill, you have been concentrating first on speed, then on comprehension and ability to organize the material mentally and recall it when needed.

You are urged to go further. Approach reading as an art as well as a skill.

You will then learn to extend the reading process in a creative way by analyzing, evaluating, and using your personal critical judgment. Your whole background of knowledge, information and experience will be brought to bear on the page in front of you. You will then read not only the words in print but the words which are implied.

While your eyes go down the printed page, your mind will be going between the lines, in and out and under and beyond the words.

A flesh and blood person with thoughts and feelings, beliefs and prejudices, the reader has his own individual reactions to everything he reads.

In general, expository prose, from the popular feature article in a current magazine to a highly specialized textbook, makes demands largely on the reader's critical sense. On a different level, modern fiction or classical literature, essays or poetry, call for a more imaginative frame of mind. Here the critical faculty must be supplemented by creative imagination.

If the creative writer writes because he has to write, the creative reader reads because he has to read.

REWARDS

The process of communication does not take place in a vacuum, but in the highly charged, rarefied atmosphere of emotions as well as intellect.

Back on the solid earth of the workday world, the plain fact that reading skill helps you to function better as a business or professional man or woman cannot be debated.

Effective communication also helps you to rise to any social occasion. All this is likely to lead to merited advancement in a chosen career with all the rewards of success.

It would be short-sighted and even cynical to stop at this point, however, and calculate all gains on the practical and material basis. Your drive toward self-improvement should also be measured by deeply rooted personal needs and the relationship of these needs to the society in which you live.

Looked at in this clear way, efficient reading brings its own reward. Only, it is not the reward of perpetual entertainment, although entertainment is wholesome and appropriate much of the time.

A deeper, richer pleasure will be found in the constant pursuit of knowledge and the eternal quest for the meaning of existence as reflected in the written word.

Neither is the reward of efficient reading necessarily the gold of the market place, although this may be desirable and appropriate. Modern man may live by bread, as well as by comfortable houses and automobiles and electronic equipment, but not by these alone.

Profits, tangible or intangible, calculable or incalculable, accrue handsomely for the individual when efficient reading becomes an integral part of his life's activities. No medium of communication has yet been discovered to surpass print in conducting the affairs of the world, passing cultural treasures on down through the generations, and providing deep and lasting personal enjoyment.

The successful reader finds so many satisfactions in unexpected places that every moment becomes an adventure of the mind and spirit.

THE ART OF READING

Once you have achieved a mastery of the art of reading and can hold your own fairly well against the daily onslaught of words in print, surprising things are likely to occur.

A genuine need for certain information will be filled by the sudden appearance of just the right book; an unanswered question by a random glance at a magazine article; a perplexing problem will be brilliantly illuminated by a chance look at a newspaper item; keys to hitherto unlocked doors of information will suddenly be in your possession through spotting a paragraph here, a phrase or even a single word there.

You will then realize with full impact that you are fully aware of not only the world of print but also the world in which you live.

REVIEW

Before continuing on to the next chapter, in which you will test yourself again, you are asked to review some of your work up to the present time.

Word recognition. Go back and look at some of the exercises which were planned to help you with recognizing words. Select a passage to read aloud to determine whether or not you have confidence in attacking all the words you meet along the way.

Reading rate and comprehension. Turn back to CHAPTER TEN and try once again the second reading test entitled "Margaret Fuller." Although you may have already filled in the answers to this test, review them anyway.

Vocabulary. Continue your review by looking over carefully the vocabulary test in CHAPTER TEN. Remember that you have but 10 seconds to complete each item on this type of test, so that speed is essential for a high score.

Finally, review and study any section of this book up to the present chapter which you feel might help you with your final test.

CHAPTER EIGHTEEN

MOVE AHEAD RAPIDLY—TEST YOURSELF

You are now going to give yourself the final test to determine your reading rate and comprehension level, your vocabulary strength, and your ability to analyze paragraphs.

A comparison with your first and second test scores will help you to judge your progress since you began this book.

Before taking the test, however, you are urged to follow the directions under the section headed "Review" in the preceding chapter, if you have not already done so.

When you are ready to go ahead with the tests, make sure that you are in a comfortable spot for working with book and pencil, and won't be interrupted for at least the next half hour.

A timing device of some kind, either a watch with a sweep hand or a stop-watch, will be needed. **Accurate Timing Is Important.**

The general directions are as follows:

Note the exact time, then begin to read the article at the rate you ordinarily use for a non-fiction piece in a magazine. **Remember that you are to answer questions about it.**

When you finish, note the number of **seconds** it has taken you. Write this information down **immediately** in the space provided.

Continue then to answer the questions **without looking back at the article.**

When you have completed the vocabulary section, continue with the paragraph analysis.

At the completion of the entire set of test exercises, you will find further instructions. Follow them carefully.

Are you ready?

Warning: If you are not ready, stop right here and postpone taking the test until you are **prepared and consider the test-taking conditions favorable.**

Time Yourself and Begin

STEPHEN CRANE

So many fantastic stories were circulated about Stephen Crane both during and after his brief lifetime that his biographers despair of ever separating the true from the false.

Some facts, however, have been reasonably well established.

The famous arthur of *The Red Badge of Courage* did not use narcotics nor did he drink to excess. His death before his twenty-ninth birthday was almost certainly due to tuberculosis. Far from being a gun-toting desperado, he was the mildest of men with a genuine love for children, dogs and horses.

He was also a known champion of the underdogs, of Bowery bums, women of the streets, homeless waifs, and down-and-outers of all types. His wife had been a so-called "fallen" woman. He even got into serious difficulties with the New York police over his stubborn defense of a chorus girl wrongfully arrested.

Undoubtedly the fact that he associated with these people created the impression that he himself was vicious and depraved and provided a stimulus for all the rumors about his life.

Stephen Crane was perhaps erratic and irresponsible. He was also the literary genius of his generation.

The fourteenth and final child of the Reverend and Mrs. Jonathan Townley Crane,

Stephen was born on November 1, 1871 in Newark, New Jersey. In this large Methodist family, he was his mother's favorite. To her, he was always "Stevie."

His earliest years were not especially eventful, except for the constant moving about which was the lot of a minister's family. His father received innumerable calls from churches in and around northern New Jersey. During his adolescence, Stephen was attending public school in Asbury Park, doing well in all studies except algebra. His ambition at that time was to be a professional baseball player.

At the age of sixteen he was entered in a Methodist private school located on the Hudson River. There he stayed for two and a half years. Crane said himself that he didn't learn anything. A classmate once remarked jokingly that at least he was good at poker and baseball. At any rate the schooling he had was enough to make him eligible to enter college.

In the fall of 1890 he was a freshman at Lafayette College in Easton, Pennsylvania. He played some intramural baseball, boxed occasionally, cut most of his classes, and got a zero in theme-writing. He left quietly at the end of the term.

The following semester found him at Syracuse University. Again he went out for baseball. In spite of his height of five feet six, his slight build, and his thin pinched face, Crane played the position of catcher. What he lacked in physique he more than made up for in stamina. Evidently he put his whole heart and soul into the game. He was elected captain of the Syracuse team.

Again he didn't do well in his studies. He wrote successfully for undergraduate publications and also sent some of his material to outside publishers, but classroom work was unbearable to him. He finally decided to give up his attempts at a formal education and become a professional writer instead.

His brother, Townley Crane, who ran a news reporting agency in Asbury Park, had helped him to get some article assignments, mostly for the *New York Tribune*. With this encouragement, Crane settled himself in New York City and tried to make a living with his pen. It was a hard struggle and he was often penniless and hungry, but he eventually did have a success. The magazine *Cosmopolitan* accepted one of his stories. Crane was just twenty-one years old at this point.

He had also completed a first novel which he had titled *Maggie: A Girl of the Streets*. Another brother, William, put up $1000 to have this work published. It was not very well received by the critics.

The following year *The Red Badge of Courage* appeared as a newspaper serial in the *Philadelphia Press*. Although Crane was not aware of it, at the age of twenty-two he was just around the corner from fame. Meanwhile he had decided to make some first-hand observations for news articles and stories. With several assignments obtained from newspaper and magazine editors, he set out for a trip to the western United States and Mexico.

Crane had a wonderful time on his travels. Seeking adventure, he discovered it almost everywhere he went. South of the border, he even experienced raw fear when a notorious Mexican bandit marked him for robbery and perhaps death. His escape was a near thing. The entire episode is immortalized in a short story entitled "Horses—One Dash."

Two other famous short stories also came out of this trip: "The Blue Hotel" and "The Bride Comes to Yellow Sky."

Back in New York, Crane continued to write, while the American reviewers were trying to decide just how to evaluate *The Red Badge of Courage*. Some of them liked it well enough, although the New York critics were hardly enthusiastic.

Then came the reports from abroad. This novel of a young man's struggle in the American Civil War received nothing but unreserved praise from the English critics. The Americans now took a second look, and a chorus of praise began to swell on both side of the Atlantic.

Thus it was that Stephen Crane, one of America's best writers, became famous.

The Red Badge of Courage was especially hailed as a masterpiece of realism. Actually, at the time the conflict so vividly described took place, the author had not even been born. Nor had he ever seen a smoking battlefield or heard a shot fired in anger.

Crane himself, however, believed that to write convincingly about events it was necessary to experience them. He had tramped the Bowery for material for his earlier works. He had also sought adventure in the West for further experiences to set down on paper. Now he felt that to know really that what he had written about was the truth, he must seek still further. In Cuba revolution and war were brewing. He decided to become a foreign correspondent.

With a belt full of gold strapped around his waist—supplied by Irving Bacheller, a famous magazine editor of the day—Crane first went to Florida, then later arranged a passage to Cuba. He never arrived, for on the way the ship sank. Out of his experiences in a lifeboat with some of the survivors, tossing in a heavy sea for thirty hours off the southern coast of the United States, came one of the great American short stories of all time, "The Open Boat."

After this harrowing escape from death by drowning, Crane never again enjoyed good health. Nevertheless, he still pursued the sound of gun-fire. When hostilities broke out between the Greeks and the Turks in 1897, he was soon on the scene of the conflict as correspondent for the *New York Journal* and the *Westminster Gazette*. It was at this time that he married Cora Taylor, a woman he had met in Florida and who had followed him across the sea.

In 1898 he was in Cuba, where war had finally broken out between Spain and the United States. He was cited in dispatches for bravery under fire. However, some of his closest friends believed that Crane had lost the desire to live and that this made him reckless.

He returned to the States and tried New York once more. But his undeserved reputation as an associate of the dregs of humanity came back to dog his footsteps around the city. Unfriendly tongues were busy, and the police hadn't forgotten him. As one of his friends, the famous music critic and writer James Huneker, said, "For a mild and melancholy kid he certainly had fallen into the garbage can of gossip . . ."

Crane's wife was living in England, perhaps to avoid the gossip and harsh public opinion in America. So now he joined her. He never again returned alive to his native land.

A broken-down manorhouse, Brede Place, was their place of residence, certainly the last spot in the world suitable for a man in poor health. But Crane seemed to like it at first, and invited many of his friends to visit him.

Crane could number among these friends at that time some of the most famous men in English letters, Joseph Conrad, H. G. Wells, and a fellow-expatriate, Henry James. They came to see him and his wife often and were hospitably entertained. But there were others lesser known who also dropped in, until the continual parade of house guests began to make his life unbearable.

Besides, Crane was failing. During this period he wrote poetry which has endured, as well as the remarkable short story, "An Episode of War." Shortly afterward he became seriously ill.

By the time the spring of 1900 arrived the doctor decided that he should go to a warmer and drier climate. His wife took him to a town called Badenweiler in the Black Mountains of Bavaria, Germany, where, on a day in May, Stephen Crane died.

Time in seconds———

Directions: Select the best answer and place the appropriate letter in the parentheses.

1. Stephen Crane was born in (a) New York City; (b) Newark, New Jersey; (c) Syracuse, New York; (d) Easton, Pennsylvania. ( )
2. Crane's father was (a) a minister; (b) a doctor; (c) a writer; (d) a college professor. ( )
3. Crane's ambition during adolescence was to become (a) a minister of the gospel; (b) a foreign correspondent; (c) a short story writer; (d) a professional baseball player. ( )
4. It is fairly sure that Crane (a) was a heavy drinker; (b) hated children and dogs; (c) was a narcotics addict; (d) died of tuberculosis. ( )
5. Crane was elected captain of the baseball team while at (a) a Methodist private school; (b) public high school; (c) Lafayette College; (d) Syracuse University. ( )
6. Crane completed his first novel when he was (a) 16 years old; (b) 19 years old; (c) 21 years old; (d) 29 years old. ( )
7. The first literary work that made Crane famous was (a) "The Open Boat"; (b) "The Blue Hotel"; (c) *The Red Badge of Courage;* (d) *Maggie: A Girl of the Streets.* ( )
8. The main reason for Crane's extensive travels was (a) he believed staying in one place too long was harmful to his literary style; (b) he wanted to escape from a desk job; (c) he wanted to obtain material to write about; (d) he wanted to run away from those who gossiped about him. ( )
9. "The Open Boat" was based on a real experience of Crane's when a boat he was on sank on the way to (a) Florida; (b) Cuba; (c) England; (d) Turkey. ( )

10. *The Red Badge of Courage* first appeared (a) in book form; (b) as a newspaper serial; (c) as a magazine serial; (d) as a short story. ( )
11. The American critics, on the whole (a) were immediately enthusiastic about *The Red Badge of Courage;* (b) gave *The Red Badge of Courage* unfavorable criticism; (c) were at first reserved about *The Red Badge of Courage* until the English critics praised it; (d) reevaluated *The Red Badge of Courage* after receiving unfavorable reports from England. ( )
12. The critics especially praised *The Red Badge of Courage* for (a) its realism; (b) its characterization; (c) its historical incidents; (d) its plot. ( )
13. "Horses—One Dash" is a story depicting Crane's narrow escape from a bandit in (a) Greece; (b) Cuba; (c) the Black Mountains of Bavaria; (d) Mexico. ( )
14. Crane's health began to fail after (a) an intense period of overwork; (b) a nervous breakdown caused by sensitivity to criticism; (c) prolonged exposure in a lifeboat; (d) his receiving wounds while under fire during the Spanish-American War. ( )
15. Crane believed that in order to write convincingly a writer must (a) receive training in newspaper work; (b) have first-hand experience of his subjects; (c) associate with successful people in the world of letters; (d) avoid being tied down by domestic cares. ( )
16. When hostilities broke out between Greece and Turkey, Crane (a) volunteered for the Greek cause; (b) was traveling in Greece on his honeymoon; (c) went to the scene of the conflict as a foreign correspondent; (d) was living in Greece. ( )
17. Two persons who helped Crane financially were (a) William Crane and Irving Bacheller; (b) Henry James and James Huneker; (c) Cora Taylor and Townley Crane; (d) Joseph Conrad and H. G. Wells. ( )
18. Crane died in (a) 1895; (b) 1900; (c) 1905; (d) 1910.
19. He died in (a) England; (b) Germany; (c) Cuba; (d) United States. ( )

20. From this brief sketch it might be concluded that history has (a) finally straightened out the details of Crane's personal life; (b) unjustly maligned Crane's reputation; (c) been critical of his literary talents without regard to his personal life; (d) fairly judged his character. ( )

VOCABULARY TEST III

Directions: Read each definition and underline the word which fits it most closely. Do not linger on any one item. Try to complete the test within five minutes. Your score will be the number correct within this time limit.

1. Sign foretelling a future event
   (a) purport; (b) omen; (c) ensign; (d) souvenir; (e) token.
2. Skill in making witty replies
   (a) sarcasm; (b) heckling; (c) mirth; (d) repartee; (e) flippancy.
3. Lacking in respect
   (a) irreverent; (b) curt; (c) callous; (d) secular; (e) abrupt.
4. To say something repeatedly
   (a) proclaim; (b) announce; (c) protest; (d) resound; (e) reiterate.
5. Expressing much meaning in few words
   (a) prolix; (b) accurate; (c) brief; (d) concise; (e) abridged.
6. Using the same standard or unit of measure
   (a) coequal; (b) commensurate; (c) plumb; (d) consistent; (e) diffuse.
7. Government by the few
   (a) tyranny; (b) parliament; (c) oligarchy; (d) triumvirate; (e) regency.
8. An act showing repentance
   (a) indulgence; (b) sacrifice; (c) prayer; (d) recompense; (e) penance.
9. Shriveled or dried up by exposure to heat
   (a) autumnal; (b) furrowed; (c) crone; (d) ochre; (e) parched.
10. Dose of a liquid drug or poison
    (a) potion; (b) pottage; (c) portion; (d) potation; (e) pottle.
11. Unable to pay one's debts
    (a) miserly; (b) indebted; (c) insolvent; (d) discredited; (e) intestate.
12. Special ability in a particular direction
    (a) intellect; (b) attribute; (c) caliber; (d) aptitude; (e) attainment.
13. To cast out
    (a) disperse; (b) doff; (c) eject; (d) suspend; (e) propel.
14. Collect literary materials into a volume
    (a) entitle; (b) garner; (c) compile; (d) translate; (e) authorize.
15. Forgive, overlook
    (a) condone; (b) remit; (c) obscure; (d) alleviate; (e) requite.
16. To study by examining separate parts of a whole (a) atomize; (b) bisect; (c) scrutinize; (d) analyze; (e) criticize.
17. A story that is not true
    (a) narrative; (b) sermon; (c) axiom; (d) fiction; (e) precept.
18. Distinguished for poetic achievement
    (a) bardic; (b) lyric; (c) laureate; (d) tragic; (e) bemused.
19. Having a biting, destructive effect
    (a) climactic; (b) drastic; (c) ascetic; (d) cryptic; (e) caustic.
20. Triangular end portion of a building under the roof
21. Yielding a profit
    (a) saleable; (b) productive; (c) remunerative; (d) marginal; (e) surplus.
22. A person whose philosophy is that pleasure is the chief goal of life
    (a) ascetic; (b) hedonist; (c) cynic; (d) plagiarist; (e) gourmet.
23. To bore or annoy
    (a) thwart; (b) vent; (c) irk; (d) fluster; (e) ingratiate.
24. Fond of being with people
    (a) gregarious; (b) courteous; (c) agreeable; (d) populous; (e) dependent.
25. Explanatory list of special words or terms included in a literary or technical work
    (a) lexicon; (b) glossary; (c) footnote; (d) appendix; (e) annotation.

26. Ability to read and write
(a) alliteration; (b) syntax; (c) literacy; (d) communication; (e) erudition
27. To strengthen by adding something else
(a) invent; (b) reinforce; (c) cultivate; (d) implement; (e) facilitate.
28. Wine poured as offering to a deity
(a) libation; (b) ritual; (c) sacrament; (d) rite; (e) tributary.
29. Office or residence of a diplomatic minister
(a) consulate; (b) envoy; (c) legation; (d) protocol; (e) delegation.
30. True to the facts
(a) literal; (b) effectual; (c) experimental; (d) conformist; (e) expert.

Directions: Read this paragraph once and then answer the questions about it. Try to complete the entire exercise within **five minutes.**

THE READING OF ADULTS

It should be recognized, however, that book reading is not the only reading in which the average man or woman indulges. We tend to forget how natural a part of our daily lives reading has become and that our society is organized on the assumption of wide-spread literacy. Nearly everyone in the United States depends upon his ability to read to see him through most of his waking day. Each of us reads—and sometimes even acts upon—such verbal information as "No Admittance," "This Way Out," "No Parking," "Sale Ends Friday," "Bus Stop" or "Today's Television Programs." As a matter of fact, it is reading on this level which has the most measurable effect upon us. Our conduct is definitely altered by our reading a traffic sign ("Right Turn on Green Arrow Only"), while it would be difficult to show that our reading of *Moby Dick* had any effect at all. Yet it is the reading of the Moby Dick type of content with which we are really concerned when we worry about the reading of adults. And when we say that Americans—by and large—are not readers, we mean that they are not sustained readers of serious content; not that they do not indulge in the simple act of deriving meaning from written symbols.

Directions: Select the best answer for each question.

1. The author of this paragraph states that by and large (a) adults are illiterate; (b) adults cannot read; (c) adults are not serious readers; (d) adults cannot act upon verbal information. ( )
2. According to the author, our conduct is definitely altered by reading (a) books; (b) traffic signs; (c) poetry; (d) newspapers. ( )
3. It might be inferred from this passage that (a) most people are incapable of following directions; (b) *Moby Dick* is much too difficult reading for the average adult; (c) traffic signs should be worded more simply; (d) since the literacy rate is so high in the United States sustained reading of serious books should be more widespread. ( )

DIRECTIONS FOR SCORING

Reading Rate. To find your reading rate in words per minute for the reading selection, turn to the TABLE FOR DETERMINING READING RATE IN WORDS PER MINUTE.

Answers to Questions. First, check the answers to the twenty multiple-choice questions for the timed reading selection in the CORRECTION KEY TO TESTS. Multiply the number you have right by **five** to get your comprehension score in percentages. For example, if you had thirteen correct out of twenty, set down your score as 65 percent.

Finally, check the answers to both the vocabulary test and the paragraph analysis test.

Progress Chart. Reading rate and all comprehension, vocabulary, and paragraph analysis scores should be entered in the places provided in your PERSONAL PROGRESS CHART.

APPENDIX

INTRODUCTION

Detailed instructions have been given concerning how to use this book for self-study, but nothing has yet been said about how to use it as a college text. If it is selected for classroom use, an immediate question arises.

What about the accessibility of the tests which measure progress, not to mention the availability of the CORRECTION KEY TO TESTS?

To answer this question and to assist in making this book an effective teaching tool in the improvement of reading, several suggestions will be made here.

To begin with, measurement of individual student ability in a college course in developmental reading can be determined by administering standardized tests, in which "norms" have been established and published.

Instruction may also include many other methods of testing and measurement, including the use of reading films, prepared slides projected with split-second timing, and devices which mechanically speed up reading.

The testing sections of this book, which include the vocabulary items and paragraph analysis, can then be used as regular assignments.

Since most permanent gains in speed and comprehension are achieved by the determined reader exposed to a great deal of print, the exercises in this book may be assigned for regular practice. The instructor may also find material in each chapter valuable for preparing classroom lectures. The material can also be a starting place for group discussion.

Finally, if the schedule of activities in the reading course is a heavy one, the entire book can be assigned as homework with the instructor reserving the right to check on progress at periodic intervals throughout the semester.

This book can be used effectively as a part of a freshman composition or communication skills course. Time is a precious commodity in these classrooms. Instructors may protest that about everything that can possibly be covered in the hours scheduled over a semester is already in the course outlines.

How can additional material in the improvement of reading be added without upsetting completely an already strict time budget?

The answer to this question must be found in some sort of compromise, so that a minimum of classroom time is consumed in taking up the skill of reading with a maximum benefit to the student.

The compromise lies in the combination of various activities.

For example, the reading exercises in this book may also be used for vocabulary work with a dictionary, or for sentence and paragraph analysis, or perhaps as theme topics for writing and speaking.

The timed exercises themselves may be assigned as homework, with the instructor making a periodic check of progress.

A final word to instructors: You might point out to students who intend to use this book as a text that not much will be gained by checking in advance the CORRECTION KEY TO EXERCISES. In fact, it would appear to be somewhat in the same category as cheating at solitaire.

A FORMULA
For Determining Reading Rate in Words per Minute

On the next few pages of the Appendix, you will find the *Tables for Determining Reading Rate in Words per Minute*, both for the tests and the exercises. A conversion is made for you from time-in-seconds to words-per-minute from the nearest 10 seconds.

Your actual reading time for a test or exercise may be either more or less than the limits of the tables. Or you may wish to compute your reading time more accurately to the exact second.

If so, you may use a formula to make your own computations. You will need this information:

- The number of words in the selection (found at the top of each column in the tables)
- The exact reading time in seconds

The formula follows:

$$\frac{\text{no. of words in selection} \times 60}{\text{time in seconds}} = \text{words per min.}$$

Note: You may use this procedure to determine your reading rate in words-per-minute for any material.

TABLES FOR DETERMINING READING RATE IN WORDS PER MINUTE

CHAPTER:	ONE	TWO	TEN	EIGHTEEN	THREE	FOUR	FOUR	FOUR
		Tests					Exercises	
Time in seconds	"The Fairy Tadpole"	"Thomas Wolfe"	"Margaret Fuller"	"Stephen Crane"	"Your Eyes"	"The Days When I Read"	"The Caliphate"	"May 1908"
60	680	1500	1500	1500	1100	735	640	435
70	582	1293	1293	1293	943	630	549	373
80	502	1128	1128	1128	825	551	480	326
90	453	1000	1000	1000	733	490	427	290
100	408	898	898	898	660	441	384	261
110	371	820	820	820	600	401	349	237
120	340	750	750	750	550	368	320	218
130	314	649	649	649	508	339	290	201
140	291	694	694	694	472	315	274	187
150	272	600	600	600	440	294	256	174
160	251	562	562	562	418	276	240	164
170	240	531	531	531	388	259	226	154
180	227	500	500	500	367	245	213	145
190	215	475	475	475	347	232	202	137
200	204	450	450	450	330	221	192	131
210	194	428	428	428	314	210	185	124
220	186	408	408	408	300	201	175	119
230	177	391	391	391	287	192	167	113
240	170	375	375	375	275	184	160	109
250	165	361	361	361	264	176	154	104
260	157	346	346	346	254	170	145	—
270	151	333	333	333	244	163	142	—
280	146	321	321	321	236	158	137	—
290	140	310	310	310	224	152	132	—
300	136	300	300	300	220	147	128	—
310	131	290	290	290	213	142	124	—
320	126	281	281	281	209	138	120	—
330	124	272	272	272	200	134	116	—
340	120	264	264	264	194	130	113	—
350	117	256	256	256	189	126	109	—

TABLES FOR DETERMINING READING RATE
IN WORDS PER MINUTE (continued)

	Tests				Exercises			
CHAPTER:	ONE	TWO	TEN	EIGHTEEN	THREE	FOUR	FOUR	FOUR
Time in seconds	"The Fairy Tadpole"	"Thomas Wolfe"	"Margaret Fuller"	"Stephen Crane"	"Your Eyes"	"The Days When I Read"	"The Caliphate"	"May 1908"
360	114	250	250	250	184	123	—	—
370	110	243	243	243	178	119	—	—
380	108	237	237	237	174	116	—	—
390	105	231	231	231	169	113	—	—
400	102	225	225	225	165	110	—	—
410	100	219	219	219	161	108	—	—
420	97	214	214	214	157	105	—	—
430	95	209	209	209	153	103	—	—
440	93	205	205	205	150	100	—	—
450	91	200	200	200	147	98	—	—
460	89	196	196	196	144	—	—	—
470	87	192	192	192	140	—	—	—
480	85	188	188	188	138	—	—	—
490	84	184	184	184	135	—	—	—
500	83	181	181	181	132	—	—	—
510	81	176	176	176	129	—	—	—
520	79	173	173	173	127	—	—	—
530	78	170	170	170	125	—	—	—
540	76	167	167	167	122	—	—	—
550	75	164	164	164	120	—	—	—
560	73	161	161	161	—	—	—	—
570	72	158	158	158	—	—	—	—
580	70	155	155	155	—	—	—	—
590	69	152	152	152	—	—	—	—
600	68	150	150	150	—	—	—	—

TABLES FOR DETERMINING READING RATE IN WORDS PER MINUTE

Exercises

CHAPTER:	FIVE	SIX	SEVEN	EIGHT	NINE	ELEVEN	TWELVE	TWELVE	THIRTEEN	FOURTEEN	FIFTEEN	SIXTEEN
Time in seconds	"Sam Johnson, Dictionary Maker"	"Speaking of Books"	"The Octopus and the Robot"	"The Inverted Pyramid"	"A Teacher Looks at Reading"	"The Art of Beginning Where You Are"	"Calculating Machine"	"How the Men From Mars Ruined a Quiet Evening"	"It's Never Good Enough"	"Sociality"	"How to Master An IN-Basket"	"The Sponge of the Present"
60	825	900	990	1050	1790	2080	800	2300	2025	1425	1115	1500
70	707	770	849	900	1543	1783	686	1970	1735	1221	956	1293
80	620	675	743	788	1342	1560	600	1725	1519	1069	836	1128
90	550	600	660	700	1193	1387	533	1533	1350	950	743	1000
100	495	540	594	630	1074	1248	480	1380	1215	855	669	898
110	450	491	540	570	976	1135	436	1255	1104	777	608	820
120	413	450	495	525	895	1040	400	1150	1013	713	558	750
130	381	415	457	484	826	960	369	1061	934	658	515	694
140	354	385	425	450	772	892	343	986	868	611	478	644
150	330	360	396	420	716	832	320	920	810	570	446	600
160	310	338	372	394	671	780	300	862	759	535	418	562
170	291	318	345	371	631	734	282	767	715	503	394	531
180 (3 mins.)	275	300	330	350	597	694	267	767	675	475	372	500
190	261	284	313	332	565	657	253	726	639	450	352	475
200	248	270	297	315	537	624	240	690	608	428	335	450
210	236	257	283	300	511	594	229	658	578	407	319	428
220	225	245	270	285	488	568	218	628	552	389	304	408
230	216	235	258	274	467	543	209	600	528	389	304	408
240	207	225	248	263	448	520	200	575	506	371	290	391
250	198	216	238	252	430	499	192	552	486	342	268	361

TABLES FOR DETERMINING READING RATE IN WORDS PER MINUTE (continued)

CHAPTER:	FIVE	SIX	SEVEN	EIGHT	NINE	ELEVEN	TWELVE	TWELVE	THIRTEEN	FOURTEEN	FIFTEEN	SIXTEEN
Time in seconds	"Sam Johnson, Dictionary Maker"	"Speaking of Books"	"The Octopus and the Robot"	"The Inverted Pyramid"	"A Teacher Looks at Reading"	"The Art of Beginning Where You Are"	"Calculating Machine"	"How the Men From Mars Ruined a Quiet Evening"	"It's Never Good Enough"	"Sociality"	"How to Master An IN-Basket"	"The Sponge of the Present"
260	190	208	229	242	413	480	185	530	467	329	258	346
270	184	200	220	233	398	462	178	511	450	317	248	333
280	177	193	213	225	386	446	171	493	434	306	239	321
290	171	186	205	217	370	430	166	476	419	295	230	310
300	165	180	198	210	358	416	160	460	405	285	223	300
310	159	174	192	203	346	403	155	446	392	276	216	290
320	155	169	186	197	336	390	150	432	379	268	209	281
330	150	164	180	191	325	378	145	418	368	259	203	272
340	146	159	173	186	316	367	141	406	358	252	197	264
350	141	154	170	180	307	357	137	396	348	244	191	256
360	138	150	165	175	299	347	134	384	338	238	186	250
370	134	146	161	170	290	337	130	373	328	231	181	243
380	131	142	157	166	283	329	127	363	319	225	176	237
390	127	138	152	161	275	320	123	353	312	219	171	231
400	124	135	149	158	269	312	120	345	304	214	168	225
410	—	—	—	—	262	304	117	337	294	209	163	219
420	—	—	—	—	256	297	115	329	289	204	160	214
430	—	—	—	—	250	290	112	321	283	199	156	209
440	—	—	—	—	244	284	109	314	276	195	152	205
450	—	—	—	—	239	277	107	307	270	190	149	200
460	—	—	—	—	234	272	105	300	264	186	145	196
470	—	—	—	—	229	266	102	294	258	182	142	192
480	—	—	—	—	224	260	100	288	253	179	140	188
490	—	—	—	—	219	255	98	282	246	174	137	184
500	—	—	—	—	215	250	96	276	234	171	134	181

189

CORRECTION KEY TO TESTS AND PERSONAL PROGRESS RECORD

CHAPTER:	TWO			TEN			EIGHTEEN		
	"Thomas Wolfe"	Vocabulary		"Margaret Fuller"	Vocabulary		"Stephen Crane"	Vocabulary	
	1. b	1. c	21. d	1. b	1. b	21. d	1. b	1. b	21. b
	2. b	2. a	22. b	2. b	2. a	22. e	2. a	2. d	22. b
	3. d	3. e	23. c	3. a	3. c	23. d	3. d	3. a	23. c
	4. a	4. c	24. b	4. a	4. b	24. a	4. d	4. e	24. a
	5. d	5. a	25. a	5. b	5. d	25. c	5. d	5. d	25. b
	6. c	6. b	26. b	6. d	6. e	26. d	6. c	6. b	26. c
	7. b	7. b	27. c	7. c	7. c	27. b	7. c	7. c	27. b
	8. d	8. e	28. a	8. d	8. a	28. a	8. c	8. e	28. a
	9. a	9. d	29. d	9. d	9. d	29. e	9. b	9. e	29. c
	10. c	10. a	30. c	10. a	10. e	30. d	10. b	10. a	30. a
	11. b	11. b	—o—	11. d	11. b	—o—	11. c	11. c	—o—
	12. d	12. e	"Books"	12. c	12. a	"The Passive Reader"	12. a	12. d	"The Reading of Adults"
	13. a	13. a	1. c	13. c	13. c	1. b	13. d	13. c	1. c
	14. a	14. a	2. b	14. c	14. e	2. c	14. c	14. c	2. b
	15. d	15. c	3. a	15. d	15. b	3. a	15. b	15. a	3. d
	16. d	16. b	Comprehension	16. b	16. a	Comprehension	16. c	16. d	Comprehension
	17. c	17. d	____%	17. c	17. c	____%	17. a	17. d	____%
	18. b	18. e		18. b	18. b		18. b	18. c	
	19. a	19. b		19. a	19. a		19. b	19. e	
	20. c	20. d		20. c	20. d		20. b	20. a	
	Rate ___w.p.m.	Number of Vocabulary Items Correct in 5 Min. ___		Rate ___w.p.m.	Number of Vocabulary Items Correct in 5 Min. ___		Rate ___w.p.m.	Number of Vocabulary Items Correct in 5 Min. ___	

CORRECTION KEY TO COMPREHENSION EXERCISES AND PERSONAL PROGRESS RECORD

CHAPTER:	THREE	FOUR	FOUR	FOUR	FIVE	SIX	SEVEN	EIGHT
Question	"Your Eyes"	"The Days When I Read"	"The Caliphate"	"May 1908"	"Sam Johnson, Dictionary Maker"	"Speaking of Books"	"The Octopus and the Robot"	"The Inverted Pyramid"
1.	c	c	d	d	d	c	c	b
2.	a	b	c	a	d	b	a	c
3.	c	d	b	b	a	d	b	d
4.	a	c	a	x	d	a	d	d
5.	d	d	a	x	a	c	a	c
6.	d	x	x	x	c	c	b	a
7.	b	x	x	x	d	a	a	d
8.	d	x	x	x	c	c	a	a
9.	a	x	x	x	c	c	a	d
10.	b	x	x	x	b	a	d	b
RATE	___ w.p.m.	___ w.p.m.	___ w.p.m.	___ w.p.m.	___ w.p.m.	___ w.p.m.	___ w.p.m.	___ w.p.m.
COMPREHENSION	___%	___%	___%	___%	___%	___%	___%	___%

CORRECTION KEY TO COMPREHENSION EXERCISES
AND PERSONAL PROGRESS RECORD

CHAPTER:	NINE "A Teacher Looks at Reading"	ELEVEN "Beginning Where You Are"	TWELVE "Calculating Machine"	TWELVE "Men from Mars"	THIRTEEN "It's Never Good Enough"	FOURTEEN "Sociality"	FIFTEEN "IN-Basket"	SIXTEEN "The Sponge of the Present"
Question								
1.	a	c	b	b	a	c	c	b
2.	b	a	c	d	c	b	b	b
3.	d	b	d	c	d	b	d	d
4.	b	a	d	a	c	d	a	d
5.	d	c	b	c	a	d	c	a
6.	a	d	c	a	b	d	a	d
7.	b	a	a	c	d	a	d	b
8.	b	c	b	d	d	c	c	c
9.	c	d	c	d	c	c	c	c
10.	a	d	a	b	b	c	b	a
RATE	w.p.m.	w.p.m.	w.p.m.	w.p.m.	w.p.m.	w.p.m.	w.p.m.	w.p.m.
COMPRE-HENSION	____%	____%	____%	____%	____%	____%	____%	____%

CORRECTION KEY TO VOCABULARY EXERCISES

CHAPTER:			FOURTEEN		
1. b	11. e	21. e	1. e	11. b	21. d
2. b	12. b	22. c	2. c	12. e	22. b
3. a	13. a	23. c	3. a	13. a	23. c
4. d	14. c	24. e	4. d	14. c	24. c
5. d	15. b	25. b	5. a	15. a	25. d
6. a	16. c	26. a	6. c	16. c	26. a
7. c	17. b	27. a	7. e	17. b	27. b
8. b	18. c	28. c	8. d	18. c	28. a
9. e	19. d	29. c	9. e	19. a	29. c
10. a	20. a	30. b	10. a	20. b	30. e

CORRECTION KEY TO PARAGRAPH ANALYSIS EXERCISES

CHAPTER SEVEN

I. 1. c	IV. 1. a	VII. 1. a	X. 1. b
2. c	2. a	2. c	2. b
3. b	3. b	3. b	3. a
II. 1. d	V. 1. d	VIII. 1. a	Items Correct
2. b	2. c	2. a	Out of 30
3. a	3. a	3. c	
III. 1. b	VI. 1. e	IX. 1. a	
2. b	2. a	2. b	
3. c	3. b	3. a	

GRAPH OF YOUR READING RATE PROGRESS
Exercises

When you enter your word-per-minute scores for the reading exercises in the spaces provided, you may also wish to record them in the form of a graph. Put a dot on the lines of the graph corresponding to chapter number and word-per-minute rate for each test. Connect these dots with a line. The connecting lines will not necessarily move uniformly upward. Various factors may cause fluctuations in reading speed. NOTE: *Comprehension should be at least 60% for the exercises you enter on the graph. If you have not achieved this comprehension level in a particular exercise, go back and try it again even if you have to slow down considerably in your reading.*

Words per Minute	Chapter: 1	2	4	4	4	5	6	7	8	9	11	12	12	13	14	15	16
1200																	
1175																	
1150																	
1125																	
1100																	
1075																	
1050																	
1025																	
1000																	
975																	
950																	
925																	
900																	
875																	
850																	
825																	
800																	
775																	
750																	
725																	
700																	
675																	
650																	
625																	
600																	
575																	
550																	
525																	
500																	
475																	
450																	
425																	
400																	
375																	
350																	
325																	
300																	
275																	
250																	
225																	
200																	
175																	
150																	
125																	
100																	
75																	
50																	
25																	
0																	